Hans-Jürgen Diller · Stephan Kohl · Joachim Kornelius · Erwin Otto
Gerd Stratmann (Hg.)

anglistik & englischunterricht

Band 33

Literature in English
New Territories

Verantwortlicher Herausgeber dieses Bandes
Albert-Reiner Glaap

HEIDELBERG 1987

CARL WINTER · UNIVERSITÄTSVERLAG

CIP-Titelaufnahme der Deutschen Bibliothek

Literature in English: new territories / [Hrsg.:
Hans-Jürgen Diller...]. – Heidelberg: Winter,
1987.
(Anglistik & [und] Englischunterricht;
Bd. 33)
ISBN 3-533-04011-9
NE: Diller, Hans-Jürgen [Hrsg.]; GT

Herausgeber:
Prof. Dr. Hans-Jürgen Diller · Prof. Dr. Stephan Kohl
Dr. Joachim Kornelius · Dr. Erwin Otto · Prof. Dr. Gerd Stratmann

Redaktionsassistent: Manfred Buschmeier

ISBN 3-533-04011-9
ISSN 0344-8266

Anschrift der Redaktion:
Dr. Joachim Kornelius, Ruhr-Universität Bochum, Englisches Seminar
Universitätsstraße 150 · 4630 Bochum 1
Verlag: Carl Winter Universitätsverlag · gegr. 1822 GmbH · Heidelberg
Satz und Druck: Carl Winter Universitätsverlag · Abteilung Druckerei · Heidelberg
Alle Rechte vorbehalten. © 1987
Photomechanische Wiedergabe nur mit ausdrücklicher Genehmigung durch den Verlag
Printed in Germany · Imprimé en Allemagne

anglistik & englischunterricht erscheint in drei Bänden pro Jahrgang. Der Gesamtumfang beträgt ca. 540 Seiten
Preis des Einzelbandes DM 25,–, des Jahrgangs DM 50,–, Studentenpreis DM 39,– pro Jahrgang
In diesen Preisen sind 7% Mehrwertsteuer enthalten
Porti werden zusätzlich in Rechnung gestellt
Preise und Lieferbarkeit älterer Jahrgänge auf Anfrage
Die genannten Preise gelten für 1987 und haben Gültigkeit bis auf Widerruf
Abbestellungen nur mit einmonatiger Kündigung bis zum Jahresschluß
Für unverlangte Einsendungen von Manuskripten wird nicht gehaftet
Mitarbeiter erhalten von ihren Beiträgen 30 Sonderdrucke und 2 Freiexemplare. Honorar wird nicht bezahlt
Der Verlag trägt die Kosten für die von der Druckerei nicht verschuldeten Korrekturen nur in beschränktem Maße
und behält sich vor, den Verfassern die Mehrkosten für Autorkorrekturen zu belasten

Inhalt

NEW TERRITORIES IN THE CLASSROOM

NEW TERRITORIES – ADDITIONAL MATERIAL

Introduction

When we speak of English literature these days, most of us do not merely think of the literature written in England or Great Britain. We know that elsewhere literature is written in English as well. This is why the word "literature" is increasingly used in the plural. Australian Literature, Canadian Literature, Indian Literature – each of these is a specific literature in itself, but they are all literatures in English. Their common ground is the English language, their special features stem from different regional, social or political contexts. New areas, new territories have been added to the field of English Literature.

This volume of the *anglistik & englischunterricht* series aims at giving an insight into the literatures of some of the New Territories. In the Federal Republic of Germany, the interest in these literatures has slowly but steadily grown in the course of the last two decades. Novels and short stories originating from countries outside the USA and Great Britain have been objects of both research and classroom discussion. One has to admit, however, that we are still in the initial stages of a new undertaking. Much remains to be done. A careful study of the so-called *Augsburger Informationen*, which are published semi-annually and in which lectures and courses offered by the English departments at German universities are itemized, proves that what has been done so far is encouraging, but – needless to say – not as yet anything comparable with the amount of „Lehrveranstaltungen" offered in the fields of British or US-American Literature.

The following table (p. 8) is based on the listings in fourteen successive editions of the *Augsburger Informationen*, which were published between 1981 and 1987.

What do these figures reveal about the teaching of "English Literature in New Territories" at unversity level?

1. Basically, there are two categories of „Lehrveranstaltungen": the ones on literature, and the others on what is mostly referred to as „Landeskunde".

2. The percentage of the „Landeskunde" courses varies. As far as India is concerned, 23% of the courses offered at German universities deal with "Life and Institutions" etc. For Canada the figure is 18%, for Africa 11%, for New Zealand less than 8%. Obviously different amounts of background information are needed when studying the various New Territories.

3. Judging from the number of courses offered, Africa and Canada rank first in the list.

	„Lehrveran-staltungen" (Total)	„Landeskunde"	
Africa	176	20	= 11.36%
Australia	76	7	= 9.21%
New Zealand	13	1	= 7.69%
India	30	7	= 23.33%
Canada	165	29	= 17.57%
Caribbean/ West Indies	55	5	= 9.09%
British Empire (general)	52	23	= 44.23%

4. Apart from lectures and seminars on specific English literatures – in Africa, Australia, the West Indies etc. – there are general courses on the "British Empire" and on "Commonwealth Literature".

At secondary school level, literatures in English from outside Great Britain, Ireland or the USA still play but a small role. Australia, India, Canada, Africa, New Zealand and the West Indies are more or less ignored by curriculum developers in most of the *Bundesländer*. Occasional statements in the ministerial guidelines are very general, they almost sound like alibis, e.g.:

> Gegenstand des Unterrichts sind die englische Sprache und die Kultur der englischsprachigen Völker [...]. Großbritannien und Nordamerika stehen dabei im Vordergrund, aber auch die anderen Völker des englischen Sprachraums sollen möglichst berücksichtigt werden.
>
> *(Rahmenrichtlinien Niedersachsen. Gymnasiale Oberstufe: Englisch, p. 4)*

> Über die Beschäftigung mit Sachverhalten des angloamerikanischen Sprachraums hinausgehend, ermöglicht die englische Sprache [...] die Erschließung von [...] Sachverhalten, die außerhalb des angloamerikanischen Sprachraums liegen.
>
> *(Richtlinien Nordrhein-Westfalen. Gymnasiale Oberstufe: Englisch, p. 44)*

[…] es sind auch Themenstellungen möglich zu englischsprachigen Literaturen außerhalb Großbritanniens und der USA und zu Aspekten […].

(Ibid., p. 237)

Whereas most of the *Lehrpläne* and *Richtlinien* are very explicit about British and US-American literature, they are taciturn when it comes to making practical suggestions for the teaching of "English Literature in New Territories" in EFL-courses at the level of the *Gymnasiale Oberstufe*. Understandable though this is on the one hand – students who are to acquire a working knowledge of the foreign language cannot be expected to delve into the fabric of all kinds of literatures – the young students of today must, on the other hand, somehow be integrated into the world of tomorrow. Considering the importance of education for international understanding, English-speaking countries outside Great Britain, Ireland and the USA must be given more scope in the curricula of our schools than has been the case so far.

This volume aims to give its readers an "inkling" of topics and trends in the literatures of some of the New Territories and to provide them with background information. Needless to say, a book like this cannot be anything near a complete survey. Some of the New Territories are missing; New Zealand, the West Indies and some other New Territories in Africa should have their place in a book like this. Considering the limited space available, however, it was impossible to include all literatures in English in this one volume. But there was an additional reason for a concentration on just a selection of New Territories. The alternative was to either present as many different literatures as possible or to limit oneself to some of them and use the remaining space to include suggestions for the *teaching* of these literatures at secondary school level. Considering the meagre information that teachers have so far been given in this field, the latter of the two possible approaches seemed to be the more advisable. Accordingly, the volume consists of two main parts: Part One ('New Territories in Literature') is a collection of articles on novels, poems, short stories or plays written by African, Australian, Indian or Canadian authors. Part Two ('New Territories in the Classroom') contains articles on the possibilities of *teaching* intercultural competence and English Literatures in New Territories. Reports from secondary school teachers on their own experiences in this field have also been included.

Additional materials are presented in a final section of this volume. Users of the book who would like to familiarize themselves with at least the political and cultural *framework* of the New Territories will find basic dates and facts in this part of the book. Thanks are due to the cultural departments of the embassies of the respective countries which have kindly made the materials available for this enterprise.

Dieter A. Berger, Düsseldorf

Ngugi wa Thiong'o: *Petals of Blood*

In October 1986 the Nobel Prize for Literature was awarded for the first time to an African writer, to the dramatist, poet, novelist, and essayist Wole Soyinka. This brought the world's attention similarly to the extensive development of creative writing on the black continent. In fact, since its beginnings in the 1950s, although there were of course precursors in the 18th, 19th and early 20th centuries, African literature in English has shown a speedy emancipation from trivial and provincial fetters, and has won an international reputation. In drama and poetry, but particularly in the novel, African writers have achieved outstanding successes. Which novelist, however, is to be introduced here as a representative of the new literary territory of Africa? A possible starting point lies, of course, in the choice of a region. Yet, although countries with the stamp of French, Belgian, German, and Portuguese colonization could evidently be excluded, there are in that huge continent still nearly a dozen countries with a British colonial history and acculturation. To complicate matters further, the three main areas West, Central, and East Africa – South Africa represents a different development – have all produced acclaimed novelists, among them Chinua Achebe, Wole Soyinka, and Amos Tutuola (all from Nigeria), Lenrie Peters (Gambia), Ayi Kwei Armah (Ghana), and Ngugi wa Thiong'o (Kenya). Obviously, many analogies exist between them, due above all to the fact that they are all black Africans who have internalised the educational clash between Western and African culture and are writing not in their mother tongues, but in English, a secondary acquired colonial language. Yet their voices are highly individualized and their approaches to the novel vary considerably. Thus, although the "Africanness" of themes and formal treatment is shared by all the writers, African fiction in English is not a homogeneous body but dependent on the sociocultural and historical conditions of a particular area.

The impact of East Africa is evident in all the writings of Ngugi wa Thiong'o, and will be especially manifest in his fourth novel. *Petals of Blood* (1977) was chosen because Ngugi, in an attempt at epic totality, fuses past and present, hope and disillusionment, village and town life, traits of religion and education – topics which dominate the African novel though mostly treated separately. Ngugi's story becomes an impressive painting of post-independent Kenya in the grip of neocolonialism. Furthermore, by ingeniously exploiting devices characteristic of African story-telling, Ngugi provides the European genre "novel" with a new stimulus.

Before we turn our attention to the structure and African themes of *Petals of Blood*, a quick glance at the author's career will be informative. James Ngugi was born in Limuru (near Nairobi) in 1938, and only in 1970 did he adopt the Kikuyu name Ngugi wa Thiong'o. His father was an "ahoi", a dispossessed peasant farmer forced to become a squatter on the estate of a well-to-do African landowner. He had three other wives besides Ngugi's mother, and Ngugi was one of about twenty-eight children in the family. At the age of nine he started primary school, and from 1954 to 1958 he received his secondary education at Alliance High School at Kikuyu (near Nairobi), which figures as Siriana Secondary School in his fiction. Meanwhile the years of the Mau Mau crisis and the State of Emergency, an important event in Kenya's recent history, had started in 1952. Ngugi, an outstanding young student, was then only fourteen years old, and he did not become involved in the campaign, which nourished a sense of guilt and shame in later years. In 1959 he started studying British literature at the famous Makerere University College in Kampala (Uganda) and took his degree after four years. The years 1964 to 1967 he spent at Leeds University. But as two novels, *Weep Not, Child* (1964) and *The River Between* (1965), had meanwhile been published, he lost interest in the M. A.-course and rather concentrated on *A Grain of Wheat*, published in 1967. Back in Kenya, he was appointed Lecturer in English at the University College, Nairobi in 1967, but resigned in 1969 in protest against government interference. Two years later he returned, assumed the headship of the Department of Literature in 1972, and helped integrate the study of African Literature and Language into its syllabus. 1977 was a crucial year for Ngugi, not only on account of the release of *Petals of Blood* and the immediate success of his first play in Gikuyu *Ngaahika Ndeenda* (*I Will Marry When I Want*). Ngugi's deep political commitment seemed finally to reach the people, with the consequence that the reigning elite in Kenya came to consider him a real danger. He was placed in detention but never brought to trial, and he was only released after twelve months in 1978. Ngugi retained his strategy, however, and in order to communicate more widely in his homeland, also published his next novel in Gikuyu. It appeared in his own English translation as *Devil on the Cross* (1982). His five novels, as well as numerous essays, plays, and short stories have made Ngugi known across the world not only as Kenya's leading author but as one of the "giants of African literature". He is now living in self-chosen exile in London.

Petals of Blood, published 1977, is a rather complex novel, which is particularly evident in the structure of the plot, the interplay of different time levels, the representative even symbolic concept of character, and the rather confusing appearance of several narrative voices. Its structural complexity is partly due to an autonomous approach to the novel realized by African writers, but not least to Ngugi's idiosyncratic experimenting with form. Especially the impressions of collectiveness and of simultaneity are striking for a European reader.

Let us start with the continuous shifts in time, so confusing at the beginning of the reading process. Gradually, however, they contribute to the African time experience of the simultaneity of present and past, because for Ngugi present events are organically rooted in the past. For the purpose of analysis different time levels must be distinguished. There is, first, a narrative of events occurring in the immediate present and covering only ten days. It tells of a case of arson in Ilmorog, a small provincial town in contemporary Kenya, resulting in the deaths of three prominent industrialists, and of the arrest of four suspects: Munira, a teacher and religious fanatic; Abdulla, a shabby vendor of oranges, who lost a leg in the Mau Mau risings; Wanja, a prostitute and brothel owner; and Karega, ex-teacher and convinced socialist, the strike-leader of the brewery workers. There is, secondly, the narrative of events set in the recent past, comprising a period of twelve years. It recounts the epic drama of the development of Old into New Ilmorog, of a godforsaken and drought-ridden village into a modern town. On this time level, the story unfolds with the arrival of the four protagonists Munira, Abdulla, Wanja, and Karega in Old Ilmorog. It tells of the people's journey to Nairobi, two years later, to seek assistance from their representative MP, of a short period of rebirth, both economically and emotionally, of the first brewing of Theng'eta, and of the radical change into New Ilmorog with the advent of tourism and the subsequent "blessings" of Western civilization. This time period (past 1) ends with the deaths by fire of Mzigo, Chui, and Kimeria. In addition, there is another past reaching further back. This ancient past (past 2) is intimately connected with the biographies of the four leading characters before they came to Ilmorog. In the course of their repeated recollections which lead back to Kenya's troublesome years of the Mau Mau revolt against British colonial rule the reader becomes familiar with their particular traumas and failures in youth. One can even distinguish a fourth time level which takes the reader back to colonial times, and sporadically even further back into Africa's history. In the consciousness of the several narrators all the happenings are enmeshed in Africa's web of history, which is understood as a continuum of past and present.

Petals of Blood is presented in four parts; yet by fusing the different time levels Ngugi realizes an organic interrelationship between the different parts. The plot structure, too, must be seen as an interlocking system of separate narrative layers, rather than as a main body of fiction dramatising the past which is embedded in a present-time framework.[1] Of course, the personal stories about Munira, Karega, Wanja, and Abdulla and their relationships constitute the novel's centre of interest. But the private histories are intricately connected with the village history of Ilmorog, if not also with Kenya's history. Interspersed little

13

by little, the different narrative layers gradually build up a more comprehensive understanding, thus arousing the reader's curiosity the more he progresses. The accumulating tension fed in that manner operates on different levels and borrows from different genres. At the surface there is the pervading thrill of the detective novel, and Ngugi, in fact, does not hesitate to adopt some of its characteristic techniques. The book opens with arson and murder, and only near the end, when a motive and evidence has likewise been heaped on all four suspects, is police inspector Godfrey able to charge Munira with the fire-setting.[2] What Inspector Godfrey does not know, however, is that another crime was committed immediately before, the killing of Kimeria by Wanja. This event, though not too important within the crime story, is crucial for the understanding of Wanja's life. The reader, privileged alone with this information, will immediately connect the public event with the private story. And he will find as much thrill in the remaining three biographies, which likewise border on the tragic. Munira, Wanja, Karega, and Abdulla all came from Limuru and apparently met in Ilmorog by chance. The more intimate their contact with each other, the more distinct become the contours of the deep traumas of their earlier lives which they either try to repress or come to terms with. Munira, for instance, the village schoolmaster, son of a wealthy, austere, and very Christian father, is married to a woman as frigid as she is religious. He is the black sheep in a family of successful brothers and sisters. Not understood by his family and deeply worried by the suicide of his favourite sister Mukami, he withdraws to Ilmorog, to a life of passive non-commitment. The arrival of Wanja, coming to live with her grandmother Nyakinyua, seems to give a new meaning to his life, but she also suffers from her past. The daughter of a money-grubbing father and a more patriotic mother, seduced and abandoned by Kimeria, Wanja tries a new start in life as a barmaid. Haunted by guilt because she once killed her new-born baby sired by Kimeria, she now desperately wants another child. She will have one finally not by Karega but surprisingly by Abdulla. Karega is driven away from Wanja's love, and temporarily from Ilmorog, too, by the intrigues of Munira, turning more and more into a religious fanatic. Only Abdulla, after recurring ups and downs as a freedom fighter and business man, can realize his timid hopes, not only in his love for Wanja, but also in the educational progress of his adopted son Joseph.

Obviously then, the detective aspects have become superseded by a psychological interest in the characters. But in *Petals of Blood* Ngugi does not simply present four separate biographies, spun together in a narrative web of sympathy, love, jealousy, business, and communal interests. Again the historical dimension takes effect, and the four biographies are merged into structural unity by intricate patterns of relationship. Karega becomes the focal point. As it turns out, Karega is not only a former pupil of Munira, but also the unfortunate

14

lover of Munira's sister Mukami, who was driven to suicide in her insoluble conflict between love and paternal obedience. And, likewise, Karega happens to be the younger brother of Nding'uri, Abdulla's former companion in the Mau Mau struggle who, betrayed by Kimeria, was hanged by the British. This same Kimeria who once seduced Wanja and abandoned her when pregnant, who later acquired wealth, social reputation, influence and power in post-independent Kenya, who renewed sexual contact with Wanja and was finally stabbed by her. The concatenation of characters and events does not stop here as connecting links are made apparent everywhere, sometimes directly, sometimes in a loose or even symbolic way, but always accompanying the characters' efforts to come to terms with the past.

In structural terms this means that the unification of the narrations on different time levels is achieved through the characters. But here we must take into account another important trait of African fiction, namely that the characters often represent a cultural summary. In *Petals of Blood,* too, the four protagonists are representative figures: the teacher, the barmaid and good whore, the socialist agitator, the small trader, are all individuals and types at the same time. And though newcomers to Ilmorog, Munira, Wanja, Karega, and Abdulla embody the destiny of that village. All the tensions resulting from the clash between old (African) and new (Western) values can be traced in them as well as in the village.[3] The disillusioning spectacle of Old Ilmorog developing into New Ilmorog is the general theme of the novel, Ngugi's final aim. With this realization his plot structure becomes even more convincing, although we have to depart from the Western character concept focussing on individuals. *Petals of Blood* is a characteristic example of African's situational novel, "wherein not one person but an entire group of people (a village, a tribe, a clan) becomes ultimately affected (usually for the worse) by the major event of the narration".[4] Ultimately, the interplay of detective story, private biography, and village history is presented as a symbolic history of Africa in fiction. The same circular movement dominates in the experience of individuals as well as the group. It is a cyclical pattern[5] from exploitation through resistance and partial victory to new oppression or, as Ngugi calls the phases of European imperialism: "slavery, colonialism and neo-colonialism".[6] In the novel itself, the titles of the four parts, read together, provide its symbolic encoding: "Walking/Toward Bethlehem/ To Be Born/Again... La Luta Continua". The didactic message of its committed author Ngugi calls for unabashed resistance, now against the capitalism of black neo-colonialists, with the old battle-cry of the Mozambique freedom fighters.

Although the plot of *Petals of Blood* finally reveals itself as a plot of suffering and frustration, the characters are not simply to be pitied, as an examination of their

15

literary status will bear out. First of all, there is not only one protagonist but four main characters of equal importance. Karega and Abdulla contribute in the same way to the collective experience as Wanja and Munira, though the latter's portrait may perhaps seem to be sketched in stronger outlines. A radicalization of this African group concept might even suggest that the village Ilmorog is the true protagonist. Even if one does not go so far, the assumption of a collective body standing at the centre of the novel, cannot be doubted. Understandably, individual characterization is losing importance, and often ethnological material replaces psychological insights. And yet the question remains: what makes Munira, Wanja, Karega, and Abdulla so convincing and emotionally gripping? It is too easy to brand them as failures, although they have been shipwrecked several times in their lives. But, anti-heroes as they are, they have not given up fighting, driven forward by a strong idealism. Thus, in a moment of crisis, when the drought finally seems to be forcing Ilmorog to her knees, they show impressive activity and masculine energy. Abdulla in particular, living up to his heroic ideals of Kenya's fight for freedom, when catapulting an antilope "Abdulla became the hero of the journey".[7] Although their heroic glory does not even last till Nairobi, and humiliations and defeats build up thickly, the four protagonists lead the expedition to success. Clearly not the big shots, who are rather satirized and caricatured, but the small people win the reader's sympathy by acts of generosity and humanity. This is confirmed by the novel's ending, when Karega, now the author's mouthpiece, is confirmed by a token of solidarity in his conviction that "the system and its gods and its angels had to be fought consciously, consistently and resolutely by all the working people".[8] Thus the four protagonists attain heroic greatness only momentarily and only against the background of the community. When the community breaks up, however, as in New Ilmorog, the heroic stature of the representative individuals is likewise affected. Then the cyclical process of rise and fall has come full circle and has to be stimulated into a new movement.

An outstanding structural feature of *Petals of Blood*, causing much confusion at first, is Ngugi's handling of narrative mediation. There is not one stable point of view but several perspectives, and a negligent reader will often find difficulty in identifying the particular narrating "I". The technique of employing different narrators, which is further complicated by the continuous time shifts, is distinct right from the beginning. The novel starts with uncommented "showing" mainly through dialogue. In chapter 2 the narration is carried on first by a collective "we" originating obviously from Old Ilmorog, afterwards by a relatively neutral narrator, then by Munira and Wanja acting as temporary narrators. And in chapter 3, when Inspector Godfrey visits Munira in prison and provides him with pen and paper, the reader is tricked into the illusion that the whole story is altogether presented by the religious teacher.[9] The nature and function of these multiple points of view must be further analysed before Ngugi's experiments with the novel form can be evaluated.[10]

The repeated appearance of a narrative "we" is undoubtedly most unusual, and yet it can easily be accounted for. This voice is connected with traditional Ilmorog, even traditional Africa, and it is telling and commenting on events from within. This means that on the narrative plane, too, in addition to the employment of representative characters, the reader is imbued with a communal experience. But necessarily the "we"-point of view has only limited privilege and can never survey the whole. "How could we have known that Wanja's extension to Abdulla's shop would start it all?"[11] is a question typical of the interior perspective of the collective consciousness. Therefore Ngugi needs an additional narrator equipped with information to the full. In fact, the greatest part of *Petals of Blood* is told from such a near omniscient perspective by a third-person narrator. As usual with the auctorial narrative situation, much direct commentary comes along with the story. Thus the reader gradually comes to know the narrator as a black man, highly educated, familiar with African history and European literature, embittered by colonialism and therefore highly critical of Western cultural traits, and above all deeply committed to socialist values. But Ngugi's experiments do not stop here. Not only does he employ Munira as an additional first-person narrator, but all the other main characters take on a narrative role as well. This is easily overlooked because Munira alone attains prominence as a scribbler of "a mixture of an autobiographical confessional and some kind of prison notes".[12] The fact is that the main third-person narration is again and again enlivened with integrated stories by the four protagonists, and even the nameless lawyer, when they tell other characters their past experiences in the form of long first-person reminiscences. This is a further breakup of the novel's narrative situation and similarly an imitation of traditional African conversational habits. The inserted oral tales are no flashbacks but autonomous recollections, although the telling mode of the narrative "I" is often dramatized by passages of dialogue. Highly subjective in tone and therefore of limited reliability, the first-person narrations of the characters, i.e. of insiders, bring a valuable complement to the auctorial narrator's exterior perspective. And yet we get inside views of great depth from the latter, too, sometimes reflecting the characters' consciousness directly by means of free indirect speech and even interior monologue. As a result, the narrative situation of *Petals of Blood* is characterized by a multiplicity of perspectives, by varying identities hiding behind the narrative "I", and by the employment of all three essential types of narration.[13] With these devices, bringing the novel nearer to the drama, Ngugi has found another means of emphasizing the collective consciousness and the oral habits characteristic of an African experience of life. It remains to be questioned, however, whether these experiments with the narrative form, which will result

17

in the adoption of film techniques in a later novel[14], do not also lead to distracting confusion and unnecessary incongruities.

With all its technical ingenuity *Petals of Blood* is in the first place a political novel. For, behind the characters' destinies and behind the development of Ilmorog, the picture of contemporary Kenya emerges. It is a picture drawn with harsh strokes and dark colours. And yet it cannot be called pessimistic, because in spite of the obvious betrayal of ideas propagated by the independence movement, the search for a more humane world is never abandoned. In his fourth novel Ngugi blends many of the controversial topics he had exposed more fully in former novels – topics related to education, religion, the colonial alienation of land, or the humiliating conflicts of the people. The motives behind Ngugi's urge to write appear most distinctly in an essential theme permeating all the other aspects: the relation between past and present. The historical theme with its clashing ideological values is unfolded, in addition to action, characters, and narrative comment, through impressive symbols, charging the concrete African issues with a universal meaning.

The above analysis of the novel's structure has already shown an intimate interrelation between past und present time levels. Thematically, too, Ngugi probes deeply into the various aspects of the past so that critics have even been tempted to interpret *Petals of Blood* as a historical novel. But Ngugi is never aiming at a purely nostalgic evocation of Africa's past – though seeking a counterpoint to the patronizing Western assumption of its superior civilization. He is preoccupied rather with the philosophy of history, in the same way as W. B. Yeats and Chinua Achebe were (two of his many stimulating literary influences). With the "second coming" both Yeats and Achebe asserted a cyclical concept of history[15], and the rough beast of the apocalypse waiting to be born again is perceptible even in Ngugi's subtitles and mottoes. Furthermore, history evolving in a cyclical pattern and ever again resulting in the same division of the characters into haves and have-nots, oppressors and oppressed, heroes and traitors, good and bad is shown to have been virulent in Kenya from colonial beginnings through the Mau Mau rebellion to post-independent times. Thus Ngugi strives hard to convince the reader that only by acknowledging the past can the conditions of present Kenya be understood.[16] Taking over the concept of alienation into his diagnosis, Ngugi, not surprisingly, adopts devices from Marxism and psychoanalysis. Even the future is alluded to and, unlike Orwell's horrible anticipation, there are glimpses of hope in *Petals of Blood*.

Ngugi's hope rests on "the so-called victims, the poor, the down-trodden". The "true lesson of history" is that "the masses had always struggled [...] to end their oppression and exploitation: that they would continue struggling until a human kingdom came".[17] Although this is especially Karega's vision, other characters express similar concepts. This collective view of history, the view that "history after all is not a gallery of dashing heroes"[18], which gets particular prominence in an African context, is repeated in innumerable variations. And yet there is an awareness that "Africa, after all, did not have one but several pasts which were in perpetual struggle".[19] The novelist's way of illustrating the plurality of experiences takes effect through the characters. Not only do the private biographies of the four protagonists form the web of communal history, also seemingly minor figures, like the old woman Nyakinyua talking "as if the rhythm of the historic rise and fall of Ilmorog flowed in her veins"[20], gain a particular importance. Ngugi confronts numerous experiences in order to extract from them the *truth* of Africa's past. His self-concept of a writer embraces thus both the tasks of the novelist and the historian, and therefore reaches back as far as to Fielding and Scott.

Not satisfied, however, with these roles Ngugi, as so many African authors[21], sees himself as a teacher, too. The writer "being a kind of sensible needle" has not only to *register* the conflicts and tensions in his society, he must also *expose* the distorting values of the capitalist system.[22] Obviously Ngugi's committed didacticism is heavily imbued with Marxism, and it is particularly the one-sided obtrusiveness of his message which has sometimes been felt as a weakness of *Petals of Blood.* On the other hand there is the fervent wish behind his unsparing analysis of Kenya's present condition to show the way to a state of harmony and innocence. This is Ngugi's final *homecoming* to his people and their uninterrupted communion between present and past – though it may perhaps remain a myth. No doubt, this utopian humanism is understandable for a non-African reader, too.

The interrelation between past and present confirmed the novel's organic unity because of its being embodied in both form and theme. The same fusion holds true for the symbolism, for *Petals of Blood,* after all, is a highly symbolic novel. Especially fire and blood gain a symbolic status, though equally important on the plane of action and characterization. Fire, particularly connected with Wanja and her traumatic experiences with it, is finally the means of Munira's cleansing act, leading to the deaths of the new capitalists Chui, Mzigo, and Kimeria. Blood, the liquid of life, shed in the continuous struggle of the African people against the colonizers, seems to have been spilt in vain. For is it not sucked from the suffering masses after independence as before? Again the two key symbols are not left in isolation but intricately connected with the general theme of the novel. Munira realizes it, recollecting that he was "a privileged witness of the growth of Ilmorog from its beginnings in rain and drought to the present flowering in petals of blood".[23] There is, in fact, a real red-petalled flower associated with blood and fire, the plant with which Theng'eta is brewed. Once more Ngugi's symbolism is loaded with meaningful ambiguity. On the one hand, Nyakinyua's renewal of the old art of Theng'eta brewing and its ritual magic announces a new birth to Ilmorog. The first drinking of the drug brings about visionary insights into the past, realizations of moments of failure and suffering, but also an urge for a new beginning. And it brings temporary wealth for Wanja and Abdulla. But only too soon the magic of Theng'eta turns negative: the same time as the drink degenerates into a popular means of intoxication, it is appropriated by the black capitalists and becomes an additional instrument of exploitation and power. Thus Karega's Marxist hopes are distinctly counterpoised by the symbol's rather pessimistic connotations. And another ominous charge is heaped on the red-petalled flower. It can be realized through the motto containing the novel's title, which is taken from a poem by the black Caribbean writer Derek Walcott. In "The Swamp" "petals of blood" is one among a series of images conveying rot and aberration. And though Ngugi's novel does not lead to a swampy chaos in the end, the negative impact of Walcott's title imagery is always imminent.[24]

Although much remains unsaid, it should have become clear that *Petals of Blood* is a great African novel: aesthetically, by its structural network and the reflection of content through experiment with form; historically, by providing a comprehensive understanding to Africa's crucial themes through the exploration of the past; and also – though with reservations – politically, by the clear-cut diagnosis of Kenya's present problems. In many ways *Petals of Blood* is typical of anglophone African writing, though in West-African areas identical topics, e.g. that of history, are perhaps rendered in different details. It is understandable when a writer committed to Africa's cause like Ngugi, is searching for a linguistic medium other than English.[25] With regard to an international readership, however, it can only be regretted if he in future writes in Gikuyu, although he is living now in self-chosen exile. Of course, there is always the possibility of a translation. Let us hope that Ngugi will, at least, continue to be his own translator into English.

Notes

1 The misleading term "frame" occurs in several interpretations of *Petals of Blood*, e.g. in Robson, C. B.: *Ngugi wa Thiong'o.* London, 1979, p. 95.
2 *Petals of Blood.* London, 1986 (¹1977), p. 332.
3 Cf. Pelsmaekers, K.: "A Hybrid Poetics in Ngugi's *Petals of Blood*". *The Commonwealth Novel in English* 2, 1983, 7–26.
4 Larson, C. R.: *The Emergence of African Fiction.* London, ²1978 (¹1971), p. 19.
5 Cf. Stratton, F.: "Cyclical Patterns in *Petals of Blood*". *The Journal of Commonwealth Literature* 15, 1980, 115–124.
6 Ngugi, "Author's Note" in *Homecoming.* New York, 1972, p. XV.
7 *PoB*, p. 134.
8 Ibid., p. 344.
9 Cf. *PoB*, p. 41: "Twelve years later, on a Sunday, Godfrey Munira tried to reconstruct that scene in a statement to the police [...]." "How does one tell of murder in a New Town? Murder of the spirit? Where does one begin?" (Ibid., p. 45).
10 Cf. Stratton, F.: "Narrative Method in the Novels of Ngugi". – In Jones, E. D. (Ed.): *African Literature Today 13. Recent Trends in the Novel.* London, 1983, pp. 122–135.
11 *PoB*, p. 264.
12 Cf. *PoB*, p. 190. Also pp. 44, 45, 117–118, 226, 243.
13 I.e. auctorial presentation, personal reflection, first-person narration. Cf. the system of F. K. Stanzel in *Theorie des Erzählens.* Göttingen, ²1982 (¹1979).
14 In a recent interview (conducted on 30 March 1985) Ngugi said: "In film I can combine my interest in the theatre and in fiction, to create something. In my new novel, *Matigari ma Njirugi*, I have been influenced by film technique." (From *The Journal of Commonwealth Literature* 21, 1986, 166).
15 Cf. Yeats's poem "The Second Coming" and Achebe's key novel for Africa *Things Fall Apart.*
16 In Karega's words: "To understand the present [...] you must understand the past. To know where you are, you must know where you came from." (*PoB*, p. 127f.) Cf. also Munira's vision: "There past – present – future were one [...]." (p. 212).
17 *PoB*, p. 303.
18 Ibid., p. 241.
19 Ibid., p. 214.
20 Ibid., p. 123.
21 Cf. Achebe, Ch.: "The Novelist as Teacher". – In *Morning Yet on Creation Day. Essays.* London, 1975.
22 Ngugi, *Homecoming.* Cf. esp. "Author's Note", "The Writer and His Past", and "The Writer in a Changing Society".
23 *PoB*, p. 45.
24 Cf. Killam, G. D.: "A Note on the Title of *Petals of Blood*". *The Journal of Commonwealth Literature* 15, 1980, 125–132.
25 Cf. Ngugi's recent book on "The Politics of Language in African Literature": *Decolonising the Mind.* London, 1986.

HEINZ ANTOR

The Bloomsbury Group

Its Philosophy, Aesthetics, and Literary Achievement

1986. 148 Seiten. Kartoniert DM 30,– (Forum Anglistik)

ISBN 3-533-03794-0

This book pursues a twofold aim. It provides an introduction to the Bloomsbury Group as a sociocultural phenomenon of the first half of our century. The author traces the circle's development from its origins at Cambridge University to the early 1940s, when the group had practically ceased to exist. The vivid controversy sparked off by the "Bloomsberries" and by their ideas is described from the earliest polemics of 1910 to the more sober analyses of the 1980s. The second aim of this study is to depict Bloomsbury's philosophical interests, especially in the ethics of the Cambridge philosopher G. E. Moore, and the latter's influence on the circle's aesthetic and literary theories. In this context, special reference is made to the works of Roger Fry and Clive Bell as well as those by Virginia Woolf and E. M. Forster. The reader's attention is drawn to Bloomsbury's emphasis on the interdependence of the arts and an extra chapter is devoted to modern aspects of Bloomsbury's beliefs. The book is rounded off with a chronological table covering the period from 1899 to 1981.

ANDREAS HÖFELE

Parodie und literarischer Wandel

Studien zur Funktion einer Schreibweise in der englischen Literatur des ausgehenden 19. Jahrhunderts

1986. 245 Seiten. Kartoniert DM 78,–. Leinen DM 108,–

(Anglistische Forschungen / 185)

ISBN 3-533-03713-4 / 3-533-03714-2

Wenn die Parodie im Unterhaltungsangebot der viktorianischen *periodical literature* als mehr oder weniger harmloser 'Neben-Gesang' ernster Werke eine enorme Popularität genießt, andererseits aber als prägender Bestandteil in die Werkstruktur einiger Schlüsseltexte der Moderne eingeht, so stellt sich die Frage, wie und unter welchen Bedingungen ein Formen- und Funktionswandel sich vollzieht, der die parodistische Schreibart von ihrer traditionellen Randposition ins Zentrum literarischer Innovation rücken läßt.
Die vorliegende Studie geht dieser Frage in den Werken dreier repräsentativer Autoren des englischen *fin de siècle* nach: Algernon Charles Swinburne, Oscar Wilde und Max Beerbohm. Exemplarisch tritt bei ihnen eine Ambivalenz hervor, die letztlich aus Aporien der romantischen Poetik herrührt, aber auch noch der Avantgarde des 20. Jhs. (Joyce, Eliot und ihren Nachfolgern) auferlegt bleibt: Parodie ist stets Symptom der Erschöpfung innovatorischer Möglichkeiten, zugleich aber auch die Möglichkeit, aus der Erschöpfung erneut schöpferischen Spielraum zu gewinnen.

CARL WINTER · UNIVERSITÄTSVERLAG · HEIDELBERG

Elmar Lehmann, Essen

"we will tell freedom".
Mbulelo Vizikhungo Mzamane's *The Children of Soweto*

1.

> remember
> as though motherless or even lifeless
> how we walked the night
> the loveless streets
> owned by so cruel such merciless emissaries who
> speak foreign tongues[1]

Quarry '78–'79, a magazine of contemporary South African writing, published extracts from the correspondence between editor and writer Lionel Abrahams and biographer and literary critic Ursula A. Barnett.[2] In her letters, Miss Barnett argues that only the literature written by black South Africans can really be called South African literature. Only blacks, she dismisses Mr. Abrahams' angry protest, are "part of the [South African and African] context" whereas white authors don't belong because they "can look forward and backward and across only to Europe".[3]

If Miss Barnett is right, then, of course, the West German reading public has not even realized yet that a South African literature exists. The works of some white writers such as Alan Paton and Nadine Gordimer, André Brink and Elsa Joubert have been translated into German and are taken care of by well-known publishing firms and influential reviewers. Black writers, however, Alex La Guma or Es'kia Mphahlele, Bessie Head or Lauretta Ngcobo, to name only a few, are completely unknown to the general public and to many, perhaps most, English Literature lecturers in this country.

Even if we don't subscribe to Miss Barnett's radicalism, we must at least accept that the black authors are as legitimate and competent interpreters of the South African situation as their white colleagues. They may not use our language of liberal humanism and middle-of-the-road policies, and their literature may not be up to the standards of postmodernism. But, then, they have their own language, geared to their political needs, they have preserved their own version of South Africa's history and they will certainly play the all-important role in the making of South Africa's future.

it were us it is us
who were taught by history
that terror before the will of the people
is like a sheep in the mouth of a crocodile
here we go again
we have learnt from so many cruel nights
that oppressors are guilty forever
and we know that we will move.[4]

In two autobiographical pieces, Mbulelo Mzamane, born in 1948, describes his "apprenticeship as a writer in the late 1960s".[5] The young author turns to the short story as his favoured genre and "attempt[s] to bring out the variety of life in Soweto"[6], using relatives and friends as his source of inspiration and as only thinly disguised principal characters.[7] The choice of the short story is strongly influenced by Mzamane's admiration for a group of writers of the 1950s. Most of these writers were connected with *Drum* magazine and went into exile in the 1960s.[8] Mphahlele's famous autobiography of his early life, *Down Second Avenue*[9], is (in Stephen Gray's words) "the archetypal story of the black South African intellectual of the 1950s".[10] The Johannesburg pieces of Nat Nakasa[11] and Can Themba's essay and stories[12] represent the quality of the writing of the period and reveal much of the decade's milieu.

Mzamane pays homage to the fifties' generation, and to Themba in particular, when he calls one of his stories, *Dube Train Revisited,* and thus recalls Themba's frequently anthologized story, *The Dube Train.*[13] His admiration, however, is not without qualification. Looking back on his pre-1976 writing, he comments:

> Despite what I now perceive as some positive elements in my early work, I was always painfully aware of a groping, of something lacking in my work, the absence of an ideological framework [...].[14]

This criticism is certainly meant to be extended to the black literature of the fifties. There is no ideology behind Themba's desperate cynicisms nor behind the resigned bitterness and the "sense of release"[15] experienced by Mphahlele when he left the country.

For the younger author, "the absence of an ideological framework" leads to long years of silence.[16] During most of the seventies, Mzamane seems to have been unable to reconcile his idea of literature as art with the urge to express his political commitment effectively. In 1980, when he started on a new book, the Black Consciousness Movement and the Soweto uprising of June 1976 had radically changed the situation and offered a solution to the creative writer's problems.

it were us, it is us
the children of Soweto
langa, kagiso, alexandra, gugulethu and nyanga
us
a people with a long history of resistance
us
who will dare the mighty
for it is freedom, only freedom which can quench our
   thirst –
we did learn from terror that it is us who will seize
   history
our freedom.[17]

A "Policy Manifesto" of the South African Students' Organisation (SASO) defines Black Consciousness as an "attitude of the mind", as a rejection of all the value systems "that seek to make him [the black] a foreigner in the country of his birth":

The Blackman must build up his own value systems, see himself as self-defined and not as defined by others.

And:

[...] therefore, we believe that in all matters relating to the struggle towards realizing our aspirations, Whites must be excluded [...].[18]

It is the Black Consciousness Movement that brought about an important change in the pragmatics of black South African literature. In an essay on Mongane Serote's poetry, Mzamane emphasizes the difference between the protest literature of the older generation of writers and the literature written by Serote and others. The protest literature is addressed to a primarily white audience and appeals to white readers "for a change of heart in their attitude to Blacks".[19] The younger authors, on the other hand, address themselves to the black community. Realizing that the whites have long ago brutally closed the "chapter of dialogue"[20], these writers want

[...] to foster group sentiment and solidarity among Blacks because [...] the solution to the problems of Black people in South Africa lies collectively with the Blacks themselves. [...] the use of traditional oral forms and township linguistic usages, the simplicity and the persuasive tone of the language, are a direct outcome of the process whereby Blacks are talking among themselves.[21]

In *The Children of Soweto* Mzamane follows the precept he discusses in his essay on Serote. It is the black community that is the hero and, at the same time, the addressee of the book while the writer adopts the role of the traditional African poet:

> As a chronicler, I chose the role of the traditional *griot*, who is the custodian of his people's oral tradition, their verse and songs, their history and their culture of resistance.[22]

4.

> remember
> how you or i or any of us
> with a voluptuous lust for death
> how we got drunk
> with whiskey, dagga and religions
> remember the shattering despair to feel as worthless
>   as debris[23]

Mzamane's *The Children of Soweto* is a "trilogy", consisting of three independent, yet interrelated stories: "My Schooldays in Soweto", "The Day of the Riots", "The Children of Soweto".[24] The stories are clearly separated insofar as there is a different set of characters in each of them, and there is no plot that develops from the first through the second to the last story. The trilogy is, however, more than a mere collection of stories. Taken together, these stories present an account of the student uprising in Soweto in 1976.

The first story, "My Schooldays in Soweto", gives a detailed description of the situation leading to the explosion of June 16, from the viewpoint of a group of schoolboys. "The Day of the Riots" tells the story of a white salesman and his black assistant who are trapped in Soweto after the outbreak of violence. The third and by far the longest story recounts the events of the uprising and its aftermath as seen from the inside, through the eyes of some of the leading members of the SSRC (Soweto Students' Representative Council).[25]

"My Schooldays in Soweto" is a story in the vein of Mzamane's earlier collection. As in the 'Jim comes to Jo'burg' sequence in *Mzala*[26], the narrator is, once again, the son of a minister, and the not so carefree spirit of the duel of wits between the boys and their teachers, Pakade and Phakoe (who "drank like twin sponges"; p. 3), reminds one of the resourcefulness and the "originality in surviving"[27] so characteristic of the Sowetans in the earlier stories:

> Our ability to supply dumb answers, to turn into obsequious samboes, to transform our whole personalities instantaneously when conditions so dic-

tated – these qualities had been nurtured in us very early in our youth in our daily intercourse with the white man, as caddies at his golf courses, carrierboys at his markets, illegal hawkers of sweets and peanuts in his trains and pilferers of sundry goods from his supermarkets. (p. 7)

The cleverness of the boys and the sportsmanship of their encounters with the two teachers either at school or in Shirley Scott's *shebeen* cannot, for a moment, conceal the real grievances felt by the students.

They are the victims of Bantu Education, of a systematic and legalized discrimination of the white regime against the black population: "[...] natives will be taught from childhood to realize that equality with Europeans is not for them [....]."[28] Instructed by often poorly qualified teachers in badly housed and barely equipped schools, their education has a predominantly "practical orientation" (p. 28). In this way, the 'native' is not only trained to accept the subordinate role prescribed for him in white South Africa, but it is also the kind of education that, according to Apartheid ideology, conforms to the black's 'racial qualities'. To make things worse, there is the language problem. Under the regulations of Bantu Education, the mother tongue (an African language) is used as the medium of instruction at primary school level, while English *and* Afrikaans are to be used in the secondary school. Without enough teachers with the necessary language proficiency, most schools had not been able to follow this regulation, when, in 1976, the Department of Bantu Education

[...] announced to have at least half the subjects in every school taught in Afrikaans with effect from the following year. Up to that time English had been the sole medium of instruction in our school. (p. 37)

The quality of this education is summed up by one of the story's characters:

The truly marvellous thing about our system of education [...] is not that the black child in this country gets a poor education, but that he gets any education at all. (p. 30)

The plan to enforce the introduction of Afrikaans as a medium of instruction caused unrest and strikes in Soweto and ultimately led to the demonstration of June 16 and to the uprising not only in Soweto but also in many other townships in South Africa.

"My Schooldays in Soweto" shows how difficult it is for the students to fight the system. Subjected to Bantu Education, they know next to nothing of their people's history, of African literature, of social and political theory. Isolated and left alone, they have yet to develop their organisational skills and to learn how to achieve unity. But they are eager to learn and they learn quickly whenever they get a chance.

27

Pakade and Phakoe may not be images of the respectable teacher, but they are able, in their own roundabout way, to introduce some of the great African writers to their students: Ngugi Wa Thiong'o (p. 10), Wole Soyinka (p. 20), Chinua Achebe (p. 21), and others. The teachers' allusions to some of the protest movements of the past and to Black Consciousness offer the students the opportunity to see their own frustration and their protest in perspective. More or less accidentally, the students even get hold of some socialist classics, bought long ago and perhaps never read by their parents. Although they may not be able to pronounce 'dialectical materialism' properly, let alone understand what it means, they do feel the need and find ways to "conscientise the student mass" (p. 24), and they do know how to assert their intellectual superiority and to irritate the enemy when they "adopt the state's motto – 'Een drag maak mag (Unity is Strength)'" as their own (p. 41).

5.

remember –
ask any child or mother
who are penned in the night of the system
ask any father
about the weight of despair
about the assault of fear on love
when gunfire shatters the night
and the running, terrified footsteps merge with
        the heartbeat
a heartbeat gone mad with horror[29]

The second story, "The Day of the Riots", concentrates on a black-and-white relationship in its usual South African form – between the (white) 'baas' and the (black) 'boy'.

Accompanied by Sipho, his assistant from Soweto, Johannesburg based salesman Johannes Venter canvasses north-western Transvaal. He almost completely relies on Sipho to do their business because the black speaks "all the languages of the people among whom they" work (p. 67), and it is Sipho who apparently organizes their occasional pleasure trips to Gaborone in Botswana, where Venter can enjoy black women without fearing the Immorality Act.[30]

Venter is one of those middle-of-the-road racists who adopts the prejudices of the society he lives in. He probably would not consciously maltreat a black, but he certainly would not befriend his assistant. He respects Sipho's unobtrusive efficiency, and when he discovers that Sipho has a university degree, he is even willing to recommend him for promotion. When Sipho declines the offer, Venter reacts in the conventional way, mixing prejudice with utter carelessness about his companion's motives:

> Johannes thought that there was certainly some grain of truth in what was said about the Bantu being temperamentally unsuited for positions of authority and responsibility. (p. 66)

What Venter does not care about and is perhaps unable to comprehend is that Sipho simply cannot afford to parade his qualifications. Being black, he must hide the fact that he is educated because, being educated, makes him a suspect and can cost him his job.

Sipho does not just hide his qualifications from his employer, but he generally behaves "with self-effacement in the presence of white people".[31] He accepts the role of the 'boy' and, although he knows that the 'baas' is dependent upon him, he would never dream of being the white man's equal.

The relationship between 'boy' and 'baas', its ideological and legal context and content, the way in which the characters of the oppressor and the oppressed are distorted and their lives destroyed, is of course a perennial theme in South African literature. Mphahlele's famous story, *Mrs. Plum*, and Miriam Tlali's *Muriel at Metropolitan*[32] deal with the subject from the point of view of black characters. Dan Jacobson in *The Trap*, Nadine Gordimer in *Ah, Woe Is Me* or Doris Lessing in *A Home for the Highland Cattle*[33] describe the white liberal who despite his opposition to Apartheid and his enlightened attitude towards blacks in general dismally fails to understand, let alone to help the individual black he or she is dealing with.

In Sipho's case, it is fear that dictates his behaviour, fear of losing his job, of being hurt or of seeing his wife and children hurt. When his children sing protest songs he stops them because he is afraid of the police (pp. 55f.). When he can save Venter's life as well as his own only by keeping the company car, he hesitates to do so because it is against company rules (pp. 65f., 72). For Sipho being the 'boy' is a kind of protection, a precarious safeguard against the dangers of being black.

Fear of the Apartheid system and fear of the students who fight the system almost paralyse Sipho when he and Venter drive into Soweto and meet a protest march. "Gone mad with horror" he hides Venter in his house overnight so that the students will not kill him, and drunk with liquor and with fear, early next morning he takes Venter home, hidden away in the boot of the company car. Once again, it is the black 'boy' who, to save himself, has to risk his life for the white 'baas'.

moving
the night giving us sanctuaries
the day witness but silent
it will be us
steel-taut to fetch freedom
and –
we will tell freedom
we are no more strangers now.[34]

Mzamane's *The Children of Soweto* belongs to a group of literary texts by black authors dealing with the Soweto uprising in 1976. Other works include Miriam Tlali's *Amandla*, Sipho Sepamla's *A Ride on the Whirlwind* and Mongane Serote's *To Every Birth Its Blood*.[35] Mzamane's trilogy, or at any rate its title story, differs from the works just mentioned, at least from Sepamla's and Serote's works, insofar as it can be called a non-fiction novel or story,

> [...] a day-to-day account of student activities as narrated by one of them who is writing from exile in Botswana. I have tried to limit the work to a strict time sequence by compressing all the action, which in real life took place over a year, to one week. [...] in a way, these events were so remarkable that the need to fictionalise does not arise.[36]

Richard Rive's novel, *Emergency*, recounting the events of Sharpeville in March 1960[37], or D. M. Zwelonke's *Robben Island*[38] and much of the South African prison literature belong to the same class of texts as "The Children of Soweto".

The non-fiction character of the third story is indicated, first, by the fact that the principal characters in the story are the student leaders listed in the author's "Acknowledgements" that are prefixed to the trilogy. Thus, 'Khotso' is, of course, Khotso Seathlolo, president of the SSRC during the uprising. The narrator also includes a number of documents, articles from newspapers (pp. 95–97, 237), an SSRC circular (pp. 125f.) and a pamphlet distributed by the Transvaal Chamber of Industries which attacks the students and warns the black labourers not to stay away from work (p. 222).[39] In addition, some passages of the story, although not directly taken from newspapers, read like they were written by a journalist, for example, the passage where the narrator gives an account of Chief Buthelezi's activities in 1976 (pp. 228f.).

However, in Mzamane's case the use of the term 'non-fiction' with its implications of the Western debate on the status of fiction and the nature of narrative is perhaps misleading. In his essay on "The Uses of Traditional Oral Forms" Mzamane says:

The book [*The Children of Soweto*] has been written to preserve the memory of these events, as in the 'tales' of my people I was told as a child.

And, he adds,

My book is a record of the attempt to create a new collective consciousness, for which Black Consciousness in South Africa stands.[40]

The Children of Soweto, then, is meant to be a 'history' of the events of 1976, a true account of the uprising set against the many only partially true or even false accounts. At the same time, it is a story that recreates the feeling and the state of mind of the blacks at an important point in their "long history of resistance" – and it is in itself a direct expression of this state of mind. In this last respect, the title story certainly resembles Serote's *No More Strangers* or the Soweto poems in Don Mattera's *Azanian Love Song*, or the poems in Sepamla's collection, *The Soweto I love*.[41] Take, for example, the many poems and songs in "The Children of Soweto"[42] or the following prose passage from the story and compare it with some lines from Mattera's *A New Time*...:

We were the children of the new diaspora, we, the children of Soweto, germinating everywhere we went little seeds of vengeance, hatred, bitterness, wrath, on the fertile soil of our hearts, watering our cherished seeds with our own blood, sweat and tears and that of our people. (p. 244)

Children singing from the graves:
  It is their year;
  All years belong to the Children
  The beginning years
  And the end years
  Earned with their blood...[43]

As Mzamane himself points out, "The Children of Soweto" is without doubt a "day-to-day account" of the uprising. This means, it is structured according to the chronology of events in Soweto. It is a story full of incidents, small and important, private and public, comic and tragic. It tells of the hectic life of the students in those days and weeks following June 16. It recalls the many things the students knew nothing about and the many things they had to learn, often at great cost. In the following passage they try to understand a totally biased report of their demonstration written by a black journalist:

'I've just heard it said that they've no real say in the final form a report takes,' Duke said. 'That's the job of the editor.'
'But he's also black,' Micky said.
'They say he, too, has no control over ... what do they call it? ... Something like a newspaper's manifesto.'

'Editorial policy,' Khotso said.
'Yes, that's it,' Duke said. 'The editorial policy is determined by the prop...'
'Proletarians?' Micky asked.
'No, sounds more like "property",' Duke said. (p. 100)

And this is a girl's first encounter with the police:

> '*Wat is jou naam?*' the old man at the reception desk enquired.
> 'Bella Mohlakoane.'
> [...] 'Bella Jojo Mohlakoane?'
> 'Yes, sir.'
> 'Yes, what?' the younger man asked.
> 'Yes, *Meneer.*'
> '*Meneer is 'n kaffir predikant, jong*! Yes, what?'
> 'Yes, *Baas.*' (p. 182)

The actual events of the uprising find expression in the loose and episodic structure of the title story. At the same time, however, the story is structured by a closely knit sequence of events which take place within a week. It begins with the death of one of the students, Muntu (which means 'Everyman'), who is shot by the police. It culminates in the long wake for Muntu and his funeral (pp. 193–219), and it ends with a kind of epilogue which sees the narrator and some of his friends in exile in Botswana.

It is during and through the funeral that the Sowetans express their "new collective consciousness". The parents and students unite in mourning during the funeral, and through the funeral they assert their solidarity and their will to fight. They turn the funeral into a political demonstration against the oppressive system, and they express their protest through the traditional forms of a funeral. They discover "strength in unity" during the funeral, and they achieve 'self-definition' through the funeral.

But, of course, the police brutally disperses the crowd and, one by one, the leaders of the SSRC have to flee the country. Only in exile can the narrator recreate the history and the state of mind of the Sowetans in 1976, and perhaps it reveals the cruelty and tragedy of the South African situation that a book whose hero and addressee is the community of Soweto could only be written far away from the place, in Aberystwyth (Wales) where Mzamane "found just such surroundings as I wished for".[44] As yet, it seems to be impossible "to tell freedom" within South Africa.

1 The verses are taken from Mongane Wally Serote's poem, "No More Strangers", published in Serote: *Selected Poems*. Ed. M. V. Mzamane. Johannesburg, 1982, pp. 135–137; the passage quoted is on p. 135.

2 Barnett, U. A., Abrahams, L.: "Does the White Writer Belong?" – In Abrahams, L. (Ed.): *Quarry '78–'79. New South African Writing.* Johannesburg, 1979, pp. 167–176. Abrahams has edited several collections of South African literature and is the author of a novel. Miss Barnett has written a biography of Es'kia Mphahlele (New York, 1977) and *A Vision of Order. A Study of Black South African Literature in English (1914–1980)*. London, 1983.

3 The quotations are from Miss Barnett's final letter, *Quarry '78–'79*, p. 175.

4 Serote: "No More Strangers", p. 136.

5 Mzamane has contributed a short statement to *Momentum. On Recent South African Writing*. Eds. M. J. Daymond, J. U. Jacobs, M. Lenta. Pietermaritzburg, 1984, pp. 301–304. The second autobiographical piece, "I Remember...", introduces *Mzala. The Stories of Mbulelo Mzamane* (Staffrider Series, 5). Johannesburg, n. d. [1980], pp. vii–xii. This collection was published in England as *My Cousin Comes to Jo'burg and Other Stories* (Drumbeat, 41). Harlow, 1981.

6 *Momentum*, p. 301.

7 Cf. "I remember...", p. xi.

8 Cf. Lewis Nkosi's essay, "The Fabulous Decade: The Fifties". – In Nkosi, L.: *Home and Exile*. London, 1965, pp. 3–34, and N. Chabani Manganyi: *Exiles and Homecomings. A Biography of Es'kia Mphahlele*. Johannesburg, 1983, pp. 122–130. On the early history of *Drum* cf. Anthony Sampson: *Drum: A Venture into the New Africa*. London, 1986.

9 London, 1959.

10 *Southern African Literature. An Introduction*. Cape Town, 1979, p. 195.

11 *The World of Nat Nakasa. Selected Writings of the Late Nat Nakasa*. Introduction by N. Gordimer. Ed. E. Patel. Johannesburg, 1975.

12 *The Will to Die*. Eds. D. Stuart, R. Holland. (African Writers Series, 104). London, 1972.

13 Mzamane's story was published in *Mzala*, pp. 146–152, Themba's story in *The Will to Die*, pp. 57–62.

14 *Momentum*, p. 302. – Mzamane's early work are the stories collected in *Mzala* and written in the late sixties (cf. *Momentum*, p. 301).

15 *Down Second Avenue*, p. 221.

16 For all the biographical details in this paragraph see *Momentum*, pp. 303f.

17 Serote: "No More Strangers", p. 135. – Mzamane uses these lines as the motto to his *The Children of Soweto*.

18 This undated pamphlet (1972/1974?) was published under SASO's Durban address. A copy of the pamphlet is in the large collection of documents in the Centre for Southern African Studies in the University of York. I have to thank the director of the Centre and the staff of the Borthwick Institute, where the collection is housed, for allowing me to consult the collection in September 1986, for their kind help and for supplying copies of the material whenever possible. – There is a detailed analysis of Black Consciousness in Mokgethi Motlhabi: *The Theory and Practice of Black Resistance to Apartheid. A Social-Ethical Analysis*. Johannesburg, 1984, pp. 106–153,

and a short essay by Gisela Albrecht: „Der Aufstand in den Köpfen. Steve Biko und die Bewegung der Black Consciousness". – In Albrecht, G.: *Soweto oder Der Aufstand der Vorstädte. Gespräche mit Südafrikanern.* Reinbek, 1977, pp. 228–249.

19 Mzamane's "Introduction" to Serote's *Selected Poems,* p. 10.

20 In Winnie Mandela's *Part of My Soul* (Ed. A. Benjamin. Harmondsworth, 1985) there is a passage called "The Chapter of Dialogue Is Finally Closed" (pp. 118–128).

21 "Introduction" to Serote's *Selected Poems,* p. 12.

22 *Momentum,* p. 304. Cf. Mzamane's essay, "The Uses of Traditional Oral Forms in Black South African Literature". – In White, L., Couzens, T. (Eds.): *Literature and Society in South Africa.* Harlow, 1984, pp. 147–160. On the "griot" cf. R. Finnegan: *Oral Literature in Africa* (Oxford Library of African Literature). Nairobi, 1970, pp. 96–98.

23 Serote: "No More Strangers", pp. 135f.

24 I quote from the following edition: (Drumbeat, 60), Harlow, 1982. The trilogy was also published (and banned) in South Africa as No. 13 of Staffrider Series. – Further references to the Drumbeat edition are included in parentheses in the text.

25 There is an informative account of the uprising by Reinhard Brückner: "Soweto 1976 – Der Aufstand der Vorstädte", in G. Albrecht's already mentioned *Soweto oder Der Aufstand der Vorstädte,* pp. 9–28. See also G. Davis, M. Senior: *South Africa – The Privileged and the Dispossessed.* 2 vols. Paderborn, 1983–1985, pp. 104–109 in the Students' Book and pp. 337–359 in the Teacher's Book.

26 The first part of Mzamane's collection (five stories) uses the familiar motif of the naive rural black confronted with life in Jo'burg.

27 *Momentum,* p. 301.

28 This is a quotation from a speech by the Minister of Native Affairs, Dr. H. F. Verwoerd, on 17 September 1953. There is a passage on Bantu Education in G. Davis, M. Senior: *South Africa – The Privileged and the Dispossessed,* pp. 350–359 in the Teacher's Book; the quotation from Verwoerd is on p. 351. Cf. E. H. Brookes: *Apartheid. A Documentary Study of Modern South Africa.* London, 1968, pp. 41–60, and Th. R. H. Davenport: *South Africa. A Modern History.* Toronto, 1977, pp. 347–349.

29 Serote: "No More Strangers", p. 135.

30 Cf. Brookes: *Apartheid,* pp. 179–186.

31 Ezekiel Mphahlele: *The African Image.* London, 1974 ([1]1962), p. 158.

32 *Mrs. Plum* was published in Mphahlele's collection, *In Corner B.* Nairobi, 1967, pp. 164–208. Miriam Tlali's short novel was published as No. 8 in the Drumbeat Series (Harlow, 1979).

33 *The Trap.* London, 1955. – *Ah, Woe Is Me,* now in Nadine Gordimer's collection, *Some Monday for Sure* (African Writers Series, 177). London, 1976, pp. 6–13; the short story was originally published in 1953. – *A Home for the Highland Cattle* now in Doris Lessing's *Collected African Stories.* Vol. 1. London, 1979, pp. 231–286; the short novel first appeared in 1953; although not strictly South African, I do include Doris Lessing; cf. Stephen Gray's "Introduction" to his edition of *The Penguin Book of Southern African Stories.* Harmondsworth, 1985, pp. 7–12.

34 Serote: "No More Strangers", p. 137.

35 *Amandla* (Staffrider Series, 6). Johannesburg, 1980. – *A Ride on the Whirlwind* (African Writers Series, 268). London, 1984; South African edition 1981. – *To Every Birth Its Blood* (Staffrider Series, 12). Johannesburg, 1981. – Cf. D. Barboure: "Mongane

Serote: Humanist and Revolutionary". – In Daymond, M. J., Jacobs, J. U., Lenta, M. (Eds.): *Momentum*, pp. 171–181.
36 Mzamane: "The Uses of Traditional Oral Forms", p. 159.
37 London, 1964.
38 (African Writers Series, 128). London, 1973.
39 Quite a number of these circulars and pamphlets, typed or handwritten, are in the collection of the Centre for Southern African Studies. There are some German translations in G. Albrecht's *Soweto oder Der Aufstand der Vorstädte*, pp. 47–51. N. Gordimer includes an SSRC pamphlet in her novel, *Burger's Daughter*. Harmondsworth, 1980, pp. 346f.; the novel was originally published in 1979.
40 "The Uses of Traditional Oral Forms", p. 159.
41 *Azanian Love Song* (Skotaville Series, 1). Johannesburg, 1983. – *The Soweto I Love*. London, 1977.
42 Poems by M. Langa, L. Tladi, M. Gwala and others are included on pp. 79, 125, 151, 198, 211f., 216, 217, 245.
43 *Azanian Love Song*, p. 79.
44 *Momentum*, p. 303.

anglistik & englischunterricht

Preis der Bände 3–27 DM 20,–. Ab Band 28 DM 25,–.
Jahresabonnement DM 50,–. Studentenabonnement DM 39,–.

CARL WINTER · UNIVERSITÄTSVERLAG · HEIDELBERG

Horst Prießnitz, Wuppertal

"Stray echoes from the elder sons of Song": The 'Dialogue' with British Literature in Twentieth Century Australian Poetry

The two "Prefatory Sonnets" which Henry Kendall set at the head of his 1869 volume of poems, *Leaves from an Australian Forest*, present in a half apologetic, half programmatic fashion an approach to the writing of poetry which the modern critic might call intertextual:[1]

1

[...]
I have no faultless fruits to offer you
    Who read this book; but certain syllables
    Herein are borrowed from unfooted dells,
And secret hollows dear to noontide dew;
And these at least, though far between and few,
    May catch the sense like subtle forest spells.

2

So take these kindly, even though there be
    Some notes that unto other lyres belong:
    Stray echoes from the elder sons of Song;
And think how from its neighbouring, native sea
The pensive shell doth borrow melody.
    I would not do the lordly masters wrong,
    By filching fair words from the shining throng
Whose music haunts me, as the wind a tree!
    Lo, when a stranger, in soft Syrian glooms
Shot through with sunset, treads the cedar dells,
    And hears the breezy ring of elfin bells
    Far down by where the white-haired cataract booms,
He, faint with sweetness caught from forest smells,
    Bears thence, unwitting, plunder of perfumes.[2]

The lines surprise us for two reasons: that the author should beg his reader to understand his borrowings from the "elder sons of Song" as both inevitable and natural – as inevitable, in fact, as the processes of nature; and that the author who makes this plea is a late romantic colonial poet, who, if Laurence Lerner's thesis is correct, should have no business conceding such dependency at all. For Lerner sees romanticism and realism as phases of negated intertextuality.[3] There is indeed a fundamental contradiction between the desire of romanticism to replace the highly cultivated conventions of literature with the speech of the people, expressing directly, with no visible external support, the truths of feeling, and the declaration of the colonial romantic, Kendall, for whom such support was indispensable. The dilemma can only be explained in terms of the different situation of the colonial and the British writer.

✻

The key to understanding these two different attitudes to intertextuality must lie in the cultural dependence of the colony on its mother country, and especially in the structure of the literary communication system, in which the colonial writer plays a far different role from that of his British counterpart. The relation between Britain and its colonies may be likened to that between the two components of a literary process whereby an original text is transplanted into a new communicative context and so modified by it that a transformed text, an adaptation arises.[4] If the culture of the mother country is the original text and the new communicative context is that of the colony, and if into that context the literary heritage of the original text is transplanted, with all its appetite for hegemony, but with the inevitable modifications which, in the course of time, that appetite will be obliged to undergo, then there will arise, quite naturally, a permanent situation of dialogue between the mother country and the colony; and of that situation the system of literary communication in the colonial context presents the most evident proof. Dominated variously by the British text and the Australian context, the phases of this communicative system illustrate on the one hand the indissolubility of the bond between mother country and colony, and on the other hand the permanent need of the Australian author to come to terms with the cultural import from Great Britain. In this system of mutual interdependence the forces exerted on colonial and British writer can be very different. The colonial romantic, for example, may be quite unable to sever himself from the speech, the traditions, the aesthetic instincts which he shares with the mother country, while his English namesake may well be intent on denying all reference to earlier texts within the common literary tradition.

As well as the colonial author and his immediate cultural background, the literary communication system comprises language, literary and aesthetic codes, publishing and marketing, the reading public with its tastes and preferences and the critics with their values and norms. These may each be in the hands of (British) text or (colonial) context, and the incentive to dialogue with the various elements of the original text may be, accordingly, more or less compelling. Five stages of dependence may, for the sake of the argument, be singled out in the many phases of development which characterize the relation between colony and mother country, and these five stages will illustrate various sides of the intertextual dialogue between original text and context.

1. In the early colonial phase the communication system is determined unequivocally by the original text. The colonial author may both feel and assert that he belongs to his new country, but his literary horizon is the canon of British literature, and his literary standing depends on his familiarity with it. Form as well as language reinforce and display his close links with the original text. His readers, who will as yet scarcely exist in the colony, will be those of the mother country, as will be the aesthetic norms, therefore, which his publisher in the mother country will have established for the sale of his wares. And his critics, finally, will be those of the London press, formed by the British literary tradition and the current tastes of the British reading public.

In this early phase the colonial writer will frequently wish to prove his equality, and, as evidence of his learning, intertextual references abound. An example of the gentrification process is Henry Carter's "Prologue. By a Gentleman of Leicester"[5], modelled, it seems likely, on Dr. Johnson's "Prologue spoken by Mr. Garrick". Carter's "Prologue", written for the opening of the Sydney theatre, quotes from Gay's *The Beggar's Opera* as well as Shakespeare's *Macbeth* and *Richard III*. Barron Field's attempt to capture the fascination of Australian flora in his poem "Botany-Bay Flowers" (1819) begins with a motto from Lucretius' *De Rerum Naturae* (I, 962–968) and *The Merry Wives of Windsor* (V, 5, 77). The poem abounds in references to *A Winter's Tale* (V, 4, 120), *The Tempest* (I, 2, 408), *Romeo and Juliet* (I, 4, 57) and *A Midsummer Night's Dream* (II, 1, 175; III, 2, 390; II, 1, 123–124; IV, 1, 68).[6]

2. As the cultural infrastructure of the context gradually develops, a colonial readership, a local market and local publishing houses will come into being; but the position of the writer will only very slightly improve, for in every other respect he remains bound to the leading strings of a dominant original text. The determining contours of this intertextuality differ from that of the earlier phase only in the greater number of quotable classics in the by now enlarged canon. Here too one might see the beginnings of those literary eulogies in which, right up to the present day, colonial (and post-colonial) writers express their frequent admiration for the great figures of British literary history: Marlowe, Shakespeare, but above all the contemporaries Blake, Wordsworth, Shelley, Keats, Burns, Byron, Tennyson and Browning.

3. Only when the colonial readership, the market and the publishing houses lose their exclusive fealty to the British cultural heritage does the situation of the

colonial writer materially improve. This is a gradual shift in certain areas away from the total dominance of the original text rather than a break in principle from continuing dependence. The English language and its literary forms guarantee the continuation of that dependence. Moreover both author and publisher know that they are still subject to British criticism and public taste; these are factors, Henry Lawson complains in his "A Song of Southern Writers", which neither of them can afford to ignore:

Talent goes for little here. To be aided, to be known,
You must fly to Northern critics who are juster than our own.
You may write above the standard, but your work is seldom seen
Till it's noticed and reprinted in an English magazine.
O the critics of your country will be very proud of you,
When you're recognized in London by an editor or two.
[...]
Write a story of the South, make it true and make it clear,
Put your soul in every sentence, have the volume published here,
And 'twill only be accepted by our critics in the mist
As a 'worthy imitation' of a Northern novelist.
For the volume needs the mighty Paternoster Row machine,
With a patronizing notice in an English magazine.[7]

The intertextuality of awakening consciousness in the colonial context is marked by the determination to bring out what is typical in that context, or what is thought to be typical, and to reduce or repress the effect of the original text across the whole range[8] of the communicative system. This global onslaught confirms on the one hand the persistent presence of the original text, on the other hand, however, the pressing need felt by an increasingly articulate context for its adaptation to the new environment which that context represents. Victor Daley's "Correggio Jones"[9] parodies an Australian artist who rejects Australian reality as trivial and yearns for the scenes and objects of British and European culture. Daley pleads for the replacement of British influence with a truly Australian literature and art.

4. Australian schools and universities were until quite recently almost exclusively in the hands of the British:[10] they were part of the original text. University departments of English were led by academics trained at English (and Scottish) universities, teachers whose reputations rested on their knowledge of English literature, whose syllabus was the canon of that literature, and whose critical values were – and very largely still are – those of the common room and the London press. Les A. Murray could still mock at these attitudes in 1974:

Literate Australia was British, or babu at least,
before Vietnam and the American conquest

career had overwhelmed learning most deeply back then:
a major in English made one a minor Englishman
and woe betide those who stepped off the duckboards of that.[11]

The dependence of the colonial author on various facets of the original text is not, therefore, entirely removed even when his own contextual awareness is reflected in a colonial publishing system, colonial markets, readers prepared to accept colonial material, and critics who are not only prepared to acknowledge the particular conditions of the colonial context but may actually be in a position to understand that an author is writing in, or establishing a colonial literary tradition. For the values of this system are still essentially British: not only because of the common language and cultural inheritance, nor even simply because of the permanent presence of the original text in the colonial context, but above all because of the absolute need to export the literary product if the author is to be known beyond the frontiers of the colony; the need therefore to keep pace with developments in the original text, of whose literature he can never be unaware. The need is all the more urgent if the material, economic factors of the communication system (publishers, markets, readers) are still subject to the institutions of the mother country; response to these will then, for the colonial writer, be a matter of daily bread.

5. The situation changes radically when the colonial context itself takes over the key factors in the communication system; then, as has already happened for the most part in the USA, the dependence of colonial author on original text is practically abolished. For Australia, however, this condition is still remote.

It is no doubt for this reason, too, that there has been as yet nothing like so intensive a literary dialogue between Britain and Australia as there has for a long time been between Britain and America. The one is mutual, the other still for the most part one-sided: a conversation engaged in by Australia. What has, however, changed is that Britain is no longer the only addressee of the Australian literary discourse. Modern Australian literature is indeed characterized by its loosening of the monolateral engagement with Britain and the development of multilateral relations to American, continental European and Asian sources, although the original relation to the British text still plays the most important role in the history of Australian literature. The heightened complexity of intercultural relationships in this most recent phase of the communicative system is reflected in a host of poems which respond to ancient Greek and Roman models, or address the work of German, French, Russian, American and most recently Asian poets, initiating a truly world-wide intertextuality. With this goes an intensive critical scrutiny of colonial Australian literature for the constituent structures of a native tradition, the search for identity being, as A. D.

Hope made clear in his 1958 poem "A Letter from Rome"[12], one of the main concerns of any colonial culture.

*

The "echoes from the elder sons of Song" which occur in many forms and have many functions in contemporary Australian poetry are both the natural resonance of a common literary tradition and a conscious signal set against this tradition. Sometimes the common ancestry will simply be recollected and confirmed; at other times the experience of an English poet will be contradicted and revoked; or again, the English text may be called on as reinforcement for a more topical critique of the Australian context, or yet again as a foil for the definition of specifically Australian aesthetic attitudes. Whatever the case, the reference to and modification of British models from *Beowulf* to Philip Larkin indicates both the continuing interdependence of text and context and the no less persistent endeavour to imbue the former with the latter. The poetic addresses, love poems, philosophical meditations, recompositions, contemporary critiques, satires of Australia and poetological reflections constitute *in toto* a discourse about the common heritage of experience, its binding quality and its aesthetic codification. No conclusion can be drawn as yet from the discovery that the intertextual references in modern Australian poetry seem to cluster round works of the English renaissance, neoclassicism and romanticism; but this does suggest a possible line of thought, for in each of these epochs the crucial issues were those of creating or refining an autochthonous literary language and laying bare the sources of its inspiration.

A chronological documentation of the discourse of Australian poetry with English literature would bring little new to the argument so far adduced; it would therefore seem better in what follows to concentrate on the most modern period, singling out one or two relevant types of poem in order to illustrate from a different angle the nature of that discourse within a temporally limited system of communication.

The *poetic address* directed to an English poet and invoking his peculiar gifts is a form still practised today.[13] References to his life and age are at times transfused with autobiographical or poetological comment, as when Judith Wright considers the visionary power of Thomas Traherne[14] or Philip Martin his life-after-death[15], or when David Rowbotham calls on *Samson Agonistes* and "When I consider how my life is spent" in a meditation on Milton's greatness.[16] Blake's visions have fascinated Australian poets;[17] a visit to "Wordsworth's House at Rydal"[18] gives Mark O'Connor occasion for a definition of poetry; John Croyston correlates his childhood and youthful experiences with those of Keats;[19] A. D. Hope's "The Apotelism of W. B. Yeats"[20] sets an episode from the life of the Irish poet; and Peter Kocan in "Philip Larkin"[21] remembers the poet, who had just recently died. The intertextual references are thinly scattered and are generally to the poet's life. But the names of Marlowe, Shakespeare, Donne, Traherne, Herrick, Milton, Blake, Wordsworth, Keats and Yeats indicate a markedly spiritual or metaphysical trend within the classical canon, and this predilection is carried further in the meditative and reflexive poems.

These *meditative* and *reflexive* poems are concerned with the whole thought-system of a writer: with his life, his work and his central philosophical ideas. There is marked interest in the reconciliation of contraries. Haydn Williams is thus fascinated by Robert Herrick, the "ordinary man's poet" who, as "Christ's pagan", became the living embodiment of the antithesis between a sacred calling and sensual delight.[22] 'Furnley Maurice' (Frank Wilmot) writes in his Donne poem[23] of the seemingly insuperable tension between love for a woman and love of God, a tension which does, however, yield a perfect synthesis. It was Furnley Maurice, too, who, in his poem "Paradise Regained", set on Australian soil the biblical and Miltonian dream of a second paradise, an emphatically human, antitheistic place, as Adam's words to Eve make abundantly clear:

> Come outward, Mate of mine; the Lord
> Hath trapped us; banished and denied
> The arboured walks of Eden wide [...].
>
> Come out, my Heart! What Eden-flower
> Matches those eyes with sorrow filled?
> In spite of God and all his power
> By thy soft body of caress
> Our disconcerted love shall build
> New Edens in the wilderness.[24]

Duncan Miller invokes the visionary Thomas Traherne in his search for a lost paradise. At the head of his poem "The Vision of Thomas Traherne" he places a quotation from the *Centuries of Meditation* ("The Third Century", 15–17). He concludes his poem with the lesson:

> Exiled and blind. More blind if we disdain
> As fantasy the verities you teach;
> The inner day you mirrored for our gain
> Is the flowering lost paradise which each
> May know is within reach.
> Its sun is hidden; you have seen full beam
> Reality which haunts the human dream.[25]

A. D. Hope sets out to reconcile the same Blakean opposites of good and evil[26] – the male and the female – as does D. J. Lake in his pictorial poem "Contraries".[27]

Chris Wallace-Crabbe had very quickly to withdraw[28] his remark that Australia had no *love poems*[29]: the sonnet cycle alone is a thoroughly Australian form of this genre. Recourse is often made to the English classics to depict the altered relation of the lovers to each other. For Evan Jones they have no longer anything to say to one another, and in "A Line from Keats" he quotes from "The Eve of St. Agnes" (XLII, 370–371) to underline this process of alienation:

> All stories, you once said, should have this end:
> To change the burden slightly, *long ago*
> *These lovers fled away into the calm.*
> Easily I became your 'dearest friend'
> And now am someone that you scarcely know,
> A memory that you balance in your palm.[30]

Donne's "The good-morrow" stands behind Rob Johnson's "A drawing by Leonardo recalling a poem by Donne", in which love is dissected anatomically:

> 'A man and woman copulating
> hemisected.' Hemi- as in hemisphere.
> 'Where can we find two better hemispheres?'[31]

Two of the finest love poems in modern Australian literature invoke a long tradition. Gwen Harwood's "Meditation on Wyatt I" and "II" reaches beyond Wyatt to the Petrarchan models: her first "Meditation" is a free version of Wyatt's Sonnet XI ("Whoso list to hunt I know where is an hind"), which is itself indebted, in all probability, to Petrach's *Rime* 190. Wyatt develops the hunting metaphor at the expense of the symbolic landscape and dreamlike atmosphere of his model, but Gwen Harwood restores these Petrarchan features to the foreground of her poem. Nor is the metaphor of the hunt any longer univocal as both partners feel pursued by the other: "Whose is the emblem of a running hound?"[32] The second "Meditation" quotes from Wyatt's "Song CCXVI": the poet's admonition not to forget evokes in her lines a moment of perfect, absolute love:

> 'Forget not yet, forget not this'
> We are what darkness has become:
> two bodies bathed in saffron light
> disarmed by sudden distances
> pitched on the singing heights of time
> our skin aflame with eastern airs,
> changed beyond reason, but not rhyme.

'The which so long hath thee so loved'
    counting the pulsebeats   foot to foot
    our splendid metres   limb to limb
    sweet assonance of tongue and tongue
    figures of speech to speech bemused
    with metaphors as unimproved
    as the crooked roads of genius

    but our hearts' rhymes are absolute.[33]

A fourth group of poems consists of poetic *recompositions* or *reversals* of already formulated aesthetic models, such as Andrew Taylor's parody – "The Flea"[34] – of Donne's poem of the same name. Here the symbol of an intensely intimate love, the *locus classicus* of erotic metaphysical casuistry, is reduced to the status of a performer in a flea-circus. Philip Martin's "Bequest" is a rewriting of Donne's "The Will":

    To those who never read, I leave my writings,
    Just what they never wanted, tunes for the deaf,
    Skywriting for the blind. To plagiarists,
    A style, if not the taste for it. To critics,
    Pushing aside their flagons to despatch
    The work of half a life in half an hour,
    This Christian hope: May they not wake in Limbo
    Blushing. To the politicians of my birthplace
    Who, not being God, do not provide: in time
    Of drought, a cup of muddy water. And
    To my coolest mistress, my electric blanket.[35]

Lola Jackson's sonnet "Westminster Bridge" calls explicitly on Wordsworth in order to revoke the romantic vision of his famous lines "Composed upon West-minster Bridge, September 3, 1802". The London of Jackson's poem is bleak and grey, and her admiration for Wordsworth is mingled with the feeling that he was, perhaps, being overcreative:

    What Wordsworth saw from here I couldn't find.
    Only a morning's grey and smoke filled [sic] air
    Hung out in loops across the Thames, and where
    His fields had been bleak buildings were aligned.
    Waiting I watched the tide disclose the slime,
    The gulls in smoggy grey cry out the speech
    Of waterside. Nothing in sight or reach
    Disclosed for me the beauty of my time.
    I saw a city's close conspiracy

Extend till men lived sandwiched in between
The grey above, the grey below; and made
Acknowledgment to William; found that he
Still held my mind captive to what he'd seen;
And sensed the dangers of a poet's trade.[36]

Hal Colebatch's "Macau, 1975 (After Auden)"[37] revokes Auden's "XXV.
Macao", written in 1938, line by line. T. H. Naisby's "An Australian Reply to
R. S. Thomas (His 'Welsh Landscape')"[38] contrasts the backward-looking
introversion of Thomas's Wales with the animated landscape of modern Aus-
tralia. J. R. Rowland's "Variation on a Theme of Philip Larkin"[39] is based on
Larkin's "Toads".

In the social – and sometimes also political – *critiques,* the reference to British
literature serves a variety of purposes. David Lake's "Anglo-saxon riddle"[40], in
the style of old-English rhyming verse, reveals itself as about a rocket which
laughs at the politicians who are unable to take seriously the lethal effect of
modern weapons of mass destruction. Rob Johnson's *Othello* poems[41] present
the figure of a Moor who feels misused by white society, while Peter Hopegood's "Caliban Reassayed"[42] illustrates the problematic relation of colonisers
and colonized. In his "Riposte to Jaques" A. D. Hope recalls Jaques' famous
speech from *As You Like It* (II, 7, 136–143) in order to apply the theatre metaphor to the existential abandonment of modern man, who feels himself to be a
player on a stage without director or part:

> Yes, it was quite a bright idea to say
> That all the world's a stage. But what a way
> To act: without an audience and no play!
>
> We have our entrances and exits, true!
> But while on stage nobody tells us who
> We are supposed to be or what to do.[43]

Hope's "The Alpha-Omega Song" is a critique of contemporary cosmologies
which yield more questions than answers; it contrasts John Dryden's "A Song
for St. Cecilia's Day November 22, 1687" with the modern lack of confidence
and poise:

> 'From harmony, from heavenly harmony,
> This universal frame began', so sang
> A prince of poets in an earlier day.
> In ours, although it makes no sense to me,
> Cosmologists now favour one Big Bang,
> But who exploded what they cannot say.

[...]
Yours was a rational theory, Glorious John;
Ours is more typical of this violent age
Whose music is discord and the battering drum.[44]

In Paul Kavanagh's "Tell Milton", the harmony and proximity to God which Milton had sung of in his "On the Morning of Christ's Nativity" are lamented as irrevocably lost:

And tell Milton
that the spheres have lost their harmony
that will hurt him

he thought he could recall their sound
almost hearing them himself one
Christmas morning
Christ too of course has gone.[45]

It can be no surprise that many poems which look back at English pre-texts do so in order to treat of peculiarly *Australian themes*. Thus the search for identity is the subject of Peter Porter's "On First Looking into Chapman's Hesiod"[46], with its evocation of Keats; and Frank Kermode's "Seven variations on a Theme of John Donne"[47] depicts a post-war Australia disoriented by the rival claims of east and west. Thomas Gray's "Elegy Written in a Country Churchyard", with its sense of history based on the common man, stands behind the simple pioneer figures of Hal Porter's eight-part sequence "In an Australian Country Graveyard":

All hereabout anachronism's rife:
The landscape plays at Constable and Gray
With hedgerow, hawthorn, far-off farm-house roof;
A lowing herd to wind its text-book way;
A ballad graveyard, hackneyed rhymes of yew,
Headstones set elegiacally askew.[48]

More frequently, however, the reference to an earlier, British text serves a topical and satirical purpose. Susan Hampton capitulates in her attempt to rewrite Sidney's *Arcadia* 400 years later, because his integration of a "golden world of pastoral love/and politics"[49] simply eludes her. Geoffrey Dutton criticises the fools' paradise of hedonistic Australia in his "Two Variations on a Theme of Andrew Marvell"[50], based on Marvell's "Bermudas". James McAuley's "A Letter to John Dryden"[51], which elicited an equally sharp riposte from Jack Lindsay[52], is a satirical critique of the mental and political climate of Australia in the 1950's, written from the point of view of a convinced conservative. A. D. Hope's *Dunciad Minor*[53] is a spirited recomposition of Pope's *Dunciad*, while

Swift's *Gulliver's Travels* inspired James McAuley's "The True Discovery of Australia":[54] Lemuel Gulliver's letter to Lord Peterborough contains little to flatter McAuley's contemporaries. Finally Coleridge's dream-vision, "Kubla Khan", stimulated John Blight[55] and A. D. Hope[56] to bitter satire against the Australian version of "Persons from Porlock".

By far the largest body of reference to English literary models is, however, concerned with *poetological reflection*. It would be a mistake to try to erect an Australian poetics simply out of this intertextuality; there are many other poems on poetry as well as theoretical statements which would have to be drawn on for this purpose. Reference here is not only to individual texts, but may extend to a whole system of thought or attitudes; thus James McAuley's and Harold Stewart's Ern Malley hoax[57] was an attempt to debunk the entire aesthetic stance of surrealist hermeticism and modernism. In a similar way A. D. Hope's hard-hitting parody "Sonnet on First Looking into Gerard Manley Hopkins" can only be understood in terms of its author's predilection for "that noble, candid speech / In which all things worth saying can be said..."[58] – the diction of the eighteenth century, and of Yeats. Hope's sonnet runs:

> No, WORSE there is none, for him, who heard (Hell!) Hop-
> kins at bay, bray – force I must be brief,
> Or in his coil, toil, bitched beyond belief,
> Wordwan, glue-gold-glutted, cry: Hi, stop!.
> Why, then? Who then, in such change and chop,
> Claptrap, terse-verse, groan and grunt of grief,
> For bruised bone, bashed ear (Tell, then!) gets relief?
> Goom, Moom, boom's noomb, and bloody pate goes Pop!
>
> Let Hiccup-Hop-Skip-Jump-kins bumpkins bruise
> Verse, which on foot-rot-feet, by jerk-work scans!
> Move I'll not, lurch-leg, in bold botch-bard's shoes!
> Back to the sane tongue used before this man's
> Made Constipation first an English Muse,
> And taught our numbers his St. Vitus dance.[59]

Richard Lawson[60] and R. H. Long[61] invoke, but also distance themselves from, Wordsworth's "Scorn Not the Sonnet" in their defence of that traditional form, while John A. Scott transforms the sonnet into a pictogram.[62] Vincent Buckley reviews in a single sweep the whole of English, American and Australian literary history ("Lament of the Makers")[63], calling on their most famous figures as representatives of a common tradition; and A. D. Hope exploits the impossibility of writing a classic epic to compose a modern mock (heroic) epic poem:

The proper way to start a poem
Built on the old high generous plan
Is to invoke the Muse; and, though I'm
Bound to placate the harridan,
She can't expect an epic proem:
The trick's been lost; the best she can
Look for in these degenerate times
Is an *O Thou* to start the rhymes.

'*O Thou!*' – You see it does sound silly –
'*Descend, my Muse!*' – and that sounds worse.
'Descend and –' 'Don't be Uncle Willy!'
She says, appearing just like nurse,
The antiseptic smile, the chilly:
'Well, Master Alec, writing verse?
[…][64]

Even when reference is confined to an individual text, it is less a matter of the usefulness of particular forms or traditions than of the quest for a valid poetics.[65] Romantic aesthetics seem to play a key role here, inasmuch as the acceptance or rejection of romantic premises determines the poetological discussion. J. J. Bray's "The Poetry of the Heart" has recourse to the opening sonnet of Sir Philip Sidney's *Astrophel and Stella*, the last line of which he takes as the motto for his own sonnet, but in fact he pleads for a poetry of the head, not of the heart:

('Fool', said my Muse to me, 'look in thy heart and write'.)

Not now: sir, you obeyed and saw within
Fair Stella's image gemmed with courtly love.
We see a ripe and humming rubbish-bin
Which birth uncapped and only death will move.
[…]
The heart builds Belsens for the head to staff.
A consul chained attends a drooling Goth.
This age with too much cause distrusts the heart.
The head makes finer if less melting art.[66]

To other writers, however, the romantic aesthetic is still very attractive, as W. D. Leadbeater and Susan Farmer[67] attest. Indeed, Gwen Kelly's "Sweet Poet" suggests a romantic renaissance, a rediscovery of the modernity of romanticism:

Shelley, sweet poet of our youth,
we worshipped at the shrine of your transcendence;

felt the sharp thorns of life in teenage flesh;
fed on the sickening violets, airy truth.

We swept the fields on gusts of skiey vision;
danced in the nude like nymphs to waves addressed:
And in the fainting air made dreams of love,
Antipodean, fraught with sad decision.

But Leavis told us: Disregard this singer.
He lacks the wit, the finely chiselled image,
The core of English poetry. And we listened;
forgot the soul's delight; declined to linger

With you in noonday dreams. Today I hew
the face of cold depression in your verses,
the weariness, monotony unending;
and once again I raise my hands to you.

Blow, west wind, blow.[68]

The clear diction and rational poetry demanded by A. D. Hope and others have induced a critical distance between Australian poets and W. H. Auden as well as T. S. Eliot[69], although only time and literary history will show to what extent, here too, attraction and rejection will serve the ends of poetic articulacy. As long as the discussion about the status of the poet and the essence of poetry continues to take place within the literary repertoire created and disseminated by the mother country, however, as it does in David Lake's "Shakespearean sonnet: Any poet to every reader", the cultural community of Great Britain with Australia will remain intact:

Who am I? Does it matter whether I slept
With Lesbia, Lucy, Harriet or Anne,
Or even if I scandalously crept
To W. H., or some less faceless man?
My essence is not mouldering in the dust
Of any office of dead lives' records,
Nor does my witnessed will define my lust
Immortal, but what second-best-bed affords.
But here you find me: here the living I
Rhythms the beating of my heart and brain,
My pattern, soul that may not wholly die
While capitols fall, but sonnets still remain.
    These words that pulse through man's eternity –
    Read them, and know the quintessential me.[70]

Notes

1 Cf. Broich, U., Pfister, M. (Eds.): *Intertextualität. Formen, Funktionen, anglistische Fallstudien.* Tübingen, 1985.

2 Kendall, H.: "Prefatory Sonnets", quoted from Elliott, B., Mitchell, A. (Eds.): *Bards in the Wilderness. Australian Colonial Poetry to 1920.* Melbourne, 1970, p. 75.

3 Cf. Lerner, L.: „Romantik, Realismus und negierte Intertextualität". – In Broich/Pfister (Eds.): *Intertextualität,* pp. 278–296, 283–284. – On the other hand see Webby, E.: *Early Australian Poetry. An Annotated Bibliography of Original Poems Published in Australian Newspapers, Magazines and Almanacks Before 1850.* Sydney, 1982.

4 Cf. Zander, H.: *Shakespeare 'bearbeitet'. Eine Untersuchung am Beispiel der Historien-Inszenierungen 1945–1975 in der Bundesrepublik Deutschland.* Tübingen, 1983, pp. 3–90.

5 Cf. Carter, H.: "Prologue. By a Gentleman of Leicester". – In Elliott/Mitchell (Eds.): *Bards in the Wilderness,* pp. 5–6.

6 Cf. Field, B.: "Botany-Bay Flowers" [1819]. – In Elliott/Mitchell (Eds.): *Bards in the Wilderness,* pp. 14–16; see also p. 236.

7 Lawson, H.: "A Song of Southern Writers". – In Cantrell, L. (Ed.): *The 1890s. Stories, Verse, and Essays.* St. Lucia, 1977, pp. 18–19; see also Lawson, H.: "Australian Bards and Bush Reviewers", ibid., p. 17.

8 My use of terminology is indebted to Broich, U.: „Zur Einzeltextreferenz". – In Broich/Pfister (Eds.): *Intertextualität,* pp. 48–52; Pfister, M.: „Zur Systemreferenz", ibid., pp. 52–58.

9 Cf. Daley, V.: "Correggio Jones". – In Cantrell, L. (Ed.): *The 1890s,* pp. 15–16.

10 Cf. Conell, W. F.: "British Influence on Australian Education in the Twentieth Century". – In Madden, A. W., Morris-Jones, W. H. (Eds.): *Australia and Britain. Studies in a Changing Relationship.* Sydney, 1980, pp. 162–179; Docker, J.: *In a Critical Condition: Reading Australian Literature.* Ringwood/Victoria, 1984.

11 Murray, L. A.: "Sidere Mens Eadem Mutato: a spiral of sonnets for Robert Ellis". – In id.: *Lunch and Counter Lunch.* Sydney, 1974, pp. 50–54, 51.

12 Cf. Hope, A. D.: "A Letter from Rome *For Dr Leonie Kramer*". – In id.: *Collected Poems 1930–1970.* Sydney, ³1972, (1966), pp. 129–148.

13 Cf. Scott, M.: "Marlowe". *Quadrant* 21, vii, 1977, 69; Haley, M.: "Shakespeare". *Quadrant* 9, iv, 1965, 37; Smither, E.: "Shakespeare wrote fast". *Poetry Australia* No. 77, 1981, 21; Haley, M.: "John Donne is Sick (30-11-1623)". *Quadrant* 15, ii, 1971, 10.

14 Cf. Wright, J.: "Reading Thomas Traherne". – In id.: *Collected Poems 1942–1970.* Sydney, ²1974, (1971), p. 209.

15 Cf. Martin, P.: "For the Tomb of Herrick". – In id.: *Voice Unaccompanied.* Canberra, 1970, p. 10.

16 Cf. Rowbotham, D.: "To Milton, at First Dark". – In id.: *Selected Poems.* St. Lucia, 1975, p. 167.

17 Cf. Martin, D.: "Blake". – In id.: *Poems of David Martin 1938–1958.* Sydney, 1958, p. 15; Skrzynecki, P.: "Blake". – In id.: *There, behind the Lids.* Normanhurst, 1970, p. 24; Johnson, T.: "To Blake". – In Johnson, T., Vaux, D.: *Coffee Cellar Chants.* Featherstone, 1973, p. 29.

18 Cf. O'Connor, M.: "Wordsworth's House at Rydal". *Poetry Australia* No. 76, 1981, 51–52.
19 Cf. Croyston, J.: "Keats". *Westerly* 1983, i, 21; see also Couper, J. M.: "May, 1819". *Meanjin* 27, 1968, 273.
20 Cf. Hope, A. D.: "The Apotelism of W. B. Yeats". – In id.: *Collected Poems*, pp. 227–228.
21 Cf. Kocan, P.: "Philip Larkin". *Quadrant* 30, iv, 1986, 15.
22 Williams, H.: "Herrick". *Westerly* 1973, iv, 10–11, here: 10.
23 Cf. 'Furnley Maurice' (Wilmot, F.): "John Donne". – In id.: *The Gully and Other Verses*. Melbourne, 1929, pp. 34–35; see also Martin, P.: "Doctor Donne of St. Paul's: The Statue Jack Built". – In id.: *The Bone Flute. Poems.* Canberra, 1974, p. 27.
24 'Furnley Maurice' (Wilmot, F.): "Paradise Regained". – In Lavater, L. (Ed.): *The Sonnet in Australia. A Survey and Selection.* Edited with a Foreword by Frederick T. Macartney. Sydney, revised and enlarged edition 1956 (1926), p. 43.
25 Miller, D.: "The Vision of Thomas Traherne". – In Hope, A. D. (Ed.): *Australian Poetry 1960.* Sydney, 1960, pp. 49–50, here: p. 50.
26 Cf. Hope, A. D.: "The Female Principle (A reply to Blake)". *Westerly* 1975, ii, 7. See also Hope, A. D.: *A Book of Answers.* Sidney, 1978.
27 Cf. Lake, D. J.: "Contraries. On a Picture by William Blake". *Westerly* 1970, iv, 9.
28 Cf. Wallace-Crabbe, Ch.: *Three Absences in Australian Writing.* Townsville, 1983, pp. 1–4.
29 Cf. Wallace-Crabbe, Ch.: "Unloving and Being in Love". – In Clark, A., Fletcher, J., Marsden, R. (Eds.): *The Theme of Love in Australian Writing.* Colloquium Papers. Sydney, 1983, pp. 67–77.
30 Jones, E.: "A Line from Keats". – In id.: *Understandings: Poems.* Melbourne, 1967, p. 11. In the original the line runs: " ... long ago/ These lovers fled away into the storm."
31 Johnson, R.: "A drawing by Leonardo recalling a poem by Donne". – In id.: *Caught on the Hop.* Adelaide, 1974, p. 46.
32 Harwood, G.: "Meditation on Wyatt I". – In id.: *Selected Poems.* Sydney, 1975, p. 106.
33 Harwood, G.: "Meditation on Wyatt II". –In id.: *Selected Poems*, pp. 106–107.
34 Cf. Taylor, A.: "The Flea". – In *Poets of the Month Series 2.* Sydney, 1976, p. 23.
35 Martin, P.: "Bequest". – In id.: *The Bone Flute*, p. 62.
36 Jackson, L.: "Westminster Bridge". *Quadrant* 8, ii, 1964, 32.
37 Cf. Colebatch, H.: "Macau, 1975 (After Auden)". *Quadrant* 20, i, 1976, 76.
38 Cf. Naisby, T. H.: "An Australian Reply to R. S. Thomas (His 'Welsh Landscape')". *Poetry Australia* No. 71, 1979, 54.
39 Cf. Rowland, J. M.: "Variations on a Theme of Philip Larkin". – In Thompson, J. (Ed.): *Australian Poetry 1965.* Sydney, 1965, pp. 23–24.
40 Lake, D.: "Anglo-saxon riddle". – In id.: *Hornpipes and Funerals: Forty-two Poems and Six Odes of Horace.* St. Lucia, 1973, p. 42.
41 Cf. Johnson, R.: "Othello and I", "Othello to Himself". – In id.: *Caught on the Hop*, pp. 47–48.
42 Cf. Hopegood, P.: "Caliban Reassayed". – In id.: *Snake's-eye Vision of a Serial Story.* Sydney, 1964, pp. 38–41; see also Hope, A. D.: "Man Friday". – In id.: *The Age of Reason.* Melbourne, 1975, pp. 23–27.

43 Cf. Hope, A. D.: "Riposte to Jaques". – In id.: *Antechinus: Poems 1975–1980.* Sydney, 1981, p. 52.

44 Cf. Hope, A. D.: "The Alpha-Omega Song". – In id.: *Antechinus,* p. 53; see also Lehmann, G.: "Elegy for Sonnets". – In id.: *Conversation with a Rider.* Sydney, 1972, p. 59. Criticism, from a feminist point of view, is to be found in Zwicky, F.: "The Name of the Game". *Meanjin* 29, 1970, 174, and Fahey, D.: "Remembering Ophelia". – In Kavanagh, P. (Ed.): *Instructions for Honey Ants and other poems.* Newcastle/N.S.W., 1983, pp. 24–27.

45 Kavanagh, P.: "Tell Milton". – In id.: *Wild Honey.* St. Lucia, 1974, p. 53.

46 Cf. Porter, P.: "On First Looking into Chapman's Hesiod". – In id.: *Living in a Calm Country.* London, 1975, pp. 21–23.

47 Cf. Kermode, F.: "Seven Variations on a Theme of Johne Donne". *Southerly* 6, iv, 1945, 39–41. The author of this poem seems to be identical with the Frank Kermode.

48 Porter, H.: "In an Australian Country Graveyard". – In id.: *In an Australian Country Graveyard and Other Poems.* Melbourne, 1974, pp. 3–29, 3.

49 Hampton, S.: "Spellbound at the Spider's Web (a letter to Sir Philip Sidney)". *Southerly* 38, 1978, 308.

50 Cf. Dutton, G.: "Two Variations on a Theme of Andrew Marvell". – In id.: *Antipodes in Shoes.* Sydney, 1958, pp. 65–66.

51 Cf. McAuley, J.: "A Letter to John Dryden". *Meanjin* 13, 1954, 28–38.

52 Cf. Lindsay, J.: "Unsolicited Reply to James McAuley's 'Letter to John Dryden'". *Meanjin* 13, 1954, 346–349.

53 Cf. Hope, A. D.: *Dunciad Minor: An heroick poem.* Melbourne, 1970.

54 Cf. McAuley, J.: "The True Discovery of Australia". – In id.: *Collected Poems 1936–1970.* Sydney, 1971, [3]1978, pp. 29–34; see also Jack Hibberd's one act play, "A Modest Proposal from the Minister for Employment and Youth Affairs Mrs Poppy Defarge adapted from Swift". – In id.: *Squibs: a collection of short plays.* Brisbane, 1984, pp. 195–200.

55 Cf. Blight, J.: "After Kublai Khan". *Overland* 19, 1960, 45.

56 Hope, A. D.: "Persons from Porlock". – In id.: *Collected Poems,* pp. 104–106.

57 Cf. ['Ern Malley']: *Ern Malley's Poems.* With an introduction by Max Harris. Adelaide, [1974].

58 Cf. Hope, A. D.: "William Butler Yeats". – In id.: *Collected Poems,* p. 72.

59 Hope, A. D.: "Sonnet on First Looking into Gerard Manley Hopkins". *Meanjin* 14, 1955, 508.

60 Cf. Lawson, R.: "The Sonnet". – In Lavater, L. (Ed.): *The Sonnet in Australia,* p. 98; see also Penn-Smith, F.: "The Pain of Words", ibid., p. 99.

61 Cf. Long, R. H.: "The Sonnet". – In Lavater (Ed.): *The Sonnet in Australia,* p. 99.

62 Cf. Scott, J. A.: "Three Sonnets: Parade". – In id.: *From the Flooded City.* St. Lucia/Queensland 1981, pp. 33–35; see also Lehmann, G.: "Elegy for Sonnets", ibid., p. 59.

63 Cf. Buckley, V.: "Lament of the Makers". *Meanjin* 18, 1959, 323–326; see also Hemensley, K.: "The English Tradition (*for John Hall*)". – In id.: *Love's Voyages.* St. Lucia, 1974, pp. 26–27.

64 Hope, A. D.: "Conversation with Calliope". – In id.: *Collected Poems,* pp. 177–200, 177.

65 Cf. Kavanagh, P.: "Grendel". – In id.: *Wild Honey,* p. 52.

66 Bray, J. J.: "The Poetry of the Heart". – In id.: *Poems 1961–1971*. Milton/Queensland, 1972, p. 11; see also Bray, J. J.: "Wordsworth", in id.: *Poems*. Melbourne, 1962, pp. 43–44, which is based on Wordsworth's "We Are Seven"; see also Couper, J. M.: "The Solitary Wordsworth", in *Poet's Choice*. Sydney, 1974, p. 27, which evokes Wordsworth's "The Solitary Reaper".

67 Cf. Leadbeater, W. D.: "Keats". – In id.: *The Gathered Skein: Poems 1972*. Newmarket, 1972, p. 17; Farmer, S.: "A Question about Keats". *Meanjin* 28, 1969, 348; see also Harris, M.: "Wordsworth in Barossa". – In id.: *A Window at Night*. Kensington Park/S.A., 1967, pp. 46–47.

68 Kelly, G.: "Sweet Poet". *Southerly* 45, 1985, 320.

69 Cf. Tranter, J.: "After Reading 'Four Quartets'". *Southerly* 41, 1981, 430; Nicholsen, D.: "Impression (after reading W. H. Auden's 'About the House')". *Poetry Australia* No. 19, 1967, 16; Roberts, N.: "The Quote from Auden". – In Tranter, J. (Ed.): *The New Australian Poetry*. St. Lucia, 1979, pp. 48–51.

70 Lake, D.: "Shakespearean Sonnet: Any poet to every reader". – In id.: *Hornpipes and Funerals*, p. 14; see also Grant, J.: "Hamlet to Ophelia". – In Smith, G. K., Grant, J.: *Turn Left at Any Time with Care*. St. Lucia, 1975, p. 44; Adamson, R.: "Prospero Coming Out of Himself". – In id.: *Selected Poems*. Sydney, 1977, pp. 85–86.

Albert-Reiner Glaap, Düsseldorf

Back to the Future.
Al Pittman, *A Rope Against the Sun* –
a slice of Canadiana

1.

"What is Canadian about Canadian plays?" is a question that has often been raised since professional theatre began to take shape in Canada. Should we expect Canadian playwrights to deal with universal issues like playwrights elsewhere, or should they try to account for the human conditions from a Canadian point of view? Can only those plays be considered *Canadian* plays which make specifically *Canadian* statements and are, as it were, dramatized chunks of Canadiana?

There can be no doubt that art has to have universality, but it is almost always grounded in a certain locality. The universal comes through the particular! The problem with that huge country Canada, however, is that there are so many particularities, so many different regions and ethnic groups that not one of them can claim to be "Canada in a nutshell". The prairie landscape is not more or less Canadian than the Pointe in Montreal or the coast of Labrador. This places those who try to pinpoint the Canadianness of Canadian literature, and of Canadian Drama in particular, in something of a dilemma. To go and see one more play on the generation gap, on AIDS or on the Bomb merely because it is written by a Canadian does not make sense to a European theatre-goer. On the other hand, any attempt to introduce Canadian Drama to people outside Canada through reference to one particular play that contains what one believes to be distinctive Canadian features is a dangerous undertaking. Distinctive features do not only make distinct in the sense that something unique is identified, but also in the sense that these features, because they are unique, cannot be found all over Canada. This applies especially to Newfoundland literature, which not only gives an insight into one specific segment of Canadian life but also raises questions related to life in general. Here, like elsewhere, the universal comes through the particular.

A Newfoundlander asked to describe his province is likely to answer: "Rock, fog, bog, and cod". But woe to the mainlander who dare make a similar remark. No other people in Canada have a stronger regional pride than do the people in Newfoundland. This pride is rooted in the cultural heritage and the social strata of the founding groups, i.e. of the Irish and the English. They brought with them different traditions. With the Irish it was a heritage of Roman Catholicism, poverty and hatred of their English oppressors, whereas puritanical Protestantism and social deference where the distinguishing features of the English who came mainly from the West Country.[1] Both groups had to cope with harsh physical conditions which merged them into one group. Both the English and the Irish were predominantly shore fishermen; their common interests brought them even closer together.

Newfoundland is Britain's oldest colony. John Cabot took possession of the island in the name of King Henry VII in 1497. Sir Humphrey Gilbert reaffirmed the right of British ownership when he claimed the island in the name of Queen Elizabeth I. Cabot's New Founde Isle, however, is not only Britain's first overseas colony, but also Canada's newest province. Only in 1949 did it become part of the nation. And Newfoundland is often referred to as "the cradle of white civilization in North America".

2.

When the Vikings landed in 1001 they called the island "Land of Forest". Newfoundland's most unusual place names are a mute testimony to different peoples and ethnic groups who came and went. Their origins are indicated by names like *Turk's Island, Ireland's Eye, Portugal Cove* and *English Harbour*.[2] The hardships that they had to cope with are reflected in *Misery Point, Breakheart Point, Wreck Cove, Bleak Island*.[3] Some of the immigrants gave humorous names to the natural landmarks, such as *Run-by-guess, Nancy Oh, Ha Ha Bay*.[4] Many place names cannot be found on any existing map, because they are merely used by people who live in the so-called outports, in isolation from other communities and from St. John's in particular. But these people's outlook on life was not altogether pessimistic as one can infer from place names like *Heart's Desire, Comfort Cove, Little Paradise* and *Sweet Bay*.[5] The "Bayman" was proud of his bravery and persistence, which also lies at the heart of the special brand of humour that people in Newfoundland are still famous for. Some of the buttons worn by the supporters of Greenpeace at the beginning of the 1980s read "Fog Off" and "In Cod We Trust".

Needless to say, the people in the old outports developed not only their own lifestyles, but also a folklore and a literature of their own. There are approximately 800 outports in Newfoundland, some with a population down to near zero, which were settled three or four hundred years ago. Hardly anything has changed in these secluded traditional communities which are, however, rapidly breaking up due to the influence of modern media, and, more recently, as a result of the so-called *Resettlement Programme* with its declared aim of centralization.

56

"Confederation was inevitable, centralization was not" is the conviction of many people in Newfoundland. Newfoundland's confederation with Canada in 1949 was the starting-point for a period marked by dislocation and a collision between new habits and traditional values. People changed their lifestyles and what had been an old British colony seemed to develop into something North American. The "stunned Newf" became the epitome of the large number of poor Newfoundlanders who went into other Canadian or American cities, where they were "out of water", i.e. not prepared to cope with the new situation. There were no upper class people to take the lead. "Newf" is an American tag, and "Newfie", which Newfoundlanders consider to be a derogatory term, was also coined by Americans. The antagonism between Mainlander and Newfoundlander is, no doubt, a result of Confederation.

Pat Byrne, a specialist in Newfoundland folklore at Memorial University in St. John's, with whom I conducted an interview, has identified three kinds of reaction on the part of former Newfoundlanders to what is going on in the island these days. When Newfoundland music was played in another province, there were many people in the audience who had left their native land after Confederation. Some of them *whispered* into one of the musicians' ear "I'm from Newfoundland", thereby practically denying it. Others said: "I live in Newfoundland. I'm a Newfoundlander." And there were the ones who tied a ribbon across their forehead with the word "Newfoundland" as a way of parading their descent. Pat Byrne is convinced that the only way of producing natural reactions would be to say: "I'm a Newfoundlander."[6]

Confederation and the changes in the post-Confederation period have become central topics in Newfoundland literature. Tom Cahill's play *As Loved Our Fathers* (1974) is about Confederation. Dominant themes in contemporary works are the antagonism between Townies and Baymen, the resettlement programme, anticapitalist politics, dissatisfaction with the island's government, the high rate of unemployment. Unemployment, however, is not a first priority any more, since there is a high rate of unemployment in all Canada. Newfoundland drama is a socio-centred type of drama which encapsulates specifically Newfoundland problems and a sense of change, cut clean across a sense of loss. David French, Michael Cook, Al Pittman and Tom Cahill are the most prominent dramatists. In Cook's and French's plays the old way of life and the inner life of outport characters play an important role. More than anything else, the old outport has become one of the myths of the literary scene. To Al Pittman, in particular, the outport is a pastoral which is continually being destroyed. Its people become more and more lonesome and are finally incapable of communicating with each other. These people are at once unique and universal. Michael Cook in *Jacob's Wake*[7] and David French in *Leaving Home*[8] try to explore the life of the people who have left Newfoundland to make a fortune elsewhere. Al Pittman's *A Rope Against the Sun*[9], however, is about the people who still live in Newfoundland and have to come to grips with the reality of a slowly petrifying social setting of an outport community.

3.

A Rope Against the Sun (1974)[10] (= *A Rope*) is an unconventional play which does not fit into any clear-cut structural patterns. It wasn't even meant to be a play, but has grown out of the author's feelings and knowledge.

> What actually happened was that I was asked by the CBC to write a poem for voices, and I agreed. That's what turned out to be *A Rope Against the Sun*. I didn't know where it was going to go, but I wanted to go with it, so I stayed with it. It became a play instead.[11]

A Rope elucidates the specific insolvable dilemma that Newfoundlanders find themselves in. It depicts one single day in the life of the people in Merasheen, a small fishing village in Placentia Bay. These people are fishermen, old folks, children, whimsical characters and eccentrics, and – last but not least – the parish priest and the local school teacher. They are at once unique and universal. Pittman has a strong sense of the Newfoundland identity, but he says:

> I'm not admiring or promoting separateness at all, but admitting it and saying, 'Okay, we have to become Canadians. This is what we suddenly are.' I personally promote the idea of being Canadian. One of the benefits of having written is that I've had the opportunity to travel within this country. I recognize that the Yukon is not Newfoundland, nor is Saskatoon Corner Brook, but I have a sense that I'm still in my country. If I go to Hartford, Connecticut, I have a sense that I'm not.[12]

Pittman does not see himself as a regional writer.[13] He wants to remain true to the place and the time and make people's voices as distinctive as possible. But he does not aim at capturing the exact idiom of a particular area in Newfoundland:

> I wouldn't want to insert a word that is foreign to any of the voices, but at the same time I'm not concerned whether it's a word that they would have used or not [...]. I'm also very cautious about utilizing the language in a way that becomes condescending or doesn't do it justice [...].[14]

Separateness, survival and identity are the central themes in *A Rope*. These, however, are not just Newfoundland topics but general Canadian issues.

In a prefatory note to *A Rope Against the Sun*, Al Pittman points out that the Merasheen of his play is "a fictitious place inhabited by fictitious people". But he also mentions that there is a real Merasheen, located in Placentia, Newfoundland, which until 1967 was "inhabited by very real people". Pittman dedicated *A Rope* to his father and all the other people who once lived on this island.

At the beginning of the play, Merasheen Island seems to be an idyllic place:

> The autumn sun, more brilliant than warm, has begun its angular ascent to the low heavens of Newfoundland moon. It pours its bright power over Merasheen Island, pushing the fog westward to sea (p. 5).

The first thing the audience hears is a song sung by Nell Pittman, one of the characters. She is lamenting the absence of her lover, whom she expected to be back a long time ago but who remains "so far away upon some foreign sea" (p. 1). When she has finished her song, Jake Connors appears on the stage and tells the audience who Nell is and what he thinks of her. Jake for his part is introduced by Joe Casey, and similarly seven other characters make their entrances, each of them being introduced by the next person in order of appearance. There are different groups of characters: the "natives", the newcomers and the narrator. Most of the "natives" are whimsical people who are absorbed with the idea of survival. The newcomers are Father Power, the parish priest, who loves his parishioners but has nothing in common with them, and Michael Kennedy, the new school teacher who came to Merasheen straight from college.

The narrator appears when most of the other characters have introduced one another (p. 5). He represents the epic element in the play: he provides the audience with interesting background information and both introduces and comments on the characters. Somehow the narrator is a substitute for what is normally contained in the stage directions (there are no stage directions in *A Rope*), but in the course of the play his function more and more resembles that of the stage manager in Thornton Wilder's *Our Town*. He becomes the linking element and the pivotal point, whereas Father Power and Michael Kennedy serve as counterfoils against which the attitudes and lifestyles of the people in Merasheen come even more to the fore.

A Rope is a well-crafted play. Although it is not formally divided into acts and scenes, its structure is clearly recognizable. References to the different times of the day reflect the ups and downs of the people in Merasheen and mark stages in the development of the play.

> The autumn sun [...] has begun its angular ascent [...]. The day has just begun [...]. (p. 5)

> By mid afternoon the women have retrieved their clothes from the lines, the sheep have gone single file to their quarters beneath the stages and stores [...], and the fog has come back in [...]. By mid afternoon everything has turned grey. (p. 33)

As the grey, dim-lit day dims itself down suddenly to darkness, [...] Merasheen shakes itself out of its overlong afternoon nap and begins to move
itself about. (p. 41)

Obviously what happens during the day must be seen in connection with the
appearance and disappearance of the sun and the fog. The rough sea influences
the people's life and way of thinking. The weather changes over the day, but the
life of the villagers does not change: They are involved in their routine duties
and lead the kind of life they have always lived.

It is the age-old dichotomy between superstition and Catholic belief that has
exerted a very strong influence on life in Merasheen. Experts say that there is
hardly any part of the world which is more productive of ghost stories and
legends of the supernatural as is Newfoundland. These stories, which originated
in England or Ireland, have been handed down from generation to generation.
Some are only remembered on the Newfoundland seashore. In *A Rope* superstitious beliefs can be found on different levels. There is a kind of hierarchy from
bad luck to threatening death. One should not make the Sign of the Cross while
watching the toast burning (p. 14); spilling salt means bad luck (p. 14). People in
Merasheen are convinced that "death is foretold by a dog burying some object
near one's home, by a bird entering a room, by a picture falling from a wall
[...]" (p. 12). They believe it is bad luck "to purchase a broom in May, to meet
a red-haired woman, to look over one's shoulder into a mirror, [...] to whistle
on the water" and – to coil *a rope against the sun* (p. 12).[15]

More important than these unsubstantial elements of superstition, which stem
from everyday observations and experiences, are the far-reaching beliefs, which
permeate the entire life of the people in Merasheen and which represent threatening death, connected first and foremost with the barren tree and the sunkers.

In the Virgin Cove there is a barren tree, surrounded by lots of rocks, which
have been carried separately from the beach. The tree is called *The Naked Man*
in remembrance of a young man who courted a girl from this region. The narrator in the play tells the audience that the young man "disappeared one storm-
stricken night to be found only when spring came to melt away the snow and
reveal his naked body sprawled at the base of the tree" (p. 10). According to
Jake Connors, "not a single leaf sprouted on that tree again" (p. 11). Ever since
that time people have been telling stories about the *Naked Man* which has virtually become a sanctuary. Everybody believes that one has to pay one's proper
homage, and this applies particularly to Mrs. Ennis who is expecting a baby. She
goes to church regularly, but her fright makes her go to the *Naked Man* right
after church to place one more rock on the pile of stones. Her superstitious
belief goes well hand in hand with her Catholic belief which can also be inferred
from her fear of and her attitude towards the so-called sunkers of Merasheen.

Nobody can tell who these sunkers really are. But they are believed to be monsters, the worst curse to mothers and sailors. There are, as it were, living and dead monuments of their power in Merasheen: mentally deranged and crippled children, and the white crosses erected on the cliffs to commemorate the sailors killed by the sunkers. As long as the sea is still and the sunkers are quiet – superstition tells the people – there is no danger. And Mrs. Ennis kneels at the altar rail of the church and prays to God "to make the Sunkers be still when my baby comes born" (p. 8).

The people in Merasheen envisage different incarnations of what seem to be dangers impending over them. They also believe in fairies and banshees, the latter being spirits whose cry is said to portend death. Suspicious creatures seem to be lurking everywhere. The various superstitious beliefs are the hinges on which life hangs in Merasheen. None of the villagers question the validity of these beliefs. Most of them cling to their Christian belief and at the same time are sunk in ignorance and superstition. They keep plodding on their way: Nell takes care of her old father, Jake Connors complains about God and the world, Joe Casey is a drunkard, who seems to live in the past. Elizabeth, his wife, says but little, and Jennifer Byrne works at the priest's house. Gossipping and gibbering appear to be their favourite diversions. Joe speaks of Jake as "a contrary old bugger" (p. 1), Father Power finds Michael Kennedy "a bit of a disappointment really" (p. 2), and Mrs. Ennis says that it would be more proper for the priest "not to have a young girl like Jennifer around" (p. 3). Obviously most people in this outport do not realize that theirs is a petrified social setting. The men talk about their work, the women mostly about their neighbours. It seems that they do not really communicate with each other, but merely talk about one another. The men go to work and, as they are sailors, are often away for a long time, whereas the women and wives stay at home and can hardly expect anything from life. As Nell puts it:

It's not fair. The Good Lord knows it's not. Not fair at all. A fine young woman like meself stuck every bit of a lifetime with an invalid to look after. It's no proper way for a woman to live. (p. 28)

There are only a few in Merasheen who at least try to direct their steps to the future – Mrs Ennis, for instance, who is expecting a baby, or Billy, who is planning a life with Jennifer, or Nell, who keeps dreaming of her lover. They are somehow future-oriented. But by and large the others cling to the past and to the traditions handed down from the past.

From the dramatic point of view, Michael Kennedy and Father Power are the most important characters in A Rope. Both are integral parts of the community, yet have remained onlookers. They are responsible for the education of the children or the furtherance of their Christian belief respectively. Michael Ken-

nedy, the school teacher, came to Merasheen with high hopes and great expectations. He likes the outport, but in the long run comes to realize that he cannot
cope with the reality of the Newfoundlanders. Similarly, Father Power becomes
disillusioned. He does love his parishioners "in the Christian sense of the word"
(p. 35), but finds it difficult to love them "in the ordinary human sense of it".
With both, hopes and illusions are finally replaced by resignation.

Michael's and the narrator's duologue (pp. 21–24) on the one hand and Father
Power's letter to the bishop (pp. 11–12) on the other hand are what could be
termed key passages of the play – in the sense that they reveal both the change of
attitudes on the part of the two characters and the well-known stereotypes
which many people – in and outside Canada – adopt when looking at Newfoundland from the outside. Michael's first impression was that Newfoundland
is "living folklore" (p. 23), "the stuff novels and poems and plays are made of"
(p. 22). But after a while he is disillusioned. The people in Newfoundland are no
longer the people of his folklore; the children, who fascinated him with their
skipping rhymes, are not cute any more. And he asks himself why he ever came
to this outport (p. 38). His unjustified optimistic view of the island is finally
replaced by a similarly unjustified pessimistic attitude towards the people,
expressed in stereotyped statements like: "They are much too petty to be fasci-
nating, too greedy to be admired, too narrow-minded to be interesting, and too
self-centred to be lovable" (p. 23). Michael is sick of the people in Merasheen
and their petty little problems (p. 38). Similarly, Father Power comes to realize
that "the sum total of his life" is "worrying about such trifling matters" (p. 56).
He, like Michael, complains about the fact that he is unsuccessful in doing what
he is supposed to do. His parishioners are ideal Christians, they come to Mass
every Sunday and the collection taken up after the sermon has not diminished
much. But they hang on to their superstitious beliefs. Therefore Father Power
asks his bishop to be transferred to another parish (p. 12). Both Michael and
Father Power fail because they believe that the best they can do for the people is
to graft their own concepts of religion and education on these people and do
away with everything that does not fit into these concepts. But there is one
important difference between the two "outsiders". Father Power does not suc-
ceed in ridding his people of their pagan idolatry. Michael fails because Father
Power's well-intentioned measures have brought about unbearable limitations
to his teaching: "How can you teach anything while you are running around
selling tickets on homemade socks and banging Bingo balls around all week
long" (p. 37). His classroom remains a classroom of his dreams; Father Power's
money-making schemes prevent Michael from being a successful teacher. In a
final dream he confronts "the monster of his misery":

> It is tall and thin with arms outspread like a crucifix. It is draped in black. It
> has a Bingo ball for a head with 0 66 where its mouth should be. It wears a

white celluloid collar around its neck, and carries in one outstretched hand a black book whose pages are dollar bills. In the other hand, it holds a whip woven out of homemade socks. The monster slides toward Michael on its one huge pulpit-shaped foot. His scream dies in the darkness with no one to hear. Suddenly there is a noise like trumpets. The Minister of Education appears and takes Michael's soul by the hand and leads it to Heaven. (p. 52)

To Father Power superstition places restrictions on a Catholic way of living. To Michael Kennedy Father Power's wrongly practised Catholicism turns out to be an insurmountable barrier to educational progress. This dichotomy reflects the playwright's own experiences. Being Catholic was an important part of his identity when he grew up. "It was as enriching as it was restrictive", Pittman said in an interview[16], and he went on to say:

[...] the kind of Catholicism I grew up with could have been a very smothering kind of thing. The institution and my allegiance to it might have been deadly, but I also grew up in a family community where those same institutionalized values were delivered to me, required of me, within the realm of real genuine warmth and love. Not love reduced to Christian love or philosophical love, but human warmth.[17]

A Rope is not only interesting because it stems from the playwright's biography, but also because it reflects Pittman's love of Dylan Thomas and his "tendencies at the time to play with language in that way".[18] He admits that what he had in mind was to depict rural life in Newfoundland in the way that Dylan Thomas does for Wales. "There's no doubt that Dylan Thomas and *Under Milk Wood* were the seeds of it", he says. The language spoken by the different characters in the play is partly rhythmic and poetical, partly sparse and earthy. There are humorous remarks and biting words – and a sprinkling of vulgarisms.

[Jake] leapt out onto the middle of the altar and bellowed 'a very merry christmas and a happy new year to ye all' before he went arse before kettle over the communion rail and landed with a plop like a flatfish in old Miss Collin's lap.[19]

First and foremost A Rope is a revealing play because it lets the audience catch a glimpse of what life is like in a Newfoundland outport, which is also a part of Canada. *Is* like? or should one say, *was* like? The play was written in 1974. Ten years later, Pittman decided to discuss it again with his students because he thought, "it would be valuable for the students to have an opportunity to talk to the person responsible for this stuff".[20] "What did they make of it?", he was asked in an interview:

I'm not sure. A lot of it was identification. Students came to me and said, 'I liked that because I know'. As a play, I have no idea what they might have thought of it.[21]

Pittman's audience still know what the outports are like in which traditional values and patterns mean more than economic growth. Whether outports like Merasheen will also exist in the future, remains to be seen. Whether Resettlement programmes will help the villagers to live a better life is a moot question. "Tomorrow and tomorrow and tomorrow creeps in its petty pace from one day to the next, or whatever it is. Tomorrow will be another day of petty pace, that's for sure", says Father Power (p. 55). So far – at least in Pittman's play – moving into the future is also a return to earlier days – *back to the future*. Pittman, as he says himself, would like to rewrite *A Rope*, but "that would be a wasted exercise because you've got to let go of it".[22]

Notes

1 Noel, S. J. R.: *Politics in Newfoundland.* Toronto, 1971, p. 4.
2 English, L. E. F.: *Historic Newfoundland.* St. John's (Tourist Services Division), [8]1975, p. 59.
3 Ibid., p. 58.
4 Ibid.
5 Ibid., p. 59.
6 Glaap, A.-R.: *Interview with Pat Byrne,* 24 September 1985 (Typescript).
7 Cook, M.: *Jacob's Wake.* Vancouver, 1975.
8 French, D.: *Leaving Home.* Toronto, 1972. Cp. also: *Of the Fields, Lately.* Toronto, 1973, and *Salt-Water Moon.* Toronto, 1985.
9 Pittman, A.: *A Rope Against the Sun.* St. John's, 1974.
10 (Pages of) quotations from the play refer to the Breakwater (St. John's) edition (cp. Note 9).
11 Garrod, A.: "Al Pittman". – In Garrod, A. (Ed.): *Speaking for Myself: Canadian Writers in Interview.* St. John's, 1986, pp. 190–207, here: p. 200.
12 Ibid., p. 197.
13 Ibid., p. 206.
14 Ibid., p. 200.
15 Cp. English, L. E. F.: *Historic Newfoundland,* p. 42.
16 Garrod, A.: "Al Pittman", p. 194.
17 Ibid., p. 195.
18 Ibid., p. 199.
19 Ibid.
20 Ibid.
21 Ibid.
22 Ibid.

Bibliography

I. Select Works of Al Pittman

Short Stories:
The Boughwolfen and Other Stories. St. John's: Breakwater Books, 1984.

Children's Books:
Down bei Jim Long's Stage. Rhymes for Children and Young Fish. Illustrated by Pam Hall. St. John's: Breakwater Books, 1976.
One Wonderful Fine Day for a Sculpin Named Sam. Illustrated by Shawn Steffler. St. John's: Breakwater Books, 1983.

Poetry:
The Elusive Resurrection. Fredericton: Brunswick Press, 1966.
Seaweed and Rosaries. Montreal: Poverty Press, 1969.
Through One More Window. St. John's: Breakwater Books, 1974.
Once When I Was Drowning. St. John's: Breakwater Books, 1978.

Drama:
A Rope Against the Sun. A Play for Voices. St. John's: Breakwater Books, 1974.

Edited:
East Coast Canada. A Poetry Anthology. Eds. Al Pittman, Raymond Fraser. Montreal: Poverty Press, 1969.
31 Newfoundland Poets. Eds. Al Pittman, Adrian Fowler. St. John's: Breakwater Books, 1979.

II. Secondary Literature

Burke, J. C.: *A Treasury of Newfoundland Humour and Wit.* St.John's, 1985.
Jackson, F. L.: *Newfoundland in Canada. A People in Search of a Polity.* St. John's, 1984.
Matthews, K.: *Our Newfoundland and Labrador Cultural Heritage,* Part 1. Scarborough/ Ontario, 1982.
Noel, S. J. R.: *Politics in Newfoundland.* Toronto, 1971.
Nowlan, M. O. (Ed.): *The Maritime Experience.* Toronto, 1975.
O'Flaherty, P.: *The Rock Observed. Studies in the Literature of Newfoundland.* Toronto, 1979.
Toy, W. (Ed.): *The Oxford Companion to Canadian Literature.* Toronto, Oxford, New York, 1983, pp. 548–552.

Vorschau auf das Programm von 1988

34. American Theater Today

    mit Beiträgen über:
    - Tendenzen des amerikanischen Theaters von den 70er bis zu den 80er Jahren;
    - die amerikanische Komödie (Neil Simon und Woody Allen);
    - *women dramatists* (Beth Henley und Marsha Norman);
    - *gay theater;*
    - experimentelles Theater;
    - David Rabe;
    - Sam Shepard;
    - David Mamet

35. Crime and Treachery – Neuere Thriller, Kriminal- und Spionageromane

    mit Beiträgen über:
    - P. D. James und die Entwicklungen des neueren englischen Kriminalromans;
    - Stanley Ellin;
    - Patricia Highsmith;
    - Entwicklungen des Spionageromans der 70er und 80er Jahre;
    - Len Deighton;
    - John Le Carré;
    - Strukturen und Wirkungsweisen des populären Thrillers (Frederick Forsyth und Robert Ludlum);
    - Kriminalroman im Unterricht

Ebenfalls in Vorbereitung

- Schottland – Literatur, Kultur, Politik
- Zweihundert Jahre amerikanische Verfassung
- Literatur und Film
- City Lyrics

CARL WINTER · UNIVERSITÄTSVERLAG · HEIDELBERG

Klaus Peter Müller, Düsseldorf

Initiations into a Canadian Identity?
Contexts of Canadian "Stories of Initiation"

US-American stories of initiation have been extensively described, analysed and defined.[1] Socially the initiation is a universal phenomenon.[2] In literature it is an equally widespread and international motif. It is, therefore, natural that one should find it in Canadian writing, too. There are, however, some peculiar characteristics and significant differences in Canadian texts, which will be outlined in the present article. The working hypotheses, based on quite an extensive reading of Canadian short stories, are as follows:

1. There are significant differences between US-American stories of initiation (as defined by the literary critics quoted in footnote 1) and comparable Canadian short stories.

2. These differences are closely related to and can often be explained by the typical Canadian context, in particular the Canadian's view(s) of the nation, its identity and historical as well as political unity.

3. This view of Canada and its position in the world, of one's self as a Canadian and of one's own place within the Canadian society often results in a young person in a Canadian story not having a definite idea, nor even any ill-defined notion, of what his/her future position should be, what maturity and adulthood should consist of, and how such an objective could be achieved. The adolescent's situation often remains vague; his/her position within society is portrayed as being very ambivalent; and there is no significant or permanent trace of an accepted or intended identity.

Such ambivalent, not clearly definable positions and attitudes may be seen as typical characteristics of modern human life. But there are also some particularly Canadian aspects of such a widespread human experience. The purpose of the article is to analyse and define these aspects as *one important part of Canadian literature,* not to claim that all Canadian writing, nor even all Canadian short stories are characterized in the same way. Indeed, it would be worthwile investigating even more of the recent narrative texts from different Canadian regions to find out whether they do not in fact reveal quite different tendencies from the one that will be defined in this article.[3] For the time being, however, it is far more important to describe this prominent part of Canadian literature, because it can be found in so much of Canadian writing and it has not yet been sufficiently investigated by literary critics.

The investigation is necessarily related to the question of the national literature(s) of Canada. It also has to ask which group(s) of Canadian society an adolescent is being initiated into in the various stories. For these reasons it is very useful to know the most important definitions of the Canadian identity which have been provided by sociologists, geographers, historians, politicians, ethnologists, literary critics, and writers of literature. The following survey of such concepts of Canadianness thus offers a frame for the understanding and evaluation of short stories and the various kinds of initiation.

The existing Canadian self-definitions also provide a way of comparing individual stories with a more general consciousness. Freese's statement concerning the relationship between a particular US-American story of initiation and the nation's self-understanding applies equally to Canada: "Inadvertently, every story of initiation turns into a commentary on central issues of American self-understanding. [...] Consequently, every story about a youth's disillusioning movement from childhood to adulthood and his or her initiation into sin and guilt implies a statement about basic American dreams and nightmares."[4]

Important Concepts and Contexts of Canadian Self-understanding and Identity

Canada did not gain its liberty and national unity in a war of independence against the European colonial nations. Autonomy was not so much fought for from within the country as granted little by little from the outside, e.g. by the 1840 Act of Union, the British North America (B. N. A.) Act of 1867, the 1931 Statute of Westminster, and in 1949 by the power given to the Canadian Parliament to amend the B. N. A. Act in matters clearly within federal jurisdiction. A Canadian "Bill of Rights" was entrenched in the B. N. A. Act in 1962. There has been a national coat of arms since 1921. In 1965 "after a protracted and bitter debate a national flag was finally adopted", and the national anthem was officially accepted in 1980, i.e. a hundred years after it had been composed.[5] Even after the "Canada Act" or "Constitution Act" of 1982 there is still no nationally accepted constitution, as the ten provinces continue to be more concerned with their provincial rights and independence than with the question of national unity.[6]

National identity and an independent self-understanding are, therefore, relatively new concepts and questions for many Canadians. Canada is going through a typically Commonwealth experience, similar to the one defined by Clark Blaise and represented by means of three different characters in his short story "A North American Education".[7] First there is a long, seemingly natural, close and unquestioned identification with the mother country, which provides the security of an identity. But with a growing awareness of distance and differences this identity becomes vulnerable and insecure. The alienation or turning away from the mother country leads to the loss of the accepted self-image which had been taken for granted. There is, as a third stage, the painful awareness that one has to create one's own identity.

Canada has been at these two latter stages of development for about a quarter of a century now. As Margaret Atwood has noted, "something changed [...] during the early 1960s. Canada ceased to be a kind of limbo you were stuck in if unlucky or not smart enough and became a real place."[8] But this new awareness led, above all, to the need to find and define one's own and the nation's identity. The noticeable new impetus and energy which was felt by many Canadians at that time did not make them smug or over-self-confident. On the contrary, it grew from and fostered a new will and desire to overcome the uncertainty of the origins, purpose and forms of a national, provincial and individual identity. Ever since that time of suspension, Canada has often been seen as a country with a weak common symbolism, unlike China and the United States for instance. It exists, "but is invisible".[9] Its past is "like the past of a psychiatric patient, something of a problem to be resolved", and the "Canadian sense of the future tends to be apocalyptic".[10]

Where for some the need to (re-)define their own identity became more and more urgent, others saw their well delineated world unnecessarily questioned. George Grant, occasionally called "'Canada's foremost political philosopher'", has been one of the loudest voices of the latter point of view in his *Lament for a Nation. The Defeat of Canadian Nationalism*. His "lament mourns the end of Canada as a sovereign state", the end of an era when people "took it for granted that they belonged to a nation", the end of a time when "the character of the country was self-evident." For Grant the nation was self-evidently "British" and at the same time "a unique species of North American".[11]

Grant's anti-American and anti-capitalist attitudes met with widespread support and sympathy. Many other aspects of his philosophy were greatly criticized, however, in particular his notion of nationalism and its premise of a pre-established order, often identified with "God as 'the limit of our right to change the world'".[12]

Nationalism implies a centralist view, the idea of a basic unity behind or beyond all divergencies and differences. Canadian nationalism failed early in the 1960s, because after almost a hundred years of indifference, neglect or repression in the wake of the Confederation of 1867, the differences suddenly became apparent. The political movement for an independent Quebec was only the most manifest representation of this development. What had only just begun as nationalism (which could easily be detected as a variant of old tendencies to establish a British hegemony) was replaced by the official policy of Biculturalism and Bilingualism.[13]

But Biculturalism was not enough. On October 8, 1971, the Prime Minister "proclaimed a policy of 'multiculturalism within a bilingual framework'".[14] The concept has been gaining strength ever since. But is it capable of supplying satisfactory answers to the individual and the national search for identity? Doubts have been raised. On the one hand, there are people who still favour a nationalist concept, arguing for a single Canadianness, and fearing that "'the fledgling Canadian Identity, already frail and wan'" will be totally destroyed by "'400 cultures in search of a people'".[15] On the other hand, there is the concern that multiculturalism may be or may become "a strategy of 'containment of the other ethnic groups, similar to that of colonial pluralism'", "'a fraud perpetrated by the British upon all other Canadians in order to keep them in their place'".[16] Two most influential concepts have, therefore, been offered as alternatives: modern technology and the land or region.

John Porter, for instance, an important advocate of a new technology, states that cultures, as they are conceived in multiculturalism, "are less and less relevant for the postindustrial society because they emphasize yesterday rather than today". The present time is characterized by "the rapidity of change" and "the shock of the future". Porter, therefore, thinks that one "can almost speak of the end of culture". As a solution to the cultural problem and an answer to the question of a national identity, he suggests that one should accept the fact that Canada has "one culture of science and technology" which helps to "enhance the self-concept of an individual" as well as the idea of a national identity.[17]

Marshall McLuhan's advocacy of a new technological culture even goes beyond the national level established by Porter. He propagates a universal culture and reduces the modern world to a "global village", where Canada would be just one house among many others.[18]

Such a universal concept is objected to by Arthur Kroker, who favours a new *national* technological culture incorporating modern technology as well as knowledge and acceptance of the past, historical awareness, and a mythical belief in the powers of the imagination. He claims that only this combination could create "a 'stable society', the survival of which would require a dynamic harmony between technology and culture". This concept excludes one-sidedness, centralism, and monolithism, because "everyone is peripheralized now by the systematic logic of technological society."[19]

Notions of modern technology are used, as we have just seen, to justify concepts of national unity or identity, global universalism as well as national and international plurality, diversification and decentralisation. Technology can be seen as a national culture, a universal culture or as a multicultural mosaic. Kroker's statement that "everyone is peripheralized" is congruent with the awareness that there is no dominant culture in Canada, and that each culture is that of a minority.[20] It is, therefore, not surprising that technology is regarded as a very important element in any modern society; in itself, however, it is hardly sufficient to define a sense of identity.

Canada is the second largest country in the world. The greater part of it is influenced by arctic and subarctic climates. It is not the easiest country to settle and live in. The facts and fictions of the land have been stressed by various concepts which are related to a Canadian identity. Northrop Frye's notion of the "garrison society" is clearly defined by both the physical aspects of the country and the colonial situation; it is a society (mainly of the 19th century, but with many visible vestiges in the 20th) characterized by "the constant fight to be clean, fully clothed, disciplined in speech and manner, to maintain [certain] standards [...] to remain a [gentleman or] gentlewoman in the backwoods", to preserve the feeling of belonging "to the gentry", and to present and embody this social status and its values to the world outside, which is often seen as a wilderness with "conditions of life that were primitive to the point of squalor".[21]

The land is so overwhelmingly large, cruel and demanding that survival is the first priority. Margaret Atwood's concept of "survival" and the "victor-victim relationship" connected with this concept were, therefore, widely accepted when they were first presented in 1972.[22] Again, however, Atwood's concept must not only be seen in relation to the land, but also to the colonial situation. She is greatly committed to the survival, revival or rather the bringing to life of a Canadian identity liberated from the long, numerous influences of colonialism, "since Canada is still in some respects a colony".[23]

This fear of the land and a concurrent clinging to colonial values characterized the Canadian mentality for a very long time and is one of the marked differences from the US-American ideology. "Accepting nature and rejecting tradition was exactly what Canada's whole history had refused to do."[24] This attitude changed when Canada became more and more of an industrial and urban society. But it is not cities that can give a sense of individual or national identity, because Canadian cities are very much "'like all cities the world over'"; it is much more the natural environment, the regional community.[25] There is an obvious need "to belong to an identifiable community", and if it is not an ethnic or social one, it is very often a community constituted by the place or region of residence. "Identity is local and regional", says Northrop Frye, and he then continues, it is "rooted in the imagination and in works of culture".[26]

It is not the country and its physical aspects alone that help to shape a sense of identity and belonging. The way the country is seen and experienced, its influence on the imagination as well as the workings of the imagination on the land are equally important. Not only does the land leave its marks on human beings,

71

it is also marked by them. This mutual relationship is stressed by areas of human interest as different as regional geography, literature, literary criticism, and sociology.

The importance of the imagination, of the mind and of language in this process of identifying (oneself with) the country makes the work of artists, in particular that of writers, especially relevant. Thus Tom Marshall is justified in saying that "Canadian poets [...] are engaged in the creation of their country", that they are in particular working on the "imaginative construction of the self, of a national sense of self".[27] E. D. Blodgett even wants to "argue that for us the place, the space of the Canadian literatures, is only real because it has been turned to fiction".[28]

The physical aspects of the country, and especially the imaginative and symbolic ones are of extreme importance for the creation of a common code, Hardin's "strong common symbolism", which is necessary for the establishment and representation of national unity and identity. Once such a common symbolism exists, the question of a national identity is easily regarded as being resolved or even unimportant. Identity is taken for granted. That is, of course, an illusion, as identity is always a question of relations, which change and have to be continually redefined. But a strong common symbolism helps to provide an important basis. Symbols like the national flag, the national anthem, etc. secure the feeling of national identity. How else would it be possible for complex societies to achieve a sense of identity? The complexity of Canadian society cannot be ignored. It is neatly described as that "of a country which is at once unicultural (represented in Anglo-Canadian dominance or – within Quebec – the *francization* policies of the Parti Quebecois), bicultural (e.g., French minorities outside Quebec or English-speaking minorities within Quebec), yet multicultural (especially in the larger cities and in the Prairie provinces)".[29]

Canadians are still working on definitions of their identity. They are for the most part experiencing the second and the beginning of the third phase of the developing Canadian culture as defined by Northrop Frye: after "the uncomplicated provincial or colonial period", which imitates traditional colonial values, the second phase takes in "more contemporary" and local influences. "The final phase, in which provincial culture becomes fully mature, occurs when the artist enters into the cultural heritage that his predecessors have drawn from, and paints or writes without any sense of a criterion external to himself and his public."[30] Frye saw beginnings of the third phase in the 1950's. A genuine culture for him depends significantly on decentralisation, interpenetration and regionalism. There is no monolithic sense of cultural identity in his concept, but one that includes ambiguities, pluralism and diversity, as is indicated in the title of his book: *Divisions on a Ground.*

Blodgett's concept of "configuration", which implies investigations of "figures and their inter-relationships", stresses even more the fact that there is no single national identity, that there are in fact "Canadian Literatures", not just one as is maintained by Ronald Sutherland for instance.[31] Blodgett strongly objects to the "mainstream" theories for Canadian literature which suggest similarities or even identities that are not really there. Such a blurring of differences between the writings of Canadian authors is compared with the political attitude of nationalism, which "only grudgingly tolerates ambiguity".[32] Ambiguity is rather deliberately cultivated in Canada; in fact, Blodgett states "that 'Canadian' must always connote ambiguity". The reason for this is simply that in Canada very different norms, values, standards, ideologies, or, as Blodgett puts it, "codes" are used to define and describe reality. Therefore, for him, "Canada is, in fact, a problem in discourse".[33] It is the problem of how language is used to "make nature what it is", to "make [our]selves real", to give a name to something in order "to identify and possess" it. The history of the Canadian land, of the settlement of the country is the history of "unnaming and renaming". Blodgett thus makes evident that "the theme of the journey to settlement is of particular value in teaching the Canadian literatures".[34]

This theme includes the initiation as the journey towards adulthood, to an awareness of one's identity and position within society. Canada has been in a phase where traditional values are criticized and conventional identities break up. The phase has been described by Clark Blaise and Northrop Frye, as presented above. Jürgen Habermas, speaking about the possibilites of a complex society to create a reasonable identity, has termed this phase "Adoleszenz-phase", adolescent phase. It is that time in a person's life when he or she becomes aware of the important distinction between norms and criteria for establishing norms.[35]

Earle Birney has his own view of this phase. His "Canada: Case History: 1973" ends with the lines: "this youth, we fear, has moved from adolescence / into what looks like permanent senescence." There seems to be no real improvement to the situation described in "Canada: Case History: 1945", which presented "the case of a high-school land, / deadset in adolescence" and asked about "this boy" with "parents unmarried and living abroad, / relatives keen to bag the estate, / schizophrenia not excluded, / will he learn to grow up before it's too late?"[36]

The search for identity, "the theme of discovery and the creation of self and country" is certainly "a major theme of Canadian literature at large". It may also be described in Margaret Atwood's words as something

> not lost or hidden / but just not found yet
> that informs, holds together / this confusion, this largeness / and dissolving:

not above or behind / or within it, but one / with it: an
identity: / something too huge and simple / for us to see.

The poem is significantly called "A Place: Fragments".[37] It is an appropriate
evocation of the atmosphere, mood, and tendency found in many Canadian
stories which are not even yet "tentative stories of initiation", because often no
attempt is made to find oneself, to seek liberation from constraints or to understand one's situation. Or, where there are such endeavours, where a youth does
indeed set out on a journey, "which seems to lift and draw [him or her] forward,
upward and inward", eventually it only too often turns out to be a journey
"forever into the vastness of the dark", with a young person not knowing where
he or she goes, nor where he or she wants to go.[38]

Contexts in Canadian Short Story Writing

Alistair MacLeod's collection of short stories, *The Lost Salt Gift of Blood,* which
is said to be "united by the theme of a sensitive consciousness brought up
against the harsher realities of life", is characterized by an atmosphere of sadness
and the feeling of having lost one's roots in the country where one was raised
(Nova Scotia in these stories).[39] The title story as well as "The Return" and
"The Boat" describe this sense of loss and the temporary returns to the "native"
land, which provide a renewed contact with nature for the persons who had left
for "the larger world" outside, for Ontario, the cities or the States. The final
journey, however (in "The Road to Rankin's Point"), is a return to home in
order "to realize and understand [...] death in all its vast diversity".[40] The
26-year-old protagonist wants to acquire this knowledge from his grandmother, who in her harsh, laborious and lonely life has had much experience of
death. The young man is suffering from a fatal illness and has only a few months
to live. A high-school teacher in Burlington and Don Mills, Ontario, he has now
returned "almost as the diseased and polluted salmon, to swim for a brief time in
the clear waters of [his] earlier stream". But like the returning salmon, which
"knows of no 'cure' for the termination of his life", there is no knowledge or
help to be had from the grandmother, who herself hoped for help from her
grandchild in her efforts to go on living. When both realize their mutual loneliness and helplessness in the face of death, they unite in a "display of weeping
weakness". The grandmother dies on the same afternoon. The young man finds
her and is now completely drawn into the "darkened void" of his life.[41]

The sense of something vital being lost and not found again, which was described above by Atwood's poem and is so strongly felt in MacLeod's short
stories, is a widespread phenomenon in Canadian literature. Pierre Spriet speaks
of a similar "failure structure" that can be detected in the novels and short stories

of Rudy Wiebe, where "plots have been moral, and the stories could be read as metaphors of Christ's sacrifice, ending as they had to in failure and death".[42]

Women are generally not an exception to this rule of failing and frustrated protagonists. The works of Alice Munro and Margaret Atwood may be mentioned in this context, and a recent collection of *Stories by Canadian Women* was reviewed as not going "beyond victimhood", as presenting initiations into "religious and sexual hypocrisy", "madness and alienation", where the women's will is "paralyzed; a symptom, perhaps, of colonization everywhere" where the women are just "More Victims".[43]

Margaret Laurence and her work, however, can be seen as belonging to a different category, one that includes (relative) success, maturity, and identity. Vanessa MacLeod, the young protagonist of eight stories gathered together in *A Bird in the House* is seen as taking "steps towards understanding or, where understanding was impossible, acceptance", thus reaching a kind of maturity that characterizes many of Laurence's female protagonists.[44] Laurence's different perspective may well have much to do with her personal experience of struggles for liberation in Africa, where she spent several years and studied the literature as well as the political situation, which largely consisted of colonial, post-colonial and tribal elements. It is interesting to see that Margaret Atwood has begun to compare more intensively the Canadian literary and political state with that of other Commonwealth nations.[45]

Mavis Gallant's story "Bernadette", about a young French Canadian servant girl in an anglophone Montreal household, describes another typical victim of ignorance, lack of concern, and terrorizing fear in the context of the French and English Canadian cultures in Quebec in the 1950s.[46] Many of Gallant's characters are, in fact, "locked into a present situation, condition, stage of personal history, from which escape is difficult, and sometimes impossible".[47] Just as Gallant's stories often describe static situations, where "individual consciences construct prisons around themselves as shields against" others[48], there are many more Canadian stories focusing on situations of stasis rather than movement, of physical and intellectual immobility or of movement back into the past or into a world of dreams and fantasy. It is, therefore, not easy to find Canadian stories which correspond in every detail with the elements of typical, acknowledged stories of initiation. Rather than setting out on a journey which leads to an *initiation as*:

1) "the Recognition of the Existence of Evil in the World",
2) "the Loss of Innocence and the Gaining of Experience and Maturity",
3) "the Introduction into the Manners and Values of a Given Society",
4) "the Process of Self-Discovery and Self-Realization"[49],

young Canadian protagonists often do not have the courage to leave, or they leave without really knowing where to go and what to look for, and having left, they fail to find what they need and eventually return to their place of departure.

Raymond Knister's "Mist Green Oats" is a fine example of the first case, a story about a young boy living on a farm, about his hard labour, his dreams of a better life in the city, and his struggle to pluck up enough courage to leave. After much wavering, the boy in the end packs his suitcase. He does not "set it plainly on the floor before the table", however, he puts "it to one side" so that his father does not see it immediately. Then, "with a beating heart he went out of the house, whistling". We do not know where he goes, but we wonder whether he will really leave on the following day. The narrator has clearly shown that the boy's dissatisfaction with his country life is understandable, but that the city is not necessarily a better place to be and is certainly misconceived in the boy's imagination.[50]

Knister's story, published in 1922, finds a sequel in Roch Carrier's "A Secret Lost in the Water" of 1979. While Knister presented a boy one year after graduation from high school and seemingly on the verge of leaving the country for the city, Carrier tells the story of a boy who did leave his native village. Years later the boy comes back and learns in dismay that "somewhere along the roads I'd taken since the village of my childhood I had forgotten my father's knowledge".[51]

Whatever this man was initiated into, it certainly was not the world of his father. He lives in a different culture now, significantly dominated by the written and not the spoken word. It has made the boy a writer with much academic knowledge, but lacking the ability to draw water from the land. Whatever symbolic meaning one may want to read into this image, it does not give the new culture more significance or value than the old one. Something was lost on the way to adulthood that the boy was never aware of. This is only known by the adult when it is already too late.

Stories in which the protagonists either remain within the society, the cultural and physical environment known to them, or come back to that society and environment as adults, cannot properly be termed "stories of initiation" in the accepted sense. They do not "lead the protagonist

– into a given society ('initiation'),
– out of a given society ('denitiation'), or
– into self-made dream and escape worlds ('victimization')".

Not even "the Reversal of the Concept" is applicable, as there are no initiations away from society, or renunciations of the accepted standards of a given society in favour of other norms and values.[52]

The differences noted so far between US-American stories of initiation and Canadian ones can, perhaps, best be shown again, in a summarized and condensed way, by a comparison of Freese's "working definition of a 'story of initiation'" with one of the best and most typical examples of the Canadian kind.

Freese's definition is:

> The protagonist of a story of initiation belongs to the transitory phase of 'adolescence'. He gains his experience in the course of a *journey* which consists of the three phases of *exit, transition,* and *(re-)entrance* and leads the protagonist from *innocence* to *experience*. During this – real or metaphorical – journey the *initiate* experiences different, mostly unexpected, bewildering, and disillusioning *confrontations* with representatives of a world hitherto unknown, and is exposed to the various temptations of a devilish *tempter* figure but can, on the other hand, find help and advice from the fatherly or motherly *mentor*. The initiate's experiences culminate in *recognition* or an *insight* bringing about an irreversible change, which often refers to the painful discovery of the disparity between *appearance* and *reality*.[53]

The story to be compared with this definition was written by Gabrielle Roy, who was born in Manitoba in 1909 and died in Quebec in 1983. Roy believed, and justifiably so, that "her upbringing as a member of a minority in Manitoba and her maturity spent as one of the majority in Quebec gave her a particular insight into what being a Canadian is and ought to mean".[54] She often in her work featured minority groups other than her own, thus dealing with a common and significant Canadian aspect. This is also the case in her short story "The Satellites", which is "based on an incident observed by Roy in 1961, while in the Ungava district of northern Quebec".[55]

It is important to notice that here one member of a significant minority group, the French Canadians, writes about a member of another important group, the natives, in this case the Eskimos. It is also a story written by a woman about a woman. In fact, there seem to be many more female protagonists whose adolescence is portrayed in Canadian stories than there are in American ones. The main topic, however, is the relationship of the Eskimo group to the dominant cultural group, which is not defined in an ethnic, political, or economic way, but as the group living in the "South". Two different cultures, two ways of living (and dying), and two distinct regions are set off against each other. The story consists of the journey which the Eskimo woman, Deborah, makes to the South and then back to her native village in the North.

Thus one important category of the traditional story of initiation is fulfilled. There is indeed a journey with its three phases of "exit", "transition", and "(re-) entrance". But it is not a journey made by a young woman. On the contrary, it is very important to be aware of the fact that Deborah belongs to the middle-aged group of Eskimos, because it is this group that is in transition. The transition is brought about by the new influence of modern life, i.e. life from the South. It is the first time that the middle-aged group has been affected by this influence. There are, in fact, three age groups or generations in the Eskimo village:

> [...] old men like Isaac, Deborah's father, reared in the old harsh ways; middle-aged men like Jonathan [Deborah's husband], divided between two influences, the ancient and the modern; and finally young men, more erect of body than their elders, slimmer too, and these were definitely inclined towards the life of today. (p. 168)

Deborah, aged forty-two, is the "victim of a swiftly progressing illness" (p. 169); in the old culture she would be prepared to die, because "from the moment one was no longer good for anything, one was always old enough for death" (ibid.). Death would be accepted quite naturally as a departure from the world; just as one came into it, out of nowhere, one leaves again, going nowhere. It is this firm belief in nature and the calm trustful acceptance of the seasons that characterizes the old culture. "What sense is it" to act differently, after all? "What is the sense of it?", Old Isaac asks, and not one of the Eskimos knows what the sense of it is and they remember the "beauty of the death of the Old One" (ibid.), who "when her hour had come" (p. 168), went on the pack-ice to die. Through the influence of the new culture, however, an effort is made to save Deborah's life. It is the pastor who takes the initiative; he thinks "that times were changing and that there was good in all these changes" (p. 171f.). The story reveals that this is not the case. The pastor is one important representative of the new culture bringing about changes in the native society through ignorance and conceit. He urges Deborah to go on living and has to admit that "the white men fear dying more than you Eskimos do". Why he asks her not to let herself die, he cannot say. He even concedes that "we [the white men] haven't learned to live in peace with one another or, for that matter, with ourselves. We haven't learned what is most essential, yet it's true that we are bent upon living longer and longer" (p. 170).

Deborah finally accepts the pastor's proposal that she should be taken to a hospital in the South, because of her wish "to recover the years that were past", "it was this good life she wanted to have once more" (p. 171).

Flying to the South she sees many new things, which she observes "with loving insistence" (p. 173) and great naiveté. The omniscient narrator presents Deborah's encounters with the new world from the Eskimo's point of view, thus creating an intriguing tension between what the reader already knows about this world and Deborah's discoveries. Deborah is at first confronted with a different land, with the physical aspects of the country, with nature and the material products of the South. These give her the impression that life in the South must be very sweet, happy, and easy. Eskimo life on the other hand "now seemed to her very cruel" (p. 175). But she never stops asking about the purpose of the things she sees, which seem to her "so slender and delicate" (p. 176), and what "the goal, so to speak, of [people's] lives" in the South is (p. 174).

After her operation, and having made some friends, Deborah learns that the whites are "no better off than the Eskimos", and "the vague hope she had maintained till then [...] that the white men would eventually manage to stretch life out forever – was extinguished once for all" (p. 178f). It is difficult for her to bear this hard truth, and the new culture of the South can now offer her only two things, for which she develops a passion: taking showers and smoking cigarettes. Deborah is not a rational person. She lives through feelings and expresses them in her actions, not by means of words, language or reason. She even asks explicitly: "Does one ever know with thoughts?" (p. 186). But even though she does not understand, and is not understood herself, by the sister for instance, she says to the latter: "Well, do I understand you? But no matter, I love you anyway." (p. 179)

Thus, when realizing that so many beautiful things from the South would not survive the journey to the North, and feeling increasingly sad and lonely, she does not know what is happening to her and simply cries. For the first time in her life, she sheds floods of tears. Only when she is told that she is lonesome does she understand what that means (p. 181).

Deborah is discharged from hospital, although her "illness may return" (ibid.). On her way home she realizes where she belongs, and that recognition fills her with new life. She is thus not initiated into a new society, but into the old one. One important change, however, is that what she took for granted earlier is now something she is acutely aware of, namely that it is her native society which gives her identity and a reason for existence (p. 182).

But her contact with the other culture has left its mark on Deborah. She has changed and cannot adapt to Eskimo life any more. She misses the "comforts of life in the South" and "especially, perhaps, that sort of friendliness – or show of friendliness – between people in the South" (p. 188). There is also a new way of thinking which has affected her and makes her face look emaciated and "marked with suffering and anxieties" in a way one did not find "in the old days on Eskimo faces" (p. 185). The narrator had warned the reader earlier on what the reason for this suffering is: "She had reached the point now of searching her mind to find imaginary solutions to hypothetical or possible evils, without the least idea, as yet, that it is through this door that sorrow enters a life." (p. 172)

This new way of thinking has a greater effect than the outward material innovations that have come with the new culture, because it is basically this attitude that destroys humanity's unity with nature. The technical innovations which sometimes also destroy the difficult balance in this vital relationship are a consequence of the mental attitude which is manifested in the technological mind trying to solve all problems set by nature, including those of illness and death.

If Deborah wants to overcome her sorrow and sadness, her dissatisfaction with life and her unwillingness to die, if she wants to die in peace with the others and with herself (unlike the white men that is, as the pastor noted above), she will have to overcome this way of thinking. She does so, when she realizes that "the better life became, the more needs it satisfied and the more new needs arose". She sees that "the others around her were, on her account, in want and deprivation" and that trying to find "a life or a place where one would lack nothing" is as impossible as trying "to satisfy the animals of the tundra, the whole of famished creation" (p. 188). This new and old awareness helps her to be reconciled with nature again. She accepts her life and its end and goes out onto the pack-ice like the Old One.

Roy's writing is very subtle and ingenious. Her use of imagery and symbols such as light, laughter, and animals are beyond the scope of this article. Neither can the structure of the story be discussed in any detail. Suffice it to say that there are six parts: the introduction with the setting, the theme, etc.; Deborah's flight to the South; Deborah in the hospital; her journey back home with the recognition of where she belongs; a discussion with the pastor; and Deborah's final recognition and her decision to die in the old way.

Roy, or the narrator, has great sympathy for the minority group. There are some positive aspects to be found in the new culture, but the negative ones clearly predominate. Roy also suggests that a concept like multiculturalism does not work, because the minority culture is too deeply affected by the new society. The influence is possibly fatal; it certainly brings disease to the old society. This is, after all, what actually happened when the colonizing nations came to the New World.[56]

Roy's story thus does not present an individual event, but the typical situation of satellite societies. The culture and identity of the satellites is being threatened; their original ways of life are being destroyed, and the shadow of death looms large over their lives.

Is there any solution suggested by the story? If returning to the old culture means dying, there certainly is not. One of the "famous last words" in Timothey Findley's novel says: "He who jumps to his death has cause [...] He who leaps has purpose."[57] Deborah has both cause and purpose. The cause is her disease and the new civilization (which probably are one and the same thing); her purpose is to die in the old way. To live in the old way is shown to be impossible. What the young Eskimos "definitely inclined towards the life of today" (p. 168) are going to do is an open question.

What is left of a story of initiation when the protagonist is initiated into an old culture which means death to her? Is it the initiation into or of a dying culture, or the reader's initiation into an awareness of the cultural situation in Canada? Should one abandon the term initiation in this context altogether or is it perhaps appropriate to speak of a typically Canadian variant? It would include in this particular case and in many other instances:

- a *transitory phase*, not of adolescence but of a later stage in life (which is easily acceptable if a story can be read as a metaphor for the historical development of the Canadian nation and its rather late concern with a national identity),

- a *journey* into a different culture, region or time,

- *experiences* which do not lead to a new acceptance of life or a change in attitude and actions,

- *confrontations* with the land and the people,

- a *tempter* who is not so much malicious as ignorant, because of his different cultural background,

- a *mentor* not present,

- a *recognition or insight* not bringing about an irreversible change in life, but leading to death, frustration, or failure,

- an acutely noticeable *disparity between appearance and reality*.

Some elements of the traditional form have been preserved; others have been significantly changed. This change is certainly not permanent, as literary forms will continue to vary and develop, just as identities change and have to be redefined again and again. However, it is very important to observe these changes and the process undergone by a culture on all of its many levels. Dominant traits must be seen and understood in literature as well as in politics, sociology, the economy, and all other sectors of society.

While on the economic level "the spectre of national disintegration will remain", and politically Trudeau's demand is still valid that "'if Canada is indeed to be a nation, there must be a national will which is something more than the lowest common denominator among the desires of provincial governments'"[58], Canadian literature also shows that identity is something that has to be fought for and is, in fact, an endless process of human existence and creation. As yet, not even a common temporary solution has been achieved in Canada in this endless journey and quest. Canada is still in a state of suspension or limen, separated from her previous condition and not yet incorporated into a new one. It, therefore, seems quite appropriate to describe the Canadian situation in terms of the adolescent phase, as has been done. This is not a unique phase, but surely a remarkable one with distinctive characteristics, even though recent studies suggest "that there is nothing *inherently* and exceptionally turbulent about the adolescent phase of development".[59] Therefore, the Canadian experience may in fact be much more representative of human life than many people are prepared to acknowledge, especially the Canadians who are often too reticent and shy to attribute international and general significance to their national and personal problems.

Notes

1 Cf. Marcus, M.: "What Is an Initiation Story?". *Journal of Aesthetics and Art Criticism* 14, 1960, 221–227, and Freese, P.: *The American Short Story. I: Initiation.* Paderborn, 1984 (student's book) and 1986 (teacher's book), where many more critical texts are quoted.

2 Cf. e.g. Levita, D. J. de: *Der Begriff der Identität.* Frankfurt/M., 1971; Erikson, E. H.: *Identity, Youth and Crisis.* New York, 1968. It should be mentioned in this context that the term "initiation" became a technical term in anthropology in 1742 when the French missionary Joseph François Lafitau called particular Canadian Indian rites celebrating maturity by that name (cf. Freese, P.: „Über die Schwierigkeiten des Heranwachsens: Amerikanische *stories of initiation* von Nathaniel Hawthorne bis Joyce Carol Oates". – In Freese, P., Groene, H., Hermes, L. (Eds.): *Die Short Story im Englischunterricht der Sekundarstufe II. Theorie und Praxis.* Paderborn, 1979, pp. 206–255, here: p. 208).

3 There are claims of such differences, put forward e.g. by Pritchard, A.: "West of the Great Divide. Man and Nature in the Literature of British Columbia". *Canadian Literature* No. 102, 1984, 36–53. He states that "the literature of British Columbia has developed in ways that strikingly contradict the 'survival' theses about Canadian literature" (p. 36). No confirmation of this has been found, however, in recent anthologies of short stories, such as: Broughton, K. M. (Ed.): *Heartland. An Anthology of Canadian Stories.* Scarborough/Ont., 1983; Flater, L., Herk, A., van Wiebe, R. (Eds.): *West of Fiction.* Edmonton, 1983; Gerson, C. (Ed.): *Vancouver Short Stories.* Vancouver, 1985; Metcalf, J. (Ed.): *Making It New. Contemporary Canadian Stories.* Toronto, 1982; Parr, J. (Ed.): *Manitoba Stories.* Winnipeg, 1981; Whitaker, M. (Ed.): *Stories from the Canadian North.* Edmonton, 1980.

4 Freese, P.: *Initiation*, 1984, p. 5.

5 McNaught, K.: *The Pelican History of Canada.* Harmondsworth, 1983, p. 310. Cf. ibid., passim and p. 131: "[...] the process of founding a continental Canadian state differed profoundly from the American [...]." Cf. also Schäfer, J.: „Auf dem Weg zur Nationalliteratur: Die Suche nach Symbolen". *Zeitschrift der Gesellschaft für Kanada-Studien* 1, iii, 1983, 28–38.

6   Roger Gibbins, Professor of political science at the University of Calgary, describes the main effect of the "Canada Act" in this way: "[...] the major impact comes from the constitutional process leading up to the act and from what it *failed* to do rather than from what it accomplished." (Gibbins, R.: "The Politics of the Canada Act". *Canadian Forum*, February 1983, 16.)

7   Blaise, C.: "A North American Education". – In Blaise, C.: *A North American Education. A book of short fiction*. Toronto, 1973, pp. 162–184. Cf. also Killam, D.: "The Customs Official and the Maple Tree". – In Breitinger, E., Sander, R. (Eds.): *Studies in Commonwealth Literature*. Tübingen, 1985, pp. 137–141. He quotes Blaise with: "It's exactly the same world that Naipaul writes about in Trinidad. It's a Commonwealth experience. The very nature of the Commonwealth is, I think, precisely that, that you feel you were created for better things but somehow the centre has receded far from you and it's not there to certify you any more so you're left with this vulnerability. And this arrogance. You've been exposed. You've come out of your shell expecting something and all you're getting is the boot." (p. 138) – Prime Minister Laurier said of Canada in a speech in London in 1897: "A colony, yet a nation – words never before in the history of the world associated together." (Quoted in Wilden, T.: *The Imaginary Canadian. An Examination for Discovery*. Vancouver, 1981, p. 217.)

8   Atwood, M.: *Second Words*. Toronto, 1982, p. 84.

9   Hardin, H.: *A Nation Unaware. The Canadian Economic Culture*. Vancouver, 1974, p. 9.

10 Frye, N.: *Divisions on a Ground. Essays on Canadian Culture*. Toronto, 1982, p. 48.

11 The first quotation is from Mandel, E.: "George Grant. Language, Nation, The Silence of God". *Canadian Literature* 83, 1979, 163–175 (here: 163); the quotations that follow are from Grant, G.: *Lament for a Nation. The Defeat of Canadian Nationalism*. Toronto, Montreal, 1971, p. 2f.

12 Keith, W. J.: *Canadian Literature in English*. London, New York, 1985, p. 207, quoting from Grant's *Philosophy in the Mass Age*, ch. 6. Cf. also Kroker, A.: *Technology and the Canadian Mind*. Montreal, 1984, p. 24 ff.

13 Cf. Anderson, A. B., Frideres J. S.: *Ethnicity in Canada. Theoretical Perspectives*. Toronto, 1981, pp. 81–98.

14 Ibid., p. 314. Cf. also pp. 99–129, 311–330.

15 Ibid., p. 326, quoting from Zolf, L.: "Mulling over Multiculturalism". *MacLean's*, April 14, 1980, 6.

16 Ibid., p. 320, quoting from Isajiw, W. W.: "Immigration and Multiculturalism – Old and New Approaches". Paper presented at the Conference on Multiculturalism and Third World Immigrants in Canada, University of Alberta, Sept. 3–5, 1975, and from Porter, J.: *The Vertical Mosaic*. Toronto, 1965.

17 Porter, J.: "Ethnic Pluralism in Canada". – In Glazer, N., Moynihan, D. P. (Eds.): *Ethnicity. Theory and Experience*. Cambridge/Mass., 1975, pp. 267–304, here: pp. 302–304.

18 Cf. McLuhan, M., Fiore, Q.: *War and Peace in the Global Village*. New York, 1968.

19 Kroker: *Technology*, pp. 104, 129. Kroker finds the most appropriate expression of this concept in the theories of Harold Innis; cf. e.g. Innis, H.: "The Strategy of Culture". – In Mandel, E. (ed.): *Contexts of Canadian Criticism*. Chicago, 1971, pp. 71–92. Innis, who died in 1952, is also said to provide most useful theories for "an understanding of contemporary Canadian cultural and communications issues".

(Parker, I.: "Beyond Content. Theories and Strategies of Media Control". *Canadian Forum*, December 1986, 6–12, here: 6.)

20 Cf. Anderson: *Ethnicity in Canada*, p. 81: "Every ethnic category in the country is a statistical minority."

21 Frye: *Divisions*, p. 46. Cf. also Cook, R.: "Imagining a North American Garden. Some Parallels & Differences in Canadian & American Culture". *Canadian Literature* No. 103, 1984, 10–23, esp. 13.

22 Atwood, M.: *Survival. A Thematic Guide to Canadian Literature*. Toronto, 1972.

23 Atwood, M.: "After *Survival* . . . Excerpts from a Speech delivered at Princeton University, April 29, 1985". – In Stanzel, F. K., Zachariesiewicz, W. (Eds.): *Encounters and Explorations. Canadian Writers and European Critics*. Würzburg, 1986, pp. 132–138, here: p. 137.

24 Cook: "Imagining a North American Garden", 15.

25 Ibid., 16, quoting from Lismer, A.: *Foundations: Building the City of God*. Toronto, 1927, p. 74. Much has been written about regionalism in Canada; cf. e. g. Adamson, A.: "Identity Through Metaphor: An Approach to the Question of Regionalism in Canadian Literature". *Studies in Canadian Literature* 5, 1980, 83–99.

26 Cook: "Imagining a North American Garden", 20; Frye, N.: *The Bush Garden. Essays on the Canadian Imagination*. Toronto, 1971, p. II.

27 Marshall, T.: *Harsh and Lovely Land. The Major Canadian Poets and the Making of a Canadian Tradition*. Vancouver, 1979, p. 176 f.

28 Blodgett, E. D.: "After Pierre Berton What? In Search of a Canadian Literature". *Essays on Canadian Writing* 30, 1984/85, 60–80, here: 62. Cf. also Blodgett, E. D.: "Gone West to Geometry's Country". – In Blodgett: *Configuration. Essays on the Canadian Literatures*. Downsview/Ont., 1982, pp. 187–218, which ends with the statement: "Thus to go west was to enter the mind's geometry, a long journey, one might say, of self-reflection, of finding one's self lost."

29 Anderson: *Ethnicity in Canada*, p. 11.

30 Frye: *Divisions*, pp. 21–23. Cf. above the three stages of liberation from the mother country.

31 Blodgett: *Configuration*, p. 8. Cf. also pp. 18 ff. and Sutherland, R.: "Canadian Literature – The Pieces and the Whole". *Zeitschrift der Gesellschaft für Kanada-Studien* 1, iii, 1983, 19–27.

32 Blodgett: *Configuration*, p. 17.

33 Blodgett: "After Pierre", 74, 62. On p. 74 Blodgett speaks of "a conflict of codes" and "the conflict of ideologies".

34 Ibid., 68, 64, 69, 78, 70.

35 Habermas, J.: „Können komplexe Gesellschaften eine vernünftige Identität ausbilden?" – In Habermas, J., Henrich, D.: *Zwei Reden*. Frankfurt/M., 1974, pp. 23–84, here: p. 29.

36 The quotations are from Birney's poems as reprinted in Foley, J. (Ed.): *The search for Identity*. Toronto, 1976, pp. 94, 77.

37 Marshall: *Harsh and Lovely Land*, pp. 159, 156. Atwood's poem is reprinted in her *Selected Poems*. New York, 1976, pp. 40–43.

38 Cf. Marcus: "What Is an Initiation Story?" for his distinctions between "tentative", "uncompleted" and "decisive initiations". The quotations are from MacLeod, A.: "The Vastness of the Dark". – In MacLeod, A.: *The Lost Salt Gift of Blood*. Toronto, 1976, pp. 33–62, here: p. 62.

39 Keith: *Canadian Literature in English*, p. 172.
40 MacLeod: *The Lost Salt Gift of Blood*, p. 170. The expression "the larger world" is used on p. 157.
41 Ibid., pp. 174, 184. Cf. also p. 187.
42 Spriet, P.: "Structure and Meaning in Rudy Wiebe's *My Lovely Enemy*". – In Kroetsch, R., Nischik, R. M. (Eds.): *Gaining Ground. European Critics on Canadian Literature*. Edmonton, 1985, pp. 53–63, here: pp. 53, 54.
43 Erlichman, S.: "More Victims". *Canadian Forum*, March 1985, 38–39. The book reviewed is Sullivan, R. (Ed.): *Stories by Canadian Women*. Oxford, 1985. As the Canadian situation seems to be different from the American one (with more female characters in Canadian stories), it is worth taking account of the discussions about female (stories of) initiation in Freese: *Initiation*, 1986, pp. 32–34; Dahmen-Eisenberg, A., et al.: „'Satin Slippers' und 'Electric Boots'. Literaturdidaktische Überlegungen zum Thema Initation und Geschlecht". *Gulliver* No. 18, 1985, 7–28; and White, B. A.: *Growing Up Female: Adolescent Girlhood in American Fiction*. Westport/Conn., 1985.
44 Thomas, C.: *The Manawaka World of Margaret Laurence*. Toronto, 1975, p. 104. Cf. also p. 192f. Similar views are expressed in Maeser, A.: "Finding the Mother: The Individuation of Laurence's Heroines". *Journal of Canadian Fiction* 27, 1980, 151–166.
45 Cf. Atwood: "After *Survival*", and her novel *Bodily Harm*. London, 1981. The Commonwealth aspect is now widely stressed. Cf. Dennis Lee's "Afterword" in Brown, R. (Ed.): *The Collected Poems of Al Purdy*. Toronto, 1986, pp. 371–391, esp. p. 390: "[...] the challenge of speaking native among English-speaking writers in Africa, India, Canada, Australia, the Carribean and elsewhere has been fundamentally the same as that faced by a Neruda or a Senghor in *their* situations."
46 Gallant, M.: "Bernadette". – In Gallant, M.: *My Heart Is Broken*. Toronto, 1982, pp. 14–41. Cf. also Hango, A. R.: *Truthfully Yours*. Toronto, 1948, about a 16-year-old French-Canadian girl wondering where babies come from and her prude Catholic environment.
47 O'Rourke, D.: "Exiles in Time. Gallant's 'My Heart is Broken'". *Canadian Literature* No. 93, 1982, 98–107, here: 98.
48 Grady, W. (Ed.): *The Penguin Book of Canadian Short Stories*. Harmondsworth, 1980, p. 206 (in his introduction to "Bernadette").
49 Freese: *Initiation*, 1986, pp. 24–26.
50 Knister, R.: "Mist Green Oates". – In Grady: *The Penguin Book of Canadian Short Stories*, pp. 106–124, here: p. 124.
51 Carrier, R.: "A Secret Lost in the Water". – In Grady: *The Penguin Book of Canadian Short Stories*, pp. 339–341, here: p. 341.
52 Freese: *Initiation*, 1986, pp. 48, 28.
53 Ibid., p. 52.
54 Marshall, J.: "Gabrielle Roy 1909–1983. Some Reminiscences". *Canadian Literature* No. 101, 1984, 183–184, here: 184.
55 Grady: *The Penguin Book of Canadian Short Stories*, p. 166, in his introduction to "The Satellites". The story is printed ibid., pp. 167–189. Page numbers of this story will from now on be inserted in the main text in brackets.

56 Cf. Nagler, M.: *Natives Without a Home.* Don Mills/Ont., 1975; Patterson, E. P.: *The Canadian Indian: The History Since 1500.* Toronto, 1972; and Ferguson, J.: "Eskimos in a Satellite Society". – In Elliot, J. L. (Ed.): *Minority Canadians I.* Scarborough/Ont., 1971, pp. 15–28.

57 Findley, T.: *Famous Last Words.* New York, 1981, p. 2.

58 Phillips, P.: *Regional Disparities.* Toronto, 1982, p. 7; Trudeau as quoted in McNaught: *The Pelican History of Canada,* p. 353.

59 Grixti, J.: "Images of adolescence. A stormy subject". *University Quarterly* 40, 1986, 171–189, here: 171.

Klaus H. Börner, Duisburg

Indian Poetry in English

Our present time which is seemingly so prosaic and matter-of-fact occasionally produces strange blossoms. One – I find – is the popularity of modern poetry. An encouraging thought even with regard to poetry in our own mother tongue, let alone to the import of foreign language poetry and let alone if the muse appears in totally outlandish garb, sari and dhoti, as it were.

Poetry in India – in the vernacular languages as well as in English – is the most prolific literary genre. For the so-called Commonwealth Literature Studies in the West, Indian poetry in English is the relevant one, unless we know Indian languages. But even in this accessible segment of Indian poetry the enormous number of published anthologies and of individual publications plus the critical appraisal is ample proof of an impressive output and of a trend of growing importance and popularity during the last decades.[1]

India has always had a firm and uninterrupted poetic tradition in her own languages, and it has even had a firm poetic tradition in English which goes back as far as the early 19th century. The latter has never been without controversy, for obvious political and ideological reasons. It was regarded as a lamentable anglomania, a pitiable "courting the Muse of Albion" and Buddhadeva Bose felt that Indo-Anglian poetry was "a blind alley, lined with curio shops, leading nowhere". And very often Indo-Anglian poets, after their return from the West, felt at home in neither language and their poetry to be of imitative mediocrity.[2] The reception of Indian poetry in English in the West was likewise controversial, if not downright damning: an Indian sensibility trying to come to grips with an idealized Western norm of poetry was very often felt to be inadequate, sentimental, odd, even ridiculous.

The important turning-point in the history of Indian poetry in English – and this is a very recent one! – was the foundation of the Calcutta Writers Workshop by P. Lal in 1958. The publication of the new poets' manifesto in 1959 formulated new ideas of poetry and poetics which made the question of language – English or vernacular – far less relevant for judging the quality of poetry. This was indeed a revolutionary change of attitude in India insofar, as the age-old, highly emotional controversy of the language problem gave way to a more sober and more objective way of evaluating literary productions. English has by now generally been accepted as a world language, and the discussion amongst a whole generation of Indian writers and critics was, and still is, not so much on vague and emotional questions of cultural identity as on the fact that they practise a craft and have a great responsibility towards the much more vital problem of adequately and lucidly giving form to the concrete experience of modern man in modern India. For the new writers and the new critics this entailed a radical condemnation of their poet ancestors: the poetry of Sri Aurobindo, Manmohan Ghose, Toru Dutt, Sarojini Naidu, and even of Rabindranath Tagore, irrespective of their international acclaim, was regarded as a mixture of Western romanticism and Eastern mysticism, an embarrassing mixture for the new poets with a distinctly false ring, and palatable for Western readers only for those who have an escapist sentimental mind or an ineradicable penchant for exoticism.

The spectrum of modern Indian poetry in English is vast. So even for introductory purposes only a small choice can be made. Any kind of selective presentation, however, is subjective and is representative only insofar as it mirrors sensibilites and affinities which, hopefully, other readers can share with the critic. I won't go into the complicated question of the reception of non-European literatures in the West[3], but generally speaking I should think that reading, evaluating, let alone teaching Indian poetry in English in the West is justified and rewarding only if this kind of poetry contains an element of familiarity and an element of the unfamiliar, the alien, which may open up new vistas for us. Otherwise, why should we not abide by our own literature? (Exotic images of the fabled, mysterious and spiritual India I would not regard as something new. The occidental mind has for centuries in regular intervals been infected with this disease of image-making which says more about "us" than "them".) Prerequisite – to repeat – for our reception and appreciation of Indian poetry in English is something which is accessible and which, in very general terms, I should like to call anthropological universals, *and* something new or different from Western poetry which is geographically, historically and culturally conditioned. The familiar element may make for a kind of existential encounter with Indian poetry, the latter may sharpen our sensibilities for cross-cultural differences and may increase our awareness of a hitherto lesser known corpus of literature in English (!) beyond our own small well-known world. It may very well be that Indian poetry holds one or the other surprise in store for the jaded Western palate.

With the little space available I suggest to provide an equally short introduction into two well-known contemporary Indian poets: Kamala Das and Nissim Ezekiel.

Kamala Das

Kamala Das was born in southern Malabar in 1934. She is the daughter of the well-known Malayali poetess Balamani Amma. At the age of fifteen she was married to K. Madhava Das, and she has three children. Kamala Das is a bilingual writer; she has published various short story collections in Malayalam under the pseudonym Madhavikutty. Four collections of her poetry in English have appeared so far: *Summer in Calcutta* (New Delhi, 1965); *The Descendants* (Calcutta, 1976); *The Old Playhouse and Other Poems* (New Delhi, 1973); *Tonight, This Savage Rite: The Love Poems of Kamala Das and Pritish Nandy* (New Delhi, 1979). A longer story, *A Doll for the Child Prostitute*, appeared in New Delhi in 1977. And a year earlier she published her autobiography *My Story* (New Delhi, 1976) after her first onset of a serious heart-disease. *My Story*, which has been translated into fourteen languages, was an immediate sensational success and at the same time a great scandal.[4] It is – for an Indian public – an exceptionally candid autobiography and it develops in logical consistency all the myth-exploding themes of her highly confessional poetry without feeling bound by reputation, morality or other limiting codes.

Confessional poetry is by necessity and definition highly subjective and personal, and the interrelationship between immediate deep-felt experience and poetic rendering is a very close one. Kamala Das' poetry is one of conversational casual tones which in many cases little betrays the condensation of thought, it is a spontaneous language of the mind and the emotions, a medium of self-awareness. This self-exploratory poetry "is committed to raw-nerve experience [...] and works through the various layers of memories to pare it down to its most painful and naked psychological causes".[5] Kamala Das is very sceptical as to whether she can make herself understood with her poetry, but the therapeutical urge is always stronger:

> [...] To spread myself across wide highways
> of your thoughts, stranger, like a loud poster
> was always my desire, but all I
> Do is lurk in shadows of culs de sac [...]
> [...] I've stretched my two dimensional
> Nudity on sheets of weeklies, monthlies,
> Quarterlies, a sad sacrifice [...]
>
> ("Loud Posters")

And yet her poetic confessions are far from being mere pathological morbid moods; they do indulge in heart-baring, it is true, they try to find solutions in personal rather than in social gestures or radical rebellion against social mores in a state of ossification. But these profoundly moving poetic confessions which provide the reader with an intensely sensuous insight into one woman's life with its longing for love, its loneliness, suffering, unfulfilment, deprivation and ever new hope, these confessions are symptomatic and of general and existential relevance. They provide us with a kaleidoscope of scenes and reflections and experiences of what it means to be a woman even in a post-Independence middle class Indian society and in the institution of the joint family and the arranged marriage. "Many of Kamala Das' poems epitomise the dilemma of the modern Indian woman who attempts to free herself, sexually and domestically, from role bondage sanctioned by the past."[6]

And it is Kamala Das's obsessive power of confessional writing which conveys a sense of almost overwhelming immediacy of pain, pain in relation to sex and the family, which transcends her individual experience to more archetypal patterns of human predicament. Syd Harrex has called this a "dual vocalism, a kind of fusion of autobiographical 'I' and archetypal 'I'".[7] Kamala Das writes on a variety of subjects ranging from childhood experiences to philosophic reflections on suicide, but at the core of her poetic nerve is the utter loneliness, the utter despair of a woman in her sexual relationship with a man. But what has become of a hopeful long summer of love?

> [...] I came to you but to learn
> What I was, and by learning, to learn to grow, but every
> Lesson you gave was about yourself [...]
> [...] You called me wife,
> I was taught to break saccharine into your tea and
> To offer at the right moment the vitamins. Cowering
> Beneath your monstrous ego I ate the magic loaf and
> Became a dwarf [...]
>
> ("The Old Playhouse")

"The Old Playhouse" is a resumé of years of female good will and curiosity being smothered by male egocentricity and utter lack of sensibility. The tone of disillusionment has become very bitter: "There is / No more singing, no more a dance, my mind is an old / Playhouse with all its lights put out." A burnt-out case almost, she gathers the lessons life has taught her in a series of ever more disillusioning love affairs, where her soul is not wanted, just the body. With cool aloofness and bitter irony she observes her own dégout and the sham of mechanical love-making, which seems to be the lot of many women seeking some kind of passion and happiness:

> [...] I must
> most deliberately
> Whip up a froth of desire,
> a passion to suit the occasion.
>
> ("Composition")

The mustering-up of sentiments becomes a bitter farce when in fact there is nothing. And yet the longing persists:

> [...] his right
> Hand on my knee, while our minds
> Are willed to race towards love;
> But, they only wander, tripping
> Idly over puddles of
> Desire ... Can this man with
> Nimble finger-tips unleash
> Nothing more alive than the
> Skin's lazy hungers? [...]
> The heart,
> An empty cistern, waiting
> Through long hours, fills itself
> With coiling snakes of silence [...]
> ("The Freaks")

The longing persists, and yet the intense feeling of pain and misery in happiness is better than cold indifferent death in life. Very often, however, love is not much more than a "skin-communicated thing" ("In Love") or a mixture of aggression and indifference:

> And we asked each other, what is
> The use, what is the bloody use?
> That was the kind of love,
> This hacking at each other's parts
> Like convicts hacking, breaking clods
> At noon.
> ("Convicts")

Sometimes, very rarely though, Kamala Das shows courage, tries to overcome her longing for an absent lover, to liberate herself from self-destructive dependence. "There was a time when I / Was sad in Calcutta...". And then she opens her eyes and mind and soul to the world around her and gains peace of mind and freedom:

> [...] I walked, I saw and
> I heard, the city tamed
> Itself for me, and then my hunger for a
> Particular touch waned
> And one day I sent him some roses and slept
> Through the night, a silent
> Dreamless sleep and woke up in the morning free.
> ("The Wild Bougainvillae")

But peace of mind and soul is not to be had once and for all. Passionate hunger for life grips her again and again like a "Forest Fire". This makes her open to the world, open to new love *and* it makes her vulnerable and leads to unhappiness and despair again. Prayers to husband or lover go unheard:

> Fond husband, ancient settler in the mind,
> Old fat spider, weaving webs of bewilderment,
> Be kind. You turn me into a bird of stone, a granite
> Dove, you build round me a shabby drawing room,
> And stroke my pitted face absent-mindedly while
> you read. With loud talk you bruise my pre-morning sleep,
> You stick a finger into my dreaming eye [...]
>
> ("The Stone Age")

Again and again she has to tell herself that everything will be allright, that she is the type that endures. But all the incantatory repetitions of self-deceptive consolation reveal even more her utter despair and loneliness:

> [...] It will be all right, it will be all right
> It will be all right between the world and me.
> It will be all right if I don't remember
> The last of the days together... [...]
>
> ("Substitute")

Nothing will be all right. The only freedom to forget and dissolve, without the slightest hope of reincarnation, lies in the thought of death. In a fine and rhythmic dialogue with the sea Kamala Das strongly feels the temptation of a suicide that seems to promise peace and freedom:

> [...]
> You swing and you swing,
> O sea, you play a child's game.
>
> But,
> I must pose.
> I must pretend
> I must act the role
> Of happy woman,
> Happy wife [...]
>
> O sea, I am fed up
> I want to be simple
> I want to be loved
> And
> If love is not to be had,
> I want to be dead, just dead [...]
>
> ("The Suicide")

Who is this Kamala Das? She is her unmistakable self and she is you and me. She is an Indian poetess writing in English, creating an Indian world we may not have been familiar with before, *and* she sings of fundamental human predicaments we all can share with her:

> [...] I am Indian, very brown, born in
> Malabar, I speak three languages, write in
> Two, dream in one [...]
> [...] The language I speak
> Becomes mine, its distortions, its queernesses
> All mine, mine alone, It is half English, half
> Indian, funny perhaps, but it is honest,
> It is as human as I am human [...]
>
> [...] Who are you, I ask each and everyone,
> The answer is, it is I. [...]
>
> [...] I am sinner,
> I am saint. I am the beloved and the
> Betrayed. I have no joys which are not yours, no
> Aches which are not yours. I too call myself I.
>
> ("An Introduction")

Nissim Ezekiel

Nissim Ezekiel was born in 1924 in Bombay of liberal Jewish parents. His education in English led to the loss of his mother tongue, Marathi. He went to England in 1948 for three years. He is editor, critic of the arts and literature, university professor, and one of the foremost Indian poets in English. His first book of poems *A Time to Change* was published in London in 1952. After his return to Bombay he has published the following poetry collections: *Sixty Poems* (1963), *The Third* (1959), *The Unfinished Man* (1960), *The Exact Name* (1965), *Hymns in Darkness* (1976), *Latter-Day Psalms* (1982).

Nissim Ezekiel is a cosmopolitan intellectual. He may have a strong sense of belonging to India and to the city of Bombay – and his poems of Indian topography and society are ample proof of his "Indianness" – but, as he says himself, "[...] there is a trap in identifying one's audience in terms of specific geographical location. I write my poems for anyone who is likely to enjoy them in any part of the world, in any time."[8] For himself he has decided to stay in Bombay, to seek his identity in his country with all its incongruities, but, versatile a poet as he is, the mere range of themes of his poetry goes beyond any nationally limited literature. His major themes, he says, are "love, personal integration, the Indian contemporary scene, modern urban life, spiritual values".[9] He described himself once as a religious-philosophical poet and at the same time as one who

93

attaches a great deal of importance to the worldliness of the world. But both his ceaseless attempt to define himself as man and poet and his quest for meaning as well as his endless explorations of the mind and the world of the senses are never static; they are existential attempts to fathom the self and the world, and these attempts are never final. Nissim Ezekiel is the "unfinished man".

Out of the wide range of themes in Nissim Ezekiel's poetry I should like to select three and illustrate them very briefly in a few poems.

1. Indian reality in the widest sense: not only the kaleidoscope of topography and society, but of what it feels to live in India. And this is made accessible, particularly for a Western reader, in a poetry which is both inward and detached. The "Very Indian Poems in English" are in a seemingly lighter and entertaining vein but they also betray an acute insight into the frailties of man and the shortcomings of social and political reality, genre-scenes capturing the particular flavour of different facets of Indian reality and gaining comic effect through the idiom of imperfect Indian English. There is the patriot, standing for peace and non-violence, the old man who does not like the young ones – "Too much going for fashion and foreign thing" – babbling on and on:

> [...] What you think of prospects of world peace?
> Pakistan behaving like this,
> China behaving like that,
> It is making me very sad, I am telling you.
> Really most harassing me.
> All men are all brothers, no?
> In India also
> Gujaraties, Maharashtrians, Hindiwallahs
> All brothers –
> Though some are having funny habits [...]
> ("The Patriot")

Or the old professor, prattling on Indian "progress is progressing. Old values are going, new values are coming" ("The Professor"). Many stills of Indian everyday life add up to a panorama of urban reality, carefully staged, revealing human mediocrity but without bitterness or sarcasm. Whether it is the memory of a "Hangover", or the cool, honest, almost dissecting description of his own "Jewish Wedding in Bombay", whether it is glimpses into different religious groups:

> [...] The Roman Catholic Goan boys
> Confessed their solitary joys
> Confessed their games with high-heeled toys
> And hastened to their prayers [...]
> ("In India")

Whether it is the very funny and yet embarrassingly formal "Goodby Party for Miss Pushpa T. S.", or the experiences of a young girl who does not want to learn English but get married instead, "How the English Lessons Ended", all these poems add up to a vivid, colourful and ironically captured Indian reality and the fundamental human condition. But there is open criticism, too, in "The Truth About the Floods", which gives the truth not about a catastrophe but about the incompetence and indifference of government officials. And there are the serious and touching vignettes of personal experiences, conjuring up, in the masterfully applied technique of foregrounding, intensely felt scenes of child-hood in "Night of the Scorpion", or the clichéd and yet irritating little conver-sation with a foreign lady about beggars:

> [...] We sipped the coffee, found it good [...]
> [...] She didn't know beggars in India
> smile only at white foreigners.
> 'Indians are friendly people, anyway'
> she said. 'So they are', I agree,
> 'so they are'. She stares at me
> dubiously. I listen to the buzzing air.
> Perhaps she thinks it best
> not to argue. I think so too.
>
> ("Poverty Poem")

2. Aspects of love: It has been observed that in many of Nissim Ezekiel's poems there is a tender balance between a sensual, existential involvement with life and an intellectual detached quest for committment. This inevitably shar-pens the awareness for conflicts, especially in the relationship between man and woman, a recurring theme in Ezekiel's poetry which comprises portraits, de-scriptions, encounters of a mostly desillusioning and even depressive character and candid reflections on the poet's own personal crises.

Men and women do have more clearly defined roles in Indian society,

> [...] the wives of India sit apart.
> They do not drink,
> They do not talk,
> of course, they do not kiss.
> The men are quite at home
> among the foreign styles [...]
>
> ("In India")

but a Western reader certainly would not agree with Emmanuel Narendra Lall who in a detailed analysis tries to show that in his relationship with women, Ezekiel "sees them filling biological and societal roles, those of mother, wife, mistress, seductress, whore, and sex object".[10] They do appear in the context which is conditioned by society and gender, but it is the poet's all-pervading humanism, however clear-sighted and disillusioned, that accepts them all in the far from ideal family of man. He may be bitter about marital relations in "Song to be Shouted Out": "Shout at me, woman! / What else are wives for?", he may have buried hopes and ideals and false images of love in "Marriage" which in the beginning always seems to deny the Primal Fall, or in "Case Study" or in "The Couple", a chance affair, a game of mutual deception, "a charade of passion and possession" which comes very close to what Kamala Das talks about. But the underlying attitude and tone is one of acceptance of life as it is with all its failures, mistakes, unrealized dreams and high ideals, it is one of acceptance of suffering with growing older and more critical. And there is very often a human tenderness, comparable to W. H. Auden's "Lullaby" which transcends mere sensuality, however precious it may be in itself, however much he celebrates the flesh, into a much more complex feeling:

> [...] I saw embarrassment and shame
> as clearly on her face
> as love, desire,
> need to know it all.
> The pathos moved me. I touched
> her feet as if in worship,
> held her breasts in adoration,
> told her she was beautiful [...]
> [...] I knew
> each part but now I saw
> the sacramental pattern, soul
> inviolate within all that
> pure being flowing from its source [...]
>
> ("Nudes 1978")

3. The "unfinished man's" religious-philosophical journey inward to define, over and over again, his constantly changing spiritual orientation and his identity as a creative poet. It is a poetic-existential pilgrimage the different stages of which define the nature of Nissim Ezekiel's quest for meaning and commitment, for strength and stability.[11] This theme in itself embraces a whole cluster of philosophical problems, since, as Linda Hess says, Ezekiel is "an endless explorer of the labyrinths of the mind, the devious delving and twisting of the ego [...]."[12]

The poem "Credo" from his *Postcard Poems* may very well be quoted as the poet's credo:

To know beneath
the depth of life
another depth begin;
blindly to sink

and be sustained
by voices, by hands,
by the human need
to hear new messages;

to describe anguish
in a soft voice,
in the simplest statements
to body forth the passions.

Poetic faith and actual experience go together to explore the true and the false in the self, to understand his own ambiguities, and to arrive, however transiently, at self-confidence and freedom from taboos and norms, even from dogmatic beliefs:

Do not choose me, O Lord,
to carry out thy purposes,
I'm quite worthy, of course,
but I have my own purposes.
You have plenty of volunteers
to choose from, Lord.
Why pick on me, the selfish one?

O well, if you insist,
I'll do your will.
Please try to make it coincide with mine.
("The Egoist's Prayers – 4")

But this seemingly independent stance is not final. It is one moment in a quest, full of ups and downs, for a sense of belonging and a meaning in and of human existence. "The more I searched, the less I found" happens again and again, as he says in the confessional poem "Background, Casually". Or he calls himself a "sad artificer, clinging / Too long to the same static vision [...] / Misled by norms, the light of reason, [...]" ("Mind") and "The Room", then, is a metaphor of life imprisoned where uncertainties, doubts, changing moods of belonging and alienation and new hope beset him. And it is in actual life as it is in the creative process of the imagination: other values and ideals than one's very own do not work. That is what he discovers in "Hymns in Darkness":

[...] Self-deception is a fact of being. How, then, to
be undeceived?

He has found too many secrets that will not work,
   too many keys that unlock no locks.
He lives in the world of desires and devices. It
   is colourful and full of poetry.
For every truth in his possession, he has a
   falsehood to go with it [...]

And then he arrives at an insight – "A single decision / is better than a hundred thoughts" – and this insight, in its definite concentration on the colourful and holy wordliness of the world of senses, seems to promise meaning, a personal one, but one that can be lived as Siddhartha found out at the end of his long spiritual quest. For the poet Nissim Ezekiel:

There is only this:
   a tarred road
   under a mild sun
   after rain,
   glowing;

   wet, green leaves
   patterned flat
   on the pavement
   around dog-shit;

   one ragged slipper
   near an open gutter,
   three crows
   pecking away at it.

And breasts, thighs, buttocks
   swinging
   now towards
   now away from him.

Notes

1 First bibliographical material can be obtained in Stiltz, G.: *Grundlagen zur Literatur in englischer Sprache*. Band 4: *Indien*. München, 1982; *ACOLIT*, a very informative kind of newsletter on teaching, research in progress, conferences, recent publications on Commonwealth Literature, edited by Dieter Riemenschneider, Martina Raßmann, Monika Trebert. Institut für England- und Amerikastudien, Universität Frankfurt, Kettenhofweg 130, 6000 Frankfurt/M.
Of the better known poetry anthologies the following selection can be recommended:
Lal, P. (Ed.): *Modern Indian Poetry in English: An Anthology and a Credo*. Calcutta, 1971 (^{1}1969); Gokak, V. K. (Ed.): *The Golden Treasury of Indo-Anglian Poetry, 1928–1965*. New Delhi, 1970 (^{2}1978, ^{3}1985); Malik, K. (Ed.): *Indian Poetry Today*. 2 vols. New Delhi, 1985; Dwivedi, A. N.: *Indian Poetry in English. A Literary History and Anthology*. New Delhi, 1980; Daruwalla, K. N. (Ed.): *Two Decades of Indian Poetry 1960–1980*. New Delhi, 1980; Ameeruddin, S. (Ed.): *New Voices in Indian Poetry in English*. Madras, 1981.

2 See: Sivaramkrishna, M.: "The 'Tongue in English Chains': Indo-English Poetry Today". – In Shahane, V. A., Sivaramkrishna, M. (Eds.): *Indian Poetry in English. A Critical Assessment*. New Delhi, 1980, p. 1.

3 I have tried to elucidate this problem in general terms in my "The Reception of Indian Literature in English in the West – A German View". *German Studies in India* 9, iv, 1985, 169–190; and in one case-study: "The Reception of Salman Rushdie's *Midnight's Children* in West Germany". *German Studies in India* 10, i, 1986, 17–26.

4 Kamala Das had to put up with a lot of ostracism and notoriety in her own country for talking so openly about sex, in her poetry as well as in her prose, thus violating strong social and moral taboos. This has led to a noticeably different reception of her poetry in India and in the West, which, again, reveals problems of cross-cultural communication because of different values, even in literary criticism. Some Indian critics have accused her of shameless immorality, the debunking of religiously sanctioned ideals, of callow exhibitionism, of a dismissive attitude toward politics etc. (See: Krewal, O.: "The Poetry of Kamala Das – A Critical Assessment". – In Sinha, K. N. (Ed.): *Indian Writing in English*. New Delhi, 1979, p. 128ff.); I. N. Agrawal ("The Language and the Limits of the Self in the Poetry of Kamala Das". – In Sinha, K. N. (Ed.): *Indian Writing in English*, p. 138ff.) calls her poetry "too private, too weak to touch off other people's sensibilities", for him it is "just a piece of trivial exhibitionism, interesting only to Women's lib crusaders"; he can discover "no sense of humour or a proper religio-social background" in her poetry. And then he closes with an observation where fundamental differences of Indian and Western approaches to literature become evident: "So long as the poet's ego remains a personal ego, it cannot attain meaning unless there is a mystical expansion of the self."

5 Brewster, A.: "The Freedom to Decompose. The Poetry of Kamala Das". *Journal of Indian Writing in English* 8, i-ii, 1980, 104.

6 Harrex, S. C.: "The Strange Case of Matthew Arnold in a Sari: An Introduction to Kamala Das". – In Harrex, S. C., O'Sullivan, V. (Eds.): *Kamala Das. A Selection with Essays on Her Work* (Centre for Research in the New Literatures in English Series, No. 1). Adelaide, 1986, p. 163. This selection is not only the first collection of Kamala Das' work outside India and thus probably more easily available to readers

99

in the West, but also provides one of the best scholarly introductions into her work which, as I said, has so far mainly been approached from different moralistic and ideological standpoints.

7 Harrex, S. C.: "The Strange Case of Matthew Arnold in a Sari", p. 165. See also: de Souza, E.: "Kamala Das". – In Shahane, V. A., Sivaramkrishna, M. (Eds.): *Indian Poetry in English. A Critical Assessment*, p. 41ff. Also: Holzmann, M.: "Indian Women Poets". – In Groß, K., Klooß, W. (Eds.): *Voices from Distant Lands. Poetry in the Commonwealth*. Würzburg, 1982, p. 130ff.

8 Beston, B.: "An Interview with Nissim Ezekiel". – In Sinha, K. N. (Ed.): *Indian Writing in English*, p. 44.

9 Quoted in Daruwalla, K. N. (Ed.): *Two Decades of Indian Poetry 1960–1980*, p. 56. This sounds cosmopolitan, it embraces the anthropological universals I mentioned earlier and that may be one of the reasons why Nissim Ezekiel is much less controversially but rather seriously and respectfully received in the East and in the West. See the two full-length studies: Karnani, C.: *Nissim Ezekiel*. New Delhi, 1974, and Rahman, A.: *Form and Value in the Poetry of Nissim Ezekiel*. New Delhi, 1981.

10 Lall, E. N.: *The Poetry of Encounter*. New Delhi, 1983, p. 92.

11 See: Singh, S.: "Journey into Self: Nissim Ezekiel: Recent Poetry". – In Shahane, V. A., Sivaramkrishna, M. (Eds.): *Indian Poetry in English. A Critical Assessment*, p. 48ff.

12 Hess, L.: "Post-Independence Indian Poetry in English". *Quest* 49, 1966, 30.

Gerhard Stilz, Tübingen

Commonwealth Literature at School – or: Can Intercultural Competence Be Taught?

I

"Great Britain – Empire – Commonwealth – Europe": A new syllabus unit for secondary schools presents a challenge and creates opportunities.* On the one hand the task of "intellectually penetrating, comprehending and ordering" the "complex interrelations" of English in a class of almost mature secondary school pupils makes demands on English teachers for which many of them are not quite prepared. On the other hand, a chance has been provided to allow young people, who in a few years will be confronted with the problems of world cultures, a deeper and more sympathetic view beyond the narrow confines of European affairs than was required or was customary in the past. But even if the individual teacher is not adequately prepared for this expansion of English as a school subject, it still must be recognized as meaningful and necessary.

We live in a world of increasing economic integration and, hopefully, of an increasingly peaceful and civilized debate about suitable measures to eliminate poverty, starvation and discrimination. Furthermore, we live in a time of increasing wanderlust – especially of Germans who travel to the remotest corners of the world – and, perhaps even more important, in a period when part of the young intelligentsia and future ruling classes still come from all over the world to train and study in Europe (not least in Germany). In such a world it is only to be welcomed if world studies do not only dwell on the surface of exotic topography but also cultivate a deep sympathy and a fundamental readiness to understand foreign cultures with every means available. Language first and foremost is one of these means, and whether in international politics, trade or commerce, English is the *lingua franca*. Yet in addition to this, concrete and palpable knowledge is necessary of those geographical and historical areas that are supposed to be correlated with one another. In fact, the three main components of the syllabus cannot be separated. First of all, there is the Empire as a historical complex, where Great Britain, as well as supplying the basic language of communication, left its mark on a multitude of public institutions and standards of behaviour; this developed into a Commonwealth of independent nations, committed to one another in an atmosphere of goodwill. Secondly, there is Great Britain itself, which has emerged from its "splendid isolation" during the last twenty-five years (more than at any time during the previous two hundred) to become involved in European affairs and particularly in the European Community. Thirdly, there is this European Community, which encompasses our German outlook, or should rather gradually integrate it. All three components belong in our lessons about world affairs which the subject of English is now capable of accommodating. Despite the facility of freely moving between these areas offered in the English language, all three components should always be kept in mind and reflected upon.

However, as already mentioned, it is not only the immediate and direct *linguistic* perception of the external reality of diverse countries, nations, economies and exotic customs which the English lesson makes possible; rather, through our linguistic approach, we find that literature, as a more essential and exceedingly sensitive indicator of intellectual culture, public awareness, and personal feeling, helps us discover those attitudes and predispositions in foreign cultures which remain hidden at first glance. This is all the more important once we have realized (and the process of realization among responsible and far-sighted politicians amounts to exactly the same thing) that it is of no sense or lasting advantage to solely ensure our economic access to foreign worlds. Instead it is ultimately worthwhile in every respect to understand, as far as possible, foreign cultures from the inside out – to get involved with them and to preserve them. We should indeed learn to question the arrogant assumption that our eurocentric view of the world should be universally valid and reliable, before the last remnants of independent and indigenous cultures are finally levelled out and made to conform to European ideologies and technologies. The imagination desirable in a future world and the diversification of thinking required for every new invention and discovery presuppose a multitude of cultural resources. The comparison is worth considering: dialect stimulates the standard language and keeps it alive – and not vice versa; likewise, it can also be expected that some of the one-sided developments and current failures in our eurocentric world may be recognized earlier and corrected in time with the aid of unconventional ways of thinking provided by exotic cultures. The English lesson can make a contribution here, by cultivating and fostering a deeper understanding of English-speaking cultures. In doing this, it would perhaps be possible to retain some of the intellectual potential of these cultures for the future.

But what shall and what can the literature class specifically contribute in this context, beyond a fact-oriented regional study? Suppose that the goal of the new world affairs component of the English lesson shall be an understanding of the world in a cultural sense; then the ability and willingness to comprehend that which is not yet a concrete fact, that which is still only intellectually anticipated and that which appears only in the guise of fiction, must extend beyond, must deepen and enlarge a merely factual knowledge of any new subject chosen from the Commonwealth area. Continuing in this vein, let us assume that literature can be regarded as a linguistic and intellectual field of experimentation in which private and political problems of everyday life are preformulated, are made tangible in everyday language and are intelligibly shaped for the common reader; let us assume that the fictional reality of literature can serve as a scenario in which difficult and complex facts may be reduced to a comprehensible form, where precarious conflicts can be settled without the necessary consequences of sanctions faced in the empirical world, and may therefore be providently discussed in the truest sense: We can then easily recognize the use and place of the literature class in our given context.

Without a doubt literature actually provides the liveliest, most imaginative and most complex connection between language and reality. Appealing and stimulating in its palpability, a literary text offers a personal, psychologically profound and thereby a livelier approach to a foreign world than an expository text. Following its author's intention, it is usually meant to create a deeper, more immediate and longer lasting impression on our minds than a report-like account, a list of facts or a documentary-type description. The great immediacy of fiction also holds its dangers, of course. The sympathy aroused in the reader with fictitious characters, his temporary identification with heroes or victims and the roleplay in which he becomes involved, tempts him to an uncontrolled emotional participation in a world of appearances unless he is equipped with a proper sense of reflection and criticism. Experimental games with reality make flights from reality possible. This, however, does not basically diminish the true value of literary fiction – that of giving an enthralling and substantial insight into foreign situations, foreign ways of thinking and foreign cultures.

II

However, before we can make this claim concrete on the basis of selected texts, we must consider which literary qualities in the text might actually facilitate and grant such a beneficial release from our own provinciality.

First of all, we must mention the ability of foreign languages to supply a new grid of possible experiences which allow the reader access to realities denied to him by his own familiar mother tongue. This observation does not, in the first place, concern the empirical reality of a foreign country or continent described in a text, but rather the different kind of access provided by the foreign language to this reality. We may indeed regard the *foreign language* and the characteristics of its *phonetics, morphology, syntax* and *semantics* as a new pair of glasses allowing a new mode of vision. However, when discussing the literature of the Commonwealth, it is not sufficient to state that our linguistic lenses will be English. Instead we are rather often faced with the problem of grasping the regional linguistic variants and registers and correlating them with Standard English. We have to point out the charm and expressive potential of these variants and see them in their historical perspective. The linguistic analysis and coordination of a text taken from the canon of Commonwealth Literature thus provides us with a sample of an intercultural experience. This demands a willingness to understand and creates an ability to perceive on a level which can not be reached by other school subjects.

A second quality makes literature a suitable exercise ground for a profound understanding of intercultural problems – namely the capability of nearly all fictional texts to present a clear, spatially and temporally concrete and plausible *view of the world seen in a unifying perspective.* The personal *narrator* who often explicitly supports the narrative viewpoint enlists our sympathy, compassion and understanding, and thus opens up a segment of the foreign world in a human light. With his authorial competence, however, he can also provide information which may be as graphic and reliable as a compendium of facts. Whereas a mere documentary study can only claim its temporary truth and validity for regional studies on the basis of its given facts, fiction can reach beyond such limitations: It wants to portray and communicate that which is characteristic, that which is not physically comprehensible and materially distinct: that which is felt to exist over and above the transient and the ephemeral. In doing so the immaterial also gains a reality which is not at hand in the world of facts. Therefore literature as fiction teaches an experience of the world, which cannot be obtained by the empirically-oriented methods of regional studies. Especially when dealing with the so-called "Third World" this characteristic reality and value of literary experience should not be underestimated.

Literature may thus help to communicate an unfamiliar view of the world. But we are, thirdly, even more dependent on fiction for the experience of previously unfamiliar *images of man.* Fictional narrative permits – and since its invention in the eighteenth century this has been one of its most important merits – the "private history" to unfold before the background of public events. Only the autobiography (whose generic classification is not easy precisely because of this) places a comparable stress on the description of *consciousness,* the feelings directing the plot, the hidden and suppressed emotional reactions – in short: the *psychological* (but no less powerfully effective) *reality.* No empirical method has yet provided us with a more subtle, more impressive, truer picture of man than literary fiction. This is not something which we can prove but rather only testify to by being fascinated and concerned in our reading. The literary *techniques of characterization,* the modes of presenting psychological insights, e.g. reporting thought processes, or describing a mental state through interior monologue, bring worlds within reach which only a literature-based regional studies programme can do. The reality of these worlds is indisputable as it usually surpasses the limited private reality of the authors who created them. Their collective relevance is valid to the extent that we recognize the individual author as a representative of his society. If we want to approach intercultural studies in our schools in terms of a well-understood humanism, then we would do well to search for and convey the image of foreign peoples in literature with the help of literary texts.

There is also a fourth factor which makes literature a particularly suitable agent of foreign cultures, namely, that a certain *conventional form* can be attributed to the vast majority of literary texts. This implies that we can, for the most part, discover by our critical reading a meaningful and productive interplay with the *literary tradition*. The author's playing with genres and sub-genres, the variation of the formal tradition, and the conflict with more or less obligatory models betrays – often demonstratively, often unconsciously – his own cultural outlook and the cultural profile of a group or of a society. Developments towards a national identity, efforts of cultural self-assertion and demonstrations of personal identity can be gaged from the implicit dialogues between individual literary works and the traditions of literary genre and form. This observation has proved to be valid in the development of the English sonnet, the Scottish border ballad, the American short story, and it is also valid for attempts to invent and impose specific Canadian, West Indian, Nigerian or Australian, Indian or New Zealand variations on traditional literary forms. In all such cases the distinctions and the interdependence of the various anglophone cultures of the world can be learned. A literary work proves to be a sensitive indicator of cultural and political relations, not only in the contents that it may communicate but also in the formal conflicts that it may embody.

III

What results from this? – The underlying theory may have become more plausible: literature lessons in foreign language teaching (and certainly not only the English class) can impart a cultural competence above that of our own empirical horizon of experience on the basis of and in connection with regional studies.

Literary education and textual analysis provide a more profound, a more direct and, at the same time, a more reflective insight into the individuality of foreign cultures than could be achieved in the fact-oriented lesson.

A more considerate and humane view of intercultural problems may be taught with the help of literature in secondary schools; but undoubtedly there still remains much to be discussed in detail by working closely with texts.

* Abbreviated form of a lecture given at the Staatliche Akademie Comburg in Schwäbisch Hall. The immediate point of reference was the consultants' report on the revision of English as a first foreign language in the ninth class in secondary schools in Baden-Württemberg (28 January 1983), which in the meantime has come into force in „Lehrplanheft" 8, 1984, „Bildungsplan für das Gymnasium" vol. 1, in the *Amtsblatt des Kultusministeriums*.

Peter O. Stummer, Munich

Bharatvarsha: Introducing Indian Prose

0. Bharatvarsha and the vision of a united sub-continent

As most readers will recall *Bharat* is the official Hindi term for the Republic of India. By using the ancient term *Bharatvarsha*[1], we hark back to the still familiar notion of a national unity on that mass of land between the ocean in the south and the snowy mountains in the north. It is true that after the two hundred years of British *Raj* (Rule), the long-striven-for Independence and *Swa Raj* (Self-Rule) brought with it the Partition of India in 1947 and the foundation of Pakistan[2], the Karachi conflict of 1965 and the Bangladesh breakaway of 1972. Nevertheless, attempts at achieving some sort of cultural unity have not been abandoned. The vision of a united sub-continent is constantly upheld at conference level by the six states concerned and is part and parcel of the present political discourse.

Indian, then, deliberately has this somewhat vague tinge to it grudgingly condoned by that grand old man of letters, Nirad Chaudhuri.[3] The etymology of *India*, country east of the river (= Indus), hints, to all appearances, at considerable Greek and Persian influence in the dawn of history.[4] The absence of all cultural suggestion in the term *Indian* might most appropriately be remembered when the implications of the post-independence debate on *Indianness* are examined or when the specific situation of modern *Indo-English* literature is discussed. (In parenthesis it should be noted that the term *Anglo-Indian* refers to writers, from Kipling to Scott and from Steel to Kaye, who were of English extraction and had lived in and had written about India.)

Fifteen per cent of the world's population live in the Republic of India, a federation that comprises twenty-two states as well as nine union territories. Fifteen languages enjoy the status of national languages under the Indian Constitution. These are: Assamese, Bengali, Gujarati, Hindi, Kannada, Kashmiri, Malayalam, Marathi, Oriya, Punjabi, Sanskrit, Sindhi, Tamil, Telugu and Urdu.[5] Division between India and Pakistan does not only rest on religious grounds, with India being predominantly Hindu, and Pakistan being mainly Muslim, the division also has a linguistic side to it. Speakers of Hindustani and Urdu can easily comprehend each other[6], yet these languages differ blatantly in the written text or on the printed page, as Hindi uses the Devanagari script, whereas Urdu is written and printed in Arabic script. As far as religion is concerned, over eighty-two per cent are Hindus, about eleven per cent Muslims, approximately two per cent

Christians, and almost just as many Sikhs. Buddhists, Jains, Parsis, and Jews do not amount to all that many in percentage, but represent significant communities in absolute numbers. But the fact that there is unity in diversity is clear from the Indian flag which has three horizontal bands of deep saffron, white and green and in their midst the chakra (wheel) symbol. It does not refer to Gandhi's spinning wheel of the same name, but conjures up connotations of the Buddhist symbol of law. Some kind of unifying factor was institutionalised as early as 1954 in the form of the Sahitya Akademi, whose literary activity sought to take care of the translation from one Indian language into another as well as the rendering of non-Indian literature into Indian languages (and most recently of Indian literature in national languages into European and other languages). As Vishnu Khare, who was with the Academy for quite a long time, recently phrased it at a symposium: what is wanted was "a bank of translators" to cope with the tremendous task that still needs doing. Insisting on Indian Literature in the singular, he explained: "Being translated into Bengali, makes a Hindi writer an Indian writer."[7]

Leading literati in India are, of course, multilingual, such as, for instance, the outstanding poets, Dilip Chitre and A. K. Ramanujan. Text material of Indian Literature will therefore include texts originally written in English as well as texts translated from national languages into English. Accessability of India through the medium of English, however, makes a virtue of necessity. Especially the context of English Language Teaching can create a facile overemphasis of the role of English, viewed from abroad, compared with its function and significance as seen from inside. Overall teaching goals should centre on post-colonial awareness and the abandonment of Euro/Ethno-centrism.[8] A purely Third World/Developing Country approach might be slightly distorting though, as India is the ninth biggest industrial power in global comparison and ranks third, after the USA and the UK, in the production of English titles, finding itself in general among the ten largest book producing countries in the world. The criteria of selection consequently are the texts' intrinsic value and, regrettably sometimes, their availability here in Western Europe. This paper, then, suggests a few self-reliant teaching units that will serve the individual teacher's envisaged purposes.

The case for the inclusion of Indian Literature in the English syllabus in Germany differs slightly from the analogous integration into English Studies in Britain. Although the problem of multi-culturalism is the same, the equivalent minorities catered for in German schools are neither Pakistani nor West Indian but Turks and Greeks. Post-modern development in narrative prose has left almost no mark on British fiction. From an Indian point-of-view, for example, recent fiction in England has certainly become more regional.[9] Indian Literature, to be sure, is not regional in the sense that it tends to be provincial or parochial. Under the influence of recent developments in African, Australian, Canadian and Caribbean literature written in English a broader understanding of *English* in English Literature is being advocated, an understanding sufficiently comprehensive to embrace: "literature written in the English language or adequately translated into it".[10] Being concerned with the acceptability of modern Indian writing, Nicholson merely concludes: "If the last definition is chosen it inevitably includes the modern literature of India."[11] As well as, we might confidently add, outstanding examples from Africa and the Caribbean, an achievement, let us face it, which this very collection of essays intends to help to further.

1. Some Suggestions for Basic Teaching Units: The Media Image of India

1.1 Woman's Plight in India as reflected in the press

Not so long ago *The Guardian* published a story about a travellers' experience in Pakistan. Under the heading 'The Unfortunate Traveller' and the title 'As we fled in the darkness to the nearest town, the nightmare continued' Nicola Earwaker recounts her and her husband's adventure at Mehar. The night watchman of a petrol station, who is supposed to offer them protection in their tent pitched nearby, suddenly takes it into his head to go after the young woman. They manage to flee in their car and to secure the help of the police. Three things are remarkable in the wording of the narration. First, there is the mention of newspaper reports on "a plague of dacoit exploits in the valley" to set the tone of threat. Second, the police's hospitality "verges on servility" and the District Magistrate assures them of his special consideration, for as British subjects, "in view of 'Pakistan's longstanding debt to Britain'", they obviously deserve special treatment. Third, after a sarcastic reference to the "well-known oriental promise" of inaction, they feel compelled to invoke Eric Newby's sentiment "after his spell in the Hindu Kush": "we longed to be back amongst 'people who mean what they say and do it'."[12] These are, no doubt, subliminal vestiges of Raj conditioning. There is an unadmitted yearning for the days of 'The White Man's Burden' behind this kind of writing, with a condescending feeling for the impertinent *wog* who, as a matter of course, always lusts after the self-assured white woman whom he seeks to dominate like his own oppressed womenfolk.

Germans, on the other hand, seem to repress their own colonial past. They therefore like to point accusing fingers at the former possessions of their erstwhile imperial competitors. The German press consequently seems to indulge in an almost gleeful treatment of details of the plight of women in India. To give but a few examples, suffice it to quote three headlines:

Böses Erwachen nach der Hochzeitsnacht[13]

1500 Inder sehen Witwenverbrennung zu[14]

Verachtet, ausgebeutet, umgebracht – Töchter gelten in Indien als Bürde: Massenmord an neugeborenen Mädchen[15]

The first implies that divorce at the woman's request is a complete novelty in Indian society, whereas, since the Hindu Marriage Act of 1955, divorce is legally possible under certain circumstances. In addition, the text indirectly denounces arranged marriages, while correctly attesting the rise of a career-oriented female middle-class. The second and the third refer to Indian sources, the daily *Times of India* and the fortnightly *India Today*[16] respectively. The second news item stresses the point that police and mayor of Umaria village in Madhya Pradesh closed their eyes to the practice of *Sati*[17] into which the husband's family is said 'to have talked' the young woman of twenty-five. The third text admits to the good intentions of the central government, but emphasizes their lack of effectiveness. "Disregard and disdain of women are omnipresent all over India", insists the author and she hastens to introduce the term 'dowry-murder' and explains it as the phenomenon where women inexplicably burn to death in their kitchens when their families refuse to make additional dowry payments. Particular stress though is laid on the 'absolute worthlessness of women', even middle-class couples, it is maintained, can no longer afford daughters. Abortion or murder are the consequences.

It might be helpful here to consult theoretical literature on the nature of prejudice and the function of (national) stereotypes.[18] Astoundingly enough, Blaicher's collection of essays does not contain a single contribution dealing with India. The one contribution on African literature[19] is in itself an example of cliché-thinking that goes off at a rather uncritical tangent. The best way to come to terms with women's role in India is, of course, the consultation of Indian specialists. Now, there is certainly no need to extenuate the problems mentioned and Indian sociologists are the first to comment critically upon them:

> Though it cannot be said that the exploitation of women in India has no parallel in any other country, it can be safely ascertained that the women had to face much cruelty and exploitation in modern India.[20]

He goes on to enumerate such things as marriage without consent, servant treatment of daughter-in-law, absence of property shares for widows, the custom of Devadasi or the lot of common prostitution, and the abuses of Sati. He is also able to document, however, the political awakening of Indian women and their unflagging endeavours to remedy these grievances. He concludes that 'certain difficulties' are the result of higher education of women and the inevitable price to pay for social reform.[21] Somewhat despondently one might add

110

that this change in female awareness through education was necessary so as to create first of all some public consciousness of this social evil. Unfortunately Sharma, too, chooses an easy way out, when he points out that in general the fate of Muslim women is much worse compared to that of their Hindu counterparts; interestingly enough, the better fortune of Christian women may, in his opinion, not be set out as a positive example because of their reputedly laxer morals. So, even if we do not on the whole contest the facts, we take umbrage at that gloatingly detailed description of disdainful mores reserved for the savage and the uncivilized.

1.2 Exotic Orientalism as exploited on the screen

Publications by the National Book Trust still find it necessary to lament a persistent tendency in 'some overseas quarters' to turn to India only in search of what used to be called 'orientalia'.[22] What looks like a cranky quirk is confirmed, however, by an authority such as the scholar-novelist Ananthamurthy, author of the famous novel *Samskara* (1965), written in Kannada. He is on record to have claimed repeatedly that writers in India are read for content, whereas in Europe they tend to be appreciated – if at all – merely for their aesthetics or – worse still – solely for some kind of 'exotic' appeal. That his view is not completely unfounded can be seen in the way journalists write, even when they purport to describe critically changing attitudes to India:

India – Janus-faced world of intellect and unreason; haughty pride and abject submission; of great riches and gross deprivation; of bodiless spirit and carnality in triumph; of many armed violence and non-violence, hands folded in a pious namas kar – has once more reduced to beggary the thin, British sense of its meanings.[23]

Tigers and temples and the Taj Mahal. Maharajahs and turbaned warriors and old men ritually wandering penniless in order to purify themselves and become holy. Snake charmers and bear tamers and wizend artisans using the simplest of tools to chisel out tiny, intricate talismans of beauty. Images of India, crossroads of the exotic East, have lingered in the Western imagination. [...] When India has broken through the legacy of its storybook history, it has emerged in Western consciousness as the land of assassination and religious riots, of chemical disaster in Bhopal and the nuclear-arms race with Pakistan. Or, more trivially, as the land of tandoori chicken and the Nehru jacket.[24]

In both cases the quotations represent the opening sentences of the two articles. The former is about Rajiv Gandhi's coming to power, the latter describes the

'Festival of India' cultural events across the United States. Stereotypes are cited with detachment but are nevertheless confirmed by using them at all. It seems difficult to rid oneself of the 'exotic appeal'.

The long tradition of countless volumes full of colourful photography has certainly contributed a great deal to the exotic appeal of this 'mysterious' country.[25] It follows that the romantic concept of India also owes quite a lot to the myth-making of films in the cinema and on the television screen. The most well-known films in that area are: *Gandhi, A Passage to India, The Far Pavilions, The Jewel in the Crown, The Man Who Would Be King, Bhowani Junction, Heat and Dust*. That this trend is far from fizzling out is, for instance, demonstrated by the showing, on BBC 2, at the end of 1986, of *Man-Eaters of Kumaon*, which is based on the memoirs of the 'great hunter', Jim Corbett. Some of these films have been of equal success in German cinemas or on German television, although on the continent they lack the motivation of Raj nostalgia. Since some material is also available on video[26], these films might serve as appetizers to whet the learners' curiosity or they can be easily used as captivating starting points for discussion. Anyway, the main points of interest are their use of 'local colour' and the characteristics of the plot. What poses as history more often than not turns out to be mere escapism; plot all too often hinges on variations of the 'miscegenation' pattern, with elements of the gender gap being 'embellished' by ethnic or racial antagonism. This ought to offer the opportunity of introducing the importance of historical circumstances in the analysis of the problems of cross-cultural communication[27], when the power relationship is not one of symmetry. Salman Rushdie has most aptly coined the phrase of 'Raj revival' for what we have been witnessing on the various screens, and he directed his criticism against the way in which "Indians get walk-ons, but remain, for the most part, bit players in their own history".[28] As if to show that Rushdie's analysis is right, *The Independent* chose the headline 'Rediscovered Empire' when it announced the showing of a lavish new film dramatisation of Priestley's novel *Lost Empires* on ITV.[29]

Another approach might be through the problematization of the Gandhi myth. The relevant material consists of biography (in print and on video[30]), autobiography, political and philosophical[31] assessments, fictional commentary in film or narrative.[32] The use of genuine Indian films could well prove a somewhat utopian idea. It seems significant though that there might occasionally be a chance of seeing films made by the Merchant-Ivory-Company (with the cooperation of Ruth Prawer Jhabvala) here, but it needs a special festival once in a lifetime to experience, say, Satyajit Ray's *Pather Panchali* or Mrinal Sen's *Parashuram*.

2. Further Suggestions for a profounder treatment in class: The Transcultural Discourse

Attention should be drawn to distinctive features of literary communication in India and Pakistan on the one side and Germany on the other. Jamal's account of the attentive and knowledgeable vast crowds a poet might attract as an audience for his outdoor readings is a good corrective for the poor reception poets find in Germany. In India literature definitely has an important socio-political function. Indian poets in Germany, by contrast, are more than frustrated by their readings to small, and sometimes far from attentive groups of listeners. It is irritating, for writers and editors alike, that Indian poetry on the German market can be found on the shelves of second-hand bookshops for half the original price only one month after publication.[33] Recitations are public events in India. In Germany the reading of poetry is a scanty affair of the closet.

In the following further intriguing confrontation with the world of India will be discussed under three headings: travelogues, fictitious Indianness, Indian classics.

2.1 Travelogues

Vidia Naipaul's[34] statements are most telling and revealing. His travelogue is based on a year's sojourn in Northern India of 1962. The darkness of the title refers to the 'featurelessness' of which he accuses the country. The analysis of more than ten years later is the result of a fifteen-month visit during Indira Gandhi's Emergency, which, for him, occasioned the insight that gave the new book its title:

> The crisis of India is not only political or economic. The larger crisis is of a wounded old civilization that has at last become aware of its inadequacies and is without the intellectual means to move ahead.[35]

Darkness tells the story of Naipaul's pilgrimage to the Cave of Amarnath in the Himalayas only to end with the rather deflating résumé that "pilgrimages were only for the devout"[36] and, one might add, not for him, the agnostic Oxford-style rationalist. In both books he goes in for a good deal of 'Gandhi-bashing', attacking the "colonial", "failed reformer" and his "mahatmahood"[37], claims that Hinduism is at the bottom of "India's intellectual second-rateness" and advocates that India should at last shed the fetters of her past.[38]

The American Robert Bohm[39] evidently does not share the self-servingness of the greater part of Naipaul's assumptions. His impressions of India go back to repeated visits, between 1968 and 1978, under the tutelage of his Indian wife,

Suman. Bohm's *Notes* are a welcome antidote to Naipaul, especially so since they concentrate on his experience in the south, in Karnataka State. He has a treatise on caste (Part II) in which he tries to put the phenomenon into perspective, instead of marvelling at the 'pariah' scavengers and sweepers or ridiculing an exaggerated sense of social differentiation and of hierarchy, viz. Naipaul's *Malhotra* episode in *Darkness*.[40] In his Part III, he gives a short survey of the political history since 1947. He tackles the persistence of various stereotypes in the West's relationship towards India, and depicts US-counterculture attitudes as a continuation of colonial stances. He gives a critical view of Mohandas Gandhi (Part IV), stresses his "unique form of psychological blackmail" and his "basically authoritarian" outlook, which is corroborated by Masselos and others. The reader who wants a more systematic look at the nature of Indian society ought to consult Dilip Hiro.[41] Those who are interested in a systematization of Western responses will find some conclusive material in K. K. Dyson.[42]

The four pieces on India by Shiva Naipaul in *Beyond the Dragon's Mouth*[43], all written in the early eighties ("The City by the Sea", "A Dying State", "The Sanjay Factor", "Bubbly"), take city-life as the springboard of reflection, Bombay, Patna, and Delhi. The astute observer notes, for instance, that "India is a bottomless reservoir of the middle- to low-range skills required by the oil-rich desert sheikdoms. Engineers, plumbers, waiters, motor-mechanics – they all want to go to the Gulf for a few years and make a small fortune."[44] He surely shares some of the hang-ups of his better-known brother, but his prose, though equally well-turned, shows the greater, (com-)passionate heart, much in evidence when he writes, for example:

> The havoc caste can wreak has been nowhere better demonstrated than in the relentless degradation imposed over the centuries on the millions of untouchables. No other tyranny has ever surpassed it in cruelty. To the pariah, the temples were forbidden; instruction of any kind was forbidden; the free use of the public highways was forbidden. He was not allowed to have in his possession – or to recite – the sacred scriptures. He had to live apart from other men and draw his water from separate wells. He was condemned to the most squalid tasks. His mere shadow was polluting and its heedless deployment could lead to his murder.[45]

When Shiva Naipaul links up Marxist false consciousness with the Hindu concept of *Maya*, he sounds as if he was being sardonic like his brother, but is not, for the simple reason that this 'bull in a china shop of perfectly glazed self-deceptions [...] was at heart a Hindu – as best as he knew how'.[46]

Nirad Chaudhuri's musings, "What divides the East from the West is neither Anglo-Saxon pride nor Hindu xenophobia. Both have indeed done their worst, but even they could not have made the division so unbridgeable without a contribution from something infinitely stronger, something which is absolutely basic to man's existence on earth – temperature"[47], sound more pessimistic than they really are. In the wake of Kipling, like Angus Wilson some twenty years later[48], he utters a warning which cherishes the idea of going against the habitual grain of cliché-thinking. In the same vein, E. M. Forster and V. S. Naipaul come in for some gentle chiding, when Wilson embarks on giving well-phrased expression to his "echantment with India". He talks of "India the mysterious", and of its "spiritual duplicity", gibes at Transcendental Meditation, but also gives the "New India of efficiency" its due. He shows sympathy for Indian distrust of "European fascination with the Hindu religious scene", sarcastically scourges several sorts of tourism, and finally comes to the conclusion:

> India, I suspect, has become the whipping boy for all the doubts and anxieties of the materialist, forward-going, outward-looking West, as it has become the ludicrous Utopia of their rebellious sons and daughters, the necessary arguing point in a tedious and, for her, largely irrelevant Western generational war. Yet this symbolic, select India seems to have infected many Indians, so that they often do not notice the elements of Western progress in their own society.[49]

2.2 Fictitious Indianness

Lastly, mention should be made of three recent (re-)publications which are well worth considering in the context of cross-cultural communication: *Karma Cola, Letters of an Indian Judge, All About H. Hatterr.*

The multi-talented Gita Mehta enhances Wilson's sly wit to write punchy satire.[50] The satirical juxtaposition of East and West actually cuts both ways. As a film-maker, she transposes the cut and countercut technique to her writing and offers a pungent sequence of relatively short, self-sufficient prose pieces. In this way "the monomania of the West" is contrasted with "the multimania of the East".[51] India, she says, is only accessible to the Western mind "after an almost total reeducation.[52] A quotation like the following,

> India as the new magnet for the new despair. When you're tired of winning come lose with us.[53]

demonstrates perfectly the underlying tone as well as the inherent tendency towards the epigrammatic. With all her tenets one should recall, however, what Wilson found so charming in many Indians: their ability to pull a foreigner's leg so ingeniously and yet so unobtrusively. A real master of the art of verbal wit and irony, by the way, is the writer, poet, and academic Nissim Ezekiel, and the actor turned editor must be applauded for including him in his otherwise rather dubious venture of an anthology about to be published under the particularly unfortunate title, *Out of India*.[54]

Letters of an Indian Judge to an English Gentlewoman, attributed to Dorothy Black and originally published in 1934, as well as the fictional autobiography by G. V. Desani under the title of *All About H. Hatterr*[55], which was published for the first time in 1948, necessitate a closer reading. The latter was enthusiastically received by T. S. Eliot among others, then, and highly praised again by Anthony Burgess, now. Desani's hero has a Scotsman for his father and a Malay woman for his mother. Up to the age of fourteen, he is brought up by the English Missionary Society, thereafter he enjoyed the education of the streets of India. The 'H' in H. Hatterr, incidentally, stands for nothing less than "Hindustaaniwallah".[56] The loose structure of the book consists of Hatterr's and his Indian friend Banerrji's visits to seven sages. Hatterr's "rigmarole English"[57] has reminded many readers, in quite a favourable way, of James Joyce. This does indeed imply that a second-language readership must needs be sufficiently 'sensitized' linguistically to appreciate the full charm of the prose. Luckily, things are much easier in the Indian Judge's case. Passages like the following may be chosen to 'prove' that the allegedly authentic letters were not written by an Indian at all, judge or no judge, but presumably by the Lady Sahib herself, who otherwise does not figure in the text as a sender of letters we get the faintest chance of reading:

> It is in the hands of the great majority now. And the mentality of the great majority, in your country, and in my country, it is not a secret, Lady Sahib. They have nothing to lose, having themselves no stake in the business, nothing saved, and nothing planned. They can afford to encourage wild-cat schemes, since if it makes them no better off, at least it cannot make them worse off than already they have allowed themselves to become. [...] Can those unable to manage their own affairs do any better for a Country, is the question I ask myself.[58]

2.3 Indian Classics

There are by now numerous publications which provide the necessary overview, whether it be Indo-English Literature in general[59] or the narrative genre in particular.[60] A special monograph on the Anglo-Indian short story also exists.[61] From the number of available and useful short story anthologies[62], two will be dealt with in greater detail.[63]

The older selection contains most of the classics. There we find twenty stories; they are, however, by thirteen authors, with only one woman amongst them.

116

From a historical point of view, it is basically the Twenties and Thirties that are contrasted with the Fifties and Sixties; but – as its most important characteristic – there are nine stories originally written in English, three that are translated from Bengali, two from Hindi and likewise from Urdu, and one each from Tamil, Marathi, Malayalam, and Telugu. The book's achievement is thus to provide a cross-section of truly Indian literature. The most recent selection again comprises twenty stories; they are by seventeen authors, six of them women. Out of these twenty, twelve are Anglo-Indian; the time-span covered stretches from Kipling to the editor.

The best story to demonstrate what white British supremacy was like is still Kipling's "Wee Willie Winkie" which has as its hero a boy of the same name, "child of the Dominant Race, aged six and three quarters".[64] More interesting and less known, especially from an Anglo-Indian point of view, are the many contributions made by women authors, some of which are included in Cowasjee's selection. Equally appealing, but more time-consuming would be a text-sequence built around the Great Mutiny/Massacre complex.[65]

As far as cross-cultural reflection in narrative form is concerned, Ruth Prawer Jhabvala's story "A Course of English Studies"[66] could be a very appropriate beginning. There, the Indian girl Nalini is sent to Britain, "where culture flourished and people were advanced and sophisticated", to get a proper education. The only desire on her part, being "a very emotional sort of person", however, is to secure love and a lover. As it turns out though, it is not only the dreary and cold climate by which she is desperately disappointed. When, therefore, she very down in the mouth writes her mother a letter, she comes to the slightly surprising conclusion: "I don't believe that Shakespeare or Keats or Shelley or any of them can have been English! I think they were Indians, at least in their previous birth!!"

On a comparable yet more serious note, Anita Desai has one of her characters in "Scholar and Gypsy"[67] ask himself "What jokes could East and West possibly share," David, with his "Vermont pride in his country wife" Pat, takes a purely ethnological interest in the people of nothern India. "Here was I, disappointed at finding them so westernized. I would have liked them a bit more primitive – at least for the sake of my thesis", he muses self-assuredly but loses his self-assertion when he discovers that he cannot make his wife waver in her resolution to stay behind with the mountain people out of sheer devotion. Otherwise much of the author's effort goes into depicting the "social bitchiness"[68] among the better-off and the well-to-do. If Jhabvala is compared to Austen then Desai ought to be put on a par with Woolf.

In Narayan's story "A Horse and Two Goats"[69] the cultural gap between American and Indian is of great importance, too, even if it is not the sole point of

117

interest. The two cannot speak to one another, as they do not understand each other's language, and, paradoxically, when they meet at the outskirts of a small Indian village, the American opens his wallet and presents his card. Behind the surface humour of the text, we feel compassion, perhaps, for the poor, who are objectively set before our eyes. At the outset, in any case, the narrator exhibits an almost god-like detachment: "Of the seven hundred thousand villages dotting the map of India, in which the majority of India's five hundred million live, flourish and die, Kritam was probably the tiniest [....]." Sly irony manifests itself, when we learn that the name of the place means 'crown' in Tamil. And yet, a serene poise certainly persists in what is generally known as 'Malgudi country', after Narayan's fictitious locale. Whereas it may be doubted that Malgudi has done "more than any other in contemporary times to make the intricacies and rhythms of Indian life accessible to people of other cultures"[70], it is probably true that many Indian readers feel "the satire is so mild as to be no more than the nip of a non-malarial mosquito" and excludes "the India of those who have managed to escape the holocausts that regularly embroil whole communities".[71] His "cunningly understated use of the English language"[72] can be studied in his novels, *The Guide* and *Waiting for the Mahatma*.[73] In both texts the *sadu* theme, the holy man topos, plays an important part; this theme is also under scrutiny in Desani, as we have seen, and is, furthermore, equally at the heart of two stories by Jhabvala and Desai.[74] They should be compared with Narayan's title story of his most recent short-story collection.[75]

Another highly relevant theme of Indian literature, especially amongst the more classical texts, could be termed the peasants' plight. Here, the most relevant stories are by the Bengali Chatterjee, the Hindi Chand, and the English writer Anand.[76] Where there is a tinge of sentimentality in Chatterjee, as in Tagore's "Cabuliwallah"[77], we encounter indirectly accusing acerbity in Prem Chand and in Mulk Raj Anand. It is not always the title stories which are the most rewarding; apart from Natwar-Singh's proposed texts, I would recommend "The Cobbler and the Machine"[78] which purports to demonstrate, parable fashion, 'the blessings of industrialisation' under Indian circumstances. As far as novels go, Anand's *Untouchable* und *Coolie*[79] as well as Markandaya's *A Handful of Rice*[80] come into this category.

Partition, as the main factor of political history, has also, of course, been reflected in literature. The best text to begin with is Singh's "The Riot".[81] Apart from Rushdie's *Midnight's Children* and Sahgal's *Rich Like Us*, a handful of novels come to mind.[82] As Robert Ross has pointed out very convincingly, a stage has been reached in the eighties when the writers' impetus no longer stem from their intention to give an exposition of 'lived-through history', but from grappling with the destructive effects of tradition.[83]

Notes

1 Singhal, D. P.: *A History of the Indian People.* London, 1983, p. 18.
2 Which caused a million dead and the 're-settlement' of over another eight millions.
3 Chaudhuri, N. C.: *The Continent of Circe. Being an essay on the peoples of India.* London, 1967, passim.
4 Cf. *English Today,* 3 July, 1985, 30.
5 Cf. Commonwealth Institute: *Commonwealth Fact Sheet, India.* London, 1982. The relationship between Sanskrit-derived languages and those of the Dravidian tradition incidentally corresponds to a North-South tension.
6 Cf. M. Jamal: *The Penguin Book of Modern Indian Poetry.* Harmondsworth, 1986. Extracts also in: *South,* October 1986, 130–132.
7 At the Frankfurt Symposium on Indian Literature, 27–28 September, 1986, documented in: Dasgupta, A., Lutze, L., Riemenschneider, D.: *... ganz unten, wie Shesha, bin ich.* Frankfurt/M., 1986.
8 Kubanek, A.: *Dritte Welt im Englischlehrbuch der Bundesrepublik Deutschland. Aspekte der Darstellung und Vermittlung.* Regensburg, 1987. The proposed term relevant for our context is "Third World Literature in English" (p. 123). India is summarily dealt with in the discussion of G. Burger who advocated the use of 'General Overseas Service of All India Radio'-material in class. He is not unduly taken to task for stressing a European advantage angle and an exaggerated 'England-centredness'. The reference (p. 43) is to „'This is the General Overseas Service of All India Radio' – Kurzwellenempfang im fortgeschrittenen Englischunterricht". *Neusprachliche Mitteilungen* 35, 1982, 16–21.
9 Jussawalla, A.: *New Writings in India.* Harmondsworth, 1974.
10 Cf. CSE mode III as indicated by E. M. Nicholson: "Indian Literature in the English Classroom -1". *Wasafiri* No. 2, Spring 1985, 25. See also P. S. Guptara: *India in the Classroom.* London, 1980.
11 "Indian Literature in the English Classroom", 25. The particular comparative angle within what used to be called Commonwealth literature is even more strongly emphasized in my introduction to a book edited by me: *The Story Must Be Told. Short Narrative Prose in the New English Literatures.*Würzburg, 1986. For a report on the actual experience with the teaching of Indian literature compare my contribution to ‚Elfter Fremdsprachendidaktiker-Kongreß, 7.–9. Oktober, 1985', edited by H. Melenk, J. Firges et al. Tübingen, 1987, pp. 133–140.
12 *The Guardian,* 17 May, 1986, 9.
13 *Süddeutsche Zeitung,* 22 September, 1986, 9.
14 *Süddeutsche Zeitung,* 7 October, 1986.
15 Venzky, G.: *Die Zeit,* No. 48, 21 November, 1986, 76.
16 Obtainable through: Nile & Mackenzie Ltd., 13 John Prince's Street, London W1M 9HB.
17 Misleadingly spelt *suttee* in books written under the spell of the imperialist past. Moreover, it should be pointed out that the term originally denotes the faithful and loving wife as an ideal and only later adopted the meaning of self-immolation of a widow through burning on the funeral pyre of her deceased husband.
18 Blaicher, G. (Ed.): *Erstarrtes Denken. Studien zu Klischee, Stereotyp und Vorurteil in englischsprachiger Literatur.* Tübingen, 1987. In particular: Six, B.: „Stereotype und Vorurteile im Kontext sozialpsychologischer Forschung", pp. 41–54.

119

19 Stoll, K.-H.: „Prospero's Erben: literarische Darstellungen des Images von Euro-
päern im heutigen Afrika". - In Blaicher, G. (Ed.): *Erstarrtes Denken*, pp. 342–349.
20 Sharma, R.: *Indian Society and Social Institutions*. New Delhi, 1980, chap. 7, "Status
of Women in India", p. 164.
21 Ibid., p. 170. It is perhaps appropriate to insert some information here on Cornelia
Sorabji (1866–1954) who pioneered the opening of the Bar in Britain to Women and
wrote two autobiographical books, *India Calling* (1934) and *India Recalled* (1936),
as well as several collections of short stories among which figures the well-known
Love and Life Behind the Purdah (1901).
22 Cf. E. W. Said: *Orientalismus*. Frankfurt/M., 1981 ([1]1978).
23 Selbourne, D.: "Rajiv Ascends his Throne". *New Statesman*, 9 November, 1984, 20–
22.
24 Henry III, W. A.: "Shining Legacy from the East". *Time*, 30 September, 1985, 46–
47.
25 Stierlin, H.: *Die Welt Indiens*. Bayreuth, 1978, is a case in point. - Dolder, U., Dolder, W., Rothermund, D.: *Indien*. Munich, 1980, combines photo appeal and text
information.
26 *Reise nach Indien*, 156 minutes, colour, VHS, Thorn Emi, Uden, The Netherlands,
1985.
27 It should be pointed out that the existing terminology is sometimes somewhat misleading, as, for instance, W. B. Gudykunst (Ed.): *Intercultural Communications
Theory*. London, 1983, and Y. Y. Kim, W. B. Gudykunst (Eds.): *Cross-Cultural
Adaptation*. London, 1987, where the main interest focuses on the 'assimilation' of
migrants within one and the same country.
28 *The Listener*, 25 September, 1986, 27.
29 *The Independent*, 24 October, 1986, 29.
30 *Mahatma Gandhi. Biografie*. Stuttgart, 1985, 24 minutes, VHS. As for the most
recent biography in print see A. Copley: *Gandhi*. Oxford, 1986.
31 Gandhi, M. K.: *An Autobiography: the story of my experiments with truth*. London,
1966. See also J. Masselos: *Indian Nationalism. A History*. New Delhi, London, 1986,
chap. 9, "Gandhi"; A. Köpcke-Duttler: *Wege des Friedens. Franziskanische Lebens-
wege – Gandhi – ökologisches Recht – Aurobindo – Tagore*. Würzburg, 1986.
32 Attenborough: *Gandhi* (film), and Narayan, R. K.: *Waiting for the Mahatma*. Chicago, London, 1981 (1955) (novel). For criticism of the film's myth-making see
F. Jussawalla: "Fact versus Fiction: Attenborough's *Gandhi* and Salman Rushdie's
Midnight's Children". *ACLALS Bulletin*, Singapore, 1986, 70–78.
33 Dasgupta, A. (Ed.): *Gelobt sei der Pfau. Indische Lyrik der Gegenwart. Anthologie*.
Munich, 1986; reviewed by Kade-Luthra, V.: *Süddeutsche Zeitung*, 3 December,
1986, 45.
34 Naipaul, V. S.: *An Area of Darkness*. Harmondsworth, 1984 (1964); *India: a Wounded Civilization*. London, 1978 (1977), pb. ed. 1983.
35 *A Wounded Civilization*, p. 18.
36 *Darkness*, p. 169.
37 *A Wounded Civilization*, p. 156.
38 Ibid., p. 174.
39 Bohm, R.: *Notes on India*. Boston/Mass., 1982.
40 *Darkness*, pp. 48–49, where he sums up the dilemma by stating that unfortunately
there are no Rastignacs in present-day India.

41 Hiro, D.: *Inside India Today*. London, 1978.
42 Dyson, K. K.: *A Various Universe*. London, Oxford, 1979.
43 London, 1984.
44 Ibid., p. 264.
45 Ibid., p. 277.
46 Cf. Madhu Jain's obituary "Angry Author". *India Today*, 31 October, 1986, 99.
47 *A Passage to England*. London, 1959, p. 26.
48 "New and Old on the Grand Trunk Road (1975)". – In idem: *Reflections in a Writer's Eye. Writings on Travel*. London, 1986, pp. 121–142.
49 Ibid., p. 133.
50 Mehta, G.: *Karma Cola. Marketing the Mystic East*. London, 1981 (1980).
51 Ibid., p. 36.
52 Ibid., p. 71.
53 Ibid., p. 79.
54 Tim Pigott-Smith, who acted in *The Jewel in the Crown*, is the editor of this anthology.
55 *Letters of an Indian Judge*. London, Sydney, [5]1982; *All About H. Hatterr*. Harmondsworth, [7]1982.
56 *All About H. Hatterr*, p. 33.
57 Ibid., p. 37.
58 *Letters of an Indian Judge*, p. 204.
59 Riemenschneider, D.: „Die indo-englische Literatur". – In Kosok, H., Prießnitz, H. (Eds.): *Literatur in englischer Sprache*. Bonn, 1977; Stilz, G.: *Grundlagen zur Literatur in englischer Sprache*. Bd. 4: *Indien*. Munich, 1982; Naik, M. K.: *Dimensions of Indian-English Literature*. New Delhi, 1983.
60 Mukherjee, M.: *The Twice-Born Fiction. Themes and Techniques of the Indian Novel in English*. New Delhi, 1971; Riemenschneider, D.: *Der moderne englischsprachige Roman Indiens*. Darmstadt, 1974; Harrex, S. C.: *The Fire and the Offering. The English-Language Novel of India 1935–1970*. 2 vols. Calcutta, 1977.
61 Stilz, G.: *Die Anglo-indische Short Story. Geschichte einer Kolonialliteratur*. Tübingen, 1980.
62 Naik, M. K. (Ed.): *The Indian English Short Story. A Representative Anthology*. New Delhi, 1984; Kumar, S. K. (Ed.): *A Portrait of India. A Selection of Short Stories*. New Delhi, 1983.
63 Cowasjee, S. (Ed.): *More Stories from the Raj and After. From Kipling to the present day*. London, 1986; Natwar-Singh, K. (Ed.): *Stories from India*. London, Sydney, Auckland, 1971 (1966).
64 Kipling, R.: *Wee Willie Winkie. Under the Deodars, The Phantom Rickshaw and Other Stories*. London, 1964 (1895).
65 Hibbert, Chr.: *The Great Mutiny*. Harmondsworth, 1978 (historical account); Flora Annie Steel: *On the Face of the Waters*. London, 1897; M. M. Kaye: *Shadow of the Moon*. London, 1957; J. Masters: *Nightrunners of Bengal*. London, 1951.
66 *How I Became A Holy Mother and Other Stories*. Harmondsworth, 1982, pp. 69–87.
67 *Games at Twilight*. Harmondsworth, 1982, pp. 108–138.
68 Ibid., "The Farewell Party", p. 86.
69 In Cowasjee, S. (Ed.): *More Stories from the Raj and After*, pp. 181–201.
70 Ram, S.: "The magical storyteller of Malgudi". *South*, April 1986, 110.
71 Desai, A.: "Malgudi". *London Review of Books*, 4 December, 1986, 24.

72 Ram, S.: "The magical storyteller of Malgudi". *South*, April 1986, 110.
73 *The Guide*. London, 1958; about to be re-published by Penguin. As for *Waiting . . .* see note 31. – For a brief but competent overview see M. K. Naik: "R. K. Narayan". – In Bock, H., Wertheim, A. (Eds.): *Essays on Contemporary Post-Colonial Fiction.* Munich, 1986, pp. 191–203.
74 Jhabvala, R. P.: "How I Became a Holy Mother". – In idem: *How I Became a Holy Mother and Other Stories*, pp. 138–153; Desai, A.: "Surface Textures". – In idem: *Games at Twilight*, pp. 34–40.
75 *Under the Banyan Tree and Other Stories.* London, 1985.
76 Chatterjee, S. Ch.: "Draught", Chand, Prem: "The Shroud", both in Natwar-Singh, K. (Ed.): *Stories from India*, which also has two stories by M. R. Anand: "The Barber's Trade Union" and "The Informer".
77 Also in Natwar-Singh, K. (Ed.): *Stories from India.*
78 In Arand, M. R.: *The Barber's Trade Union and Other Stories*. London, 1944, pp. 84–94.
79 *Untouchable*. New Delhi, 1983 (1935). For a thorough portrait of Anand see D. Riemenschneider: "Mulk Raj Arand". – In Bock, H., Wertheim, A. (Eds.): *Essays on Contemporary Post-Colonial Fiction*, pp. 173–189. For "The Making of an Indian-English Novel: *Untouchable*" see M. R. Anand in M. Butcher (Ed.): *The Eye of the Beholder. Indian Writing in English*. London, 1983, pp. 34–43.
80 *A Handful of Rice*. London, 1966.
81 In Cowasjee, S. (Ed.): *More Stories from the Raj and After*, pp. 231–235; see also: Saadat Hasan Manto: "The dog of Titual". *The Listener,* 13 August, 1987, 16–17.
82 Singh, K.: *Train to Pakistan*. New York, 1956; Malgonkar, M.: *A Bend in the Ganges*. New Delhi, 1964; Nahal, Ch.: *Azadi*. Boston, 1975; Rushdie, S.: *Shame*. London, 1983; Sidhwa, B.: *The Bride*. New York, 1983.
83 Ross, R. L.: "The Emerging Myth: Partition in the Indian and Pakistanian Novel". *ACLALS Bulletin*, Singapore, 1986, 63–69.

Ingrid Hartmann-Scheer, Ratingen

Wole Soyinka's *Death and the King's Horseman:* An Experiment in an English „Leistungskurs"

I suppose reading an African play in a German school is not yet so common as not to require some explanation. Therefore before tackling the actual play *Death and the King's Horseman* by Wole Soyinka[1] some general arguments will be given for reading such a play in class and for my choosing this particular play. After a brief summary of the play itself the basic questions which were discussed in class will be pointed out, as well as the particular problems pupils had in understanding its language, imagery and thoughts. Following this there are some suggestions, some of which were made by the students themselves, on how to overcome these problems, which age group this play is suitable for and what previous knowledge students should already have acquired or be provided with before tackling the play. Finally there will be some suggestions for further reading either to enlarge on one or other of the themes of the play or to emphasize the genre and compare it with other plays.

For the subject English the *Richtlinien für die gymnasiale Oberstufe in Nordrhein-Westfalen* offer a list of topics regarded as typical or characteristic of the Anglo-American socio-cultural background. 'The British Empire' and the 'experiences of and with the colonial heritage'[2] are two examples. When looking for writers who deal with these topics E. M. Forster's *A Passage to India* or George Orwell's *Burmese Days* quickly come to mind, to mention but two well-known fictional texts that deal with these experiences. These writers, whatever their opinions on the empire and colonialism may be, look at people and events from a European point of view.

Of course, there has always been fictional and non-fictional material written by native authors. But when reading such novels, plays or stories in school there are some basic problems which are encountered. Firstly, if these authors write in their own native language we can only make use of English translations, which in turn should be avoided if authentic English material on the same topic is available. Another difficulty is that often a lot of background information on historical and cultural aspects of the respective peoples and countries is needed in order to make the pupils understand the conflicts which the protagonists have.

Considering the above Soyinka play seemed a good choice, as it is written in English and contains familiar patterns of thought in the scenes with English protagonists. It also offers an introduction to beliefs or, as Soyinka puts it in his "Author's Note" at the beginning of the play, to "the universe of the Yoruba mind"[3] which is initially difficult for pupils to get in contact with, or even understand. This very fact puts the pupils to some extent in the position of Pilkings, a British colonial officer and a character in the play, whose way of thinking, speaking etc. the pupils can more easily identify with at the beginning of the play. For Pilkings, as for the pupils, the native customs and beliefs are strange and in some cases incompatible with the white man's point of view.

At this point a summary of the play is appropriate. The setting is an unnamed town in Nigeria during World War II. Elesin Oba[4], the native King's horseman, is about to follow his master who died some time previously. According to his people's tradition, the horseman has to follow his master a certain time after the latter's death. He is to act as emissary to enable the dead King, or rather his spirit, to fulfil his task as intermediary between the world of the living, the dead and the unborn, and he has to accompany the King to the abode of the gods and the land of the ancestors to reconfirm the connection between the two worlds.

Pilkings, the British District Officer in this part of Nigeria, and his wife Jane are about to go to a ball held in honour of H. R. H. the Prince, who is on a tour of the colonies, when Pilkings is informed about the ritual to be carried out that very same night. For various reasons, both personal and political, he is determined to prevent Elesin's death by all means and even goes out personally to arrest him. While he is out doing this, Olunde, Elesin's eldest son, arrives. Pilkings had previously helped him to go to Great Britain to study there against Elesin's will. Now he has returned from England on this very day in order to bury his father. In a conversation with Pilkings' wife Jane, Olunde tries to make her understand why this ritual has to be carried out both for the welfare of Elesin himself and for that of his people, and implores her to help hold Pilkings back. But Olunde is too late. Pilkings comes back with the arrested Elesin and is going to keep him in custody for that night. Elesin is a broken man. He is fully aware of the disaster which his failure will bring on his people. Olunde, also conscious of the implication, disowns his father and disappears. Being kept in close custody Elesin tries to understand why he failed. He finally lays the blame on himself because he had weakened in his determination to follow his King at a critical moment, and had therefore failed. He confesses his weakness to Iyaloya, the leader, speaker for the market-women and guardian of the native traditions. She has come to blame and pity Elesin as well as to announce the arrival of a messenger who has taken Elesin's place and who is to carry the important message to release the dead King's spirit, a task which Elesin himself had failed to fulfil. This messenger turns out to be the dead body of Olunde, who has taken his father's place in order to save the spiritual well-being of his people. While Elesin, forbidden to leave his cell, stands staring at his dead son, trying to transmit to him the secret message to be taken to the dead King, he suddenly strangles himself with the chain he is fettered with.

This is the basic plot of the play, which consists of five scenes. Once the pupils get into the play they become curious and fascinated. The problem is, however, getting them started, because the very first scene is particularly difficult and strange for them. It introduces the main character Elesin Oba and the task he is about to fulfil at the end of the day, and it does so with the help of rich imagery which is rooted in the social and agricultural background of the Yoruba. Explaining the words alone is not sufficient in order to grasp the meaning of the images. Unless one of the pupils has some knowledge, the teacher should take care to depict the setting to them, a market-place in an African town; it is even better to show them a picture of such a place since its importance and the out-look of its inhabitants are very different from what the pupils are acquainted with. The teacher should also give some brief information on the social and eco-nomic function of markets in rural African areas. It would be even better if some, or all, pupils had some basic knowledge of the economic conditions and the agricultural production of farmers in West-African countries. A cross-check with the geography department at school or collaboration between the two sub-jects could help to provide the material and inspire some inter-disciplinary work. The first scene is read aloud in class as this makes it easier to get its tone and the atmosphere. The pupils' questions together with those of the teacher, who draws the pupils' attention to important passages, clarify Elesin's social position and the task he has to fulfil, i. e. following his King into the world of the gods and ancestors. The images, which mainly concentrate on farming, animal life and travelling, are only explained and interpreted in as far as they give a clue to what is going on.

After this first reading in class, the pupils sum up in keywords what they have learnt about Elesin Oba and his journey. This is done at home and read out and completed in the next lesson in school. Starting from this material, all the infor-mation is collected in Scene 1 about the gods, about the world of the dead and unborn and about its importance for the living[5] and then compared with ideas and concepts of life after death which the pupils know. The pupils recognize that for Elesin and his people the world of the living and that of the dead is basic-ally the same, and that dying or being born is just a transition from one world into the other, or a return to one of the worlds. This concept creates a deep feel-ing of continuity, of belonging together whether alive or dead. As Elesin puts it: "Coiled to the navel of the world is that endless cord that links us all to the great origin."[6] 'Us' here includes the dead ancestors, the living and the generations yet to be born. This idea of continuity has to be made clear in order to understand how important Elesin's death is for maintaining this link and how disastrous his failure will be for his whole people.[7] This emphasis on society and the role each has to fulfil for the communal welfare is an important aspect of the play and explains Olunde's self-sacrifice:

There lies the honour of your household and of our race. Because he [i.e. Olunde] could not bear to let honour fly out of doors, he stopped it with his life. The son has proved the father, Elesin [...]. Your heir has taken the burden on himself. What the end will be, we are not gods to tell.[8]

The pupils can read the second and fourth scenes on their own because the language and the topics are more familiar to them. Scene 2 is set in the home of Pilkings and his wife and gives information about the two characters and their attitudes towards the native people. In Scene 4 Olunde's position is made clear. He whom his father believed lost when he went to England availed himself of the best parts of modern civilization (by studying medicine), remained deeply rooted at the same time in the native tradition, as Elesin observes in the final scene:

[...] I know now that I did give birth to a son. Once I mistrusted him for seeking the companionship of those my spirit knew as enemies of our race. Now I understand. One should seek to obtain the secrets of his enemies.[9]

When Jane Pilkings wonders what Olunde thinks about the traditions of his own people he says:

Neither did I. But I found out over there. I am grateful to your country for that. And I will never give it up.[10]

Although there is a lot about the white man's attitude towards natives and their customs and traditions and white man's insensitivity or even inability to understand or at least tolerate them in Scenes 2 and 4, it is important not to enlarge on this topic too much in order to avoid the impression that the play portrays a 'clash of cultures'. In his "Author's Note"[11] Soyinka warns the reader against such a simplification of the issue. It would belittle Elesin's failure and somehow take away his responsibility, which he gradually acknowledges in Scene 5:

[...] my weakness came not merely from the abomination of the white man [...] there was also a weight of longing on my earth-held limbs.[12] [...] My will was squelched in the spittle of an alien race, and all because I had committed the blasphemy of thought – that there might be the hand of the gods in a stranger's intervention.[13]

By letting the pupils compare Elesin in the last scene with Elesin as he presents himself in the first and third scenes, where he affirms his will-power and determination to fulfil his task, where he brushes aside Iyaloya's warnings, which she again confronts him with in the final scene, they become aware of his great downfall and of a resemblance to the classical tragic hero, whose downfall is due to some flaw in his character.

The contrast between the self-assured Elesin in the opening scene and the broken man at the end leads to a discussion of the structure of the play. The exposition in Scene 1 is followed by a presentation of the surroundings and ways of thinking of the white man, personified by Pilkings and his wife Jane. After a brief interlude of comic relief at the beginning of Scene 3 we watch the ritual, in which Elesin is to follow his dead King and where he is at the height of his will-power. This and the final scene should be read out in class for better understanding and also because of their dramatic impact. Crisis and turning-point are found in Scene 4 where the captured Elesin faces his son and is disowned by him. One pupil remarked that here two worlds, i.e. that of the natives and of the Europeans, literally meet on the same ground for the first time: Olunde, a defendant of native traditions, comes to the Resident's house, whereas Elesin is brought there by force. In the foregoing scenes these two worlds were kept apart, one being set in the market-place, the other in the Resident's area. In the final scene Elesin comes to face his failure, the consequences of which can perhaps be alleviated by his son's self-sacrifice.

Another formal element to be discussed is the function of the praise-singer, who appears in Scenes 1, 3 and 5. By making the pupils look carefully at what the praise-singer says and does, they find out that he tells about Elesin himself and his task (Scene 1), acts as the mouthpiece of the dead King and keeps the reader informed about what is going on when Elesin is falling in a trance (Scene 3). In the final scene he again acts as the speaker of the departed King, reminding Elesin of his task and his failure, and he also voices the criticism and fears of his own people.

So far I have outlined the main topics discussed in class. Some others to be considered are the different roles of women in this society, especially Iyaloya's, who is called the "Mother of the market" and is deeply respected by Elesin. Then there are Joseph and Amusa, two natives working for the white man and to a certain extent estranged from their own people. But when it comes to the point they turn out to be rooted in their native traditions.[14] The importance which a culture with its rituals and traditions has for the spiritual and common well-being of a people is an aspect of the play that some pupils regarded as very important.[15] By gradually working out the basic ideas about the worlds of the living and the dead in the first scene, and becoming aware of the fact that the images employed in the play are rooted in the environment and way of living of the native people, the pupils were made to recognize too, how much our thinking is influenced by our cultural background and were made to reflect on our traditions, which, up until then, they had not thought about very closely. They also noticed the impact of any colonial rule: namely that what looks like mere political domination can go much deeper and affect the basic ideas that hold a society spiritually together.

When asked if more information should be given to them before they began to read the play most pupils were against this, because as one pupil put it, "all you need to know is contained in the first scene". The pupils preferred rather more information on matters of religion and social and moral values after reading and interpreting the play. What helped them a lot in understanding certain ideas and formal elements in the play was their previous reading of a Shakespearean play (*Julius Caesar*; the film version of *Macbeth*) and some basic knowledge about the Elizabethan view of the world, where a strongly hierarchical structure of the universe is emphasized, containing a predestined order that cannot be upset without grave consequences for the whole universe. Some pupils saw parallels between Elesin's acceptance at the end for responsibility for his failure and Macbeth's and Brutus' end. Pilkings, they pointed out, has something of the Greek tragic hero, for by trying to prevent Elesin's death he brings about an even greater disaster, as Iyaloya makes clear at the end of Scene 5.[16] But whatever similarity of thought or form that could be found, the play gains its impact from its own plot and theme and this made it for some pupils one of the most interesting texts they had ever read.

Inspired by the "Author's Note"[17], where Soyinka points out that the play is based on historical events and comments on the changes he made, we also discussed basic differences between non-fictional and fictional texts and the functions of both from the writer's and the reader's points of view. This topic, which was also previously discussed in connection with *Julius Caesar*, gained new relevance because Soyinka himself refers to the historical event and his dramatic intention.

It is obvious that Soyinka's play is only suitable for a „Leistungskurs" because it takes about 14 lessons to read and interpret in class and preferably in classes 12/1 or 13/1 as knowledge of another modern play and a Shakespearean drama make this play more easily accessible.

The following suggestions for further reading material are in no way representative or exhaustive. They just offer other views and literary forms, e.g. Aniebo's short story "The Loneliness of the Long-Distance Traveller"[18] which deals with the encounter between a young Nigerian soldier and a young American military advisor. In "Exile", a short story by Rose Moss[19], we follow a young South African musician in his vain attempt to get used to America. Examples of colonial prejudice can be taken from Orwell's *Burmese Days*[20] or Forster's *A Passage to India*[21] or Gordimer's *A World of Strangers*[22]. Extracts from these texts can also be used for the required written tests.

In my opinion *Death and the King's Horseman* also lends itself to an interdisciplinary project, on which the teachers of English, Geography, Philosophy and Sociology could work together with the teachers of Religion to the mutual benefit of the different subjects as well as the pupils.

Notes

1 Soyinka, W.: *Six Plays*. London, 1984, pp. 143–220.
2 Der Kultusminister des Landes NRW (Ed.): *Richtlinien für die gymnasiale Oberstufe in Nordrhein-Westfalen. Englisch*. Köln, 1981, pp. 41–45.
3 Soyinka: *Death and the King's Horseman*, pp. 144–145. For information on the Yoruba cf. Davidson, B.: *The Africans. An Entry to Cultural History*. Harmondsworth, 1973; Osae, T. A., Odunsi, A. T. C.: *A Short History of West Africa*. Book II. London, 1973.
4 'Elesin Oba' is the native term for the 'King's Horseman'.
5 Soyinka: *Death and the King's Horseman*, p. 149.
6 Ibid., p. 157.
7 Ibid., p. 205.
8 Ibid., p. 218.
9 Ibid., p. 205.
10 Ibid., p. 196.
11 Ibid., pp. 144–145.
12 Ibid., p. 207.
13 Ibid., p. 212.
14 Ibid., pp. 164–165.
15 Ibid., p. 215: "We will disturb you no further, servant of the white king. Just let Elesin fulfil his oath and we will retire home and pay homage to our king."
16 Ibid., p. 219.
17 Ibid., pp. 144–145.
18 Aniebo, J. N. C.: *Of Wives, Talismans and the Dead. Short Stories*. London, Ibadan, Nairobi, 1983, pp. 103–108.
19 Gray, St. (Ed.): *The Penguin Book of Southern African Stories*. Harmondsworth, 1985, pp. 236–250.
20 Orwell, G.: *Burmese Days*. Harmondsworth, 1967.
21 Forster, E. M.: *A Passage to India*. Harmondsworth, 1961.
22 Gordimer, N.: *A World of Strangers*. Harmondsworth, 1962.

HANS W. SCHMIDT und P. WÜLFING (Hrsg.)

Antikes Denken – Moderne Schule

Beiträge zu den antiken Grundlagen unseres Denkens

1988. 321 Seiten. Kartoniert DM 65,-
(Beihefte zum Gymnasium, Heft 9)

Dieser Band ist das Ergebnis der vom Deutschen Altphilologenverband und dem internationalen Colloquium Didacticum Classicum gemeinsam veranstalteten Tagung in Tübingen 1986. Seine Beiträge umfassen jene Themen des antiken Denkens, die in der heutigen Schule Gegenstand des Unterrichts sind – oder sein können, nicht nur in den Alten Sprachen, sondern auch in Geschichte, Philosophie und Religionslehre. Der rein philosophiegeschichtliche Horizont ist überall überschritten, insofern als

– neue Antworten auf aktuelle Fragestellungen gesucht werden (besonders in den Beiträgen von I. Fetscher, K. Gaiser, A. Setaioli, F. Schwarz, J. Klowski)

– die politische Situation einbezogen wird (besonders in den Beiträgen von Mirriam Griffin, J. Malitz, B. Kytzler)

– methodische Probleme der philosophischen Interpretation behandelt werden (besonders in den Beiträgen von J. Frère, E. Lefèvre, M. McGann)

– die Behandlung im Gymnasialunterricht thematisiert wird (besonders in den Beiträgen von H. Storch, R. Thurow, J. den Boeft, G. Lagarrigue)

– nicht nur philosophische Schriften im engeren Sinn, sondern auch andere Texte als Träger philosophischer Aussagen betrachtet werden (besonders in den Beiträgen von M. McGann, M. Fuhrmann)

Eine solche Zusammenschau wird ebenso die wissenschaftliche Diskussion beleben, wie sie denen eine zuverlässige Grundlage bietet, die antikes Denken an der Zugangspforte zur heutigen Zeit, der modernen Schule, zu vermitteln haben.

CARL WINTER · UNIVERSITÄTSVERLAG
D-6900 Heidelberg · Lutherstraße 59

Ingrid Ross, Krefeld

"The influence of a place on one's writing": Margaret Laurence's Short Story "To Set Our House in Order" and her Essay "A Place to Stand On" in a Class 12 „Leistungskurs"

The following is not meant to be a systematic analysis of the two texts in question, nor is it a discussion of conceivable teaching objectives or other didactic criteria for a unit on them. It is rather meant to be a pragmatic essay in which I share with my readers my own experience of finding the texts and putting them to use in the classroom. It is by no means an idealized description of a teaching unit; I have not tried either to hide or to exaggerate difficulties that arose. My main objective in writing this is to encourage other teachers to use these texts by Margaret Laurence in their classes, and to discover "new territories" for themselves and their pupils.

In Canada, Margaret Laurence (born 1926) is counted among the foremost novelists[1], and a few years ago, a German critic dealt with her as one of "Canada's major contemporary novelists".[2] Ever since reading what is perhaps her most famous book, *The Stone Angel*, I have personally counted her among my favourites. I looked for something in that vein to give my advanced English pupils to read and study, but for some reason, Margaret Laurence's works are hard to come by in Europe. She is virtually non-existent for British booksellers. Thus, I was happy to discover two stories and an essay by Laurence in the more readily available *Anthology of Canadian Literature in English*[3], all of which texts would be quite suitable for classroom use, depending on the nature of the unit. One of the stories, "The Tomorrow-Tamer", is set in Africa, where Laurence spent several years in the 1950s, and quite convincingly adopts the tone of some actual African writing in English. The other story, called "To Set Our House in Order", is from the semi-autobiographical collection *A Bird in the House* (1970) and is set in the fictional prairie town of Manawaka, Manitoba, the special place Laurence created from elements of her own home town of Neepawa, Man., as a backdrop to several of her novels and stories. This story immediately appealed to me because of its reminiscence of *The Stone Angel*, and, as luck would have it, it made a perfect sequel to the novel my class had read that term (12.1), i.e. *To Kill A Mockingbird* by Harper Lee. Not only that, but the accompanying essay, "A Place to Stand On", which deals with some aspects of why this particular writer writes as she does, including the important aspect of regionalism as

131

opposed to parochialism, seemed an ideal text to set both fictional texts in perspective and thus add scope to the unit on the novel as well.

"To Set Our House in Order": Characterization of the text

The story is told by Vanessa MacLeod, who is ten years old at the time of the narrated events. On the surface, it is about the complications surrounding the birth of Vanessa's baby brother. Her mother has to go to hospital before the expected time, which leaves the girl alone with her grandmother for most of the day. It is probably her anxiety for her mother during this time which tenses her up and makes her unusually aware of a whole range of other feelings regarding her family.

Obviously, this is what the story is really about, and we can classify it as a kind of story of initiation[4], since at the end Vanessa shows a new awareness of values and the relationships of people.

The first definite hint as to the 'real' meaning of the story is given when Grandmother MacLeod teaches Vanessa the lesson she herself was taught by her own father, that "God wants us to set our house in order" (p. 157; cf. title). We are immediately aware of irony here, because by this time we have gathered that Grandmother MacLeod is not one for practising this rule herself, at least not in its superficial meaning, because we learn that she never helps with the housework. Instead, she has even asked her son to move in with his family, so that her daughter-in-law can keep house for her now that she can no longer afford hired help. The sense of irony is enhanced later on when she expresses pride in her family's motto: "Pleasure Arises from Work" (p. 158).

It is not until later in the story that we learn (much more consciously than the narrator herself) that the irony goes much deeper than a reference to bad housekeeping. "House" can be taken to mean "family", and the MacLeod family is indeed not in order. First of all, there is Grandmother's pretence of being a lady directly descended from the Scottish nobility, whereas in truth she is an Ontario "horse doctor's" daughter. Her husband was a Greek scholar at heart, but for some reason he worked as a (successful) country doctor in the prairie town of Manawaka. Of her two sons, one, Roderick, was killed in the First World War, and the other, Vanessa's father Ewen, has also become a doctor, although he, too, used to have other plans for his life. As the story unfolds, we learn that Ewen feels guilty of Roderick's untimely death on account of a childhood episode in which he accidentally caused his brother's partial blindness. This, in turn, seems to have made him feel permanently obliged to make up for things to his mother, who still treats him like a child when she reprimands him for using "bad language" in her presence. It also makes him give in to his mother against

132

his will when she insists on their naming the new baby Roderick. Vanessa perceives all this without really understanding it, but she has a definite feeling in the end "that whatever God might love in this world, it was certainly not order". (p. 164)

The amount of space allotted to details about Grandmother MacLeod in the first part of the story (up to the bottom of p. 159) makes her the first focus of interest. But since Vanessa is the first-person narrator of the story, it is always in some connection with her that the old lady is seen. Her introduction into the action already stresses the ladylike quality of her behaviour, "standing there in her quilted black satin dressing gown, her slight figure held straight and poised". She is shown in direct contrast to her son, who appears dishevelled and worried. It is worth looking at two similes with reference to Grandmother MacLeod on this first page. One compares her hair to "white-feathered wings in the snare of her coarse night-time hairnet", which conveys a feeling of imprisonment, or at least of something not free. The other compares her voice to "the tap of a sterling teaspoon on a crystal goblet", giving the immediate impression of quality, authority and a high living standard. (The same applies to another simile much later, on p. 162, where her voice is again compared to silver, this time including a slight touch of menace: "as pointed and precise as her silver nail-scissors.")

The idea of something not free about Grandmother is developed in the whole of the first part of the story, particularly in her treatment of Vanessa, who is not supposed to move freely throughout the house. Grandmother herself hides whatever feelings she may have behind her poise and self-discipline, and quotes the mottos of Scottish clans and religious sayings instead.

All this focus on Grandmother MacLeod serves to illustrate the way of life Vanessa has grown into, and the values she is torn between, i.e. her grandmother's old-world ones and those of her definitely more liberal-minded parents (cf. p. 156, lines 28–30; p. 157, line 1).

In the second part of the story, more of the family history is revealed. Here we cannot find one person so definitely at the centre of interest as Grandmother MacLeod is in the first part, but rather a series of details about other members of the family which all seem to accord to a pattern of contrast between illusion (or wishful thinking) and reality. One central passage is Vanessa's conversation with her father, in which she gives vent to her feelings towards Grandmother, only to be told that people's behaviour has to do with their troubles in life, and which leaves her very much confused ("I didn't know –" I stammered; p. 161).[5] Her dream of a caught sparrow (cf. the simile of Grandmother's hair!), of her mother crying, and of dead children's voices that night, mirrors this confusion.

Another episode of recognition for Vanessa near the end of the story is the conversation she overhears between her mother and her Aunt Edna. Here she realizes, or at least gets a vague idea of the part her dead uncle Roderick still plays in her family. This makes her ride away on her bicycle to think things out for herself, leading to the concluding sentence about God not loving order, which subtly, though not directly, echoes the title.

There is one speciality of detail in this story that should not go unmentioned. Margaret Laurence draws the reader's attention to a character's hair first of all, and in so doing she very subtly makes a variety of points. The contrast between Ewen running his hands through his dishevelled, sand-coloured hair, and his mother with her "feathery" white hair ensnared in a net has already been mentioned above. On the same page, Beth (Vanessa's mother) is shown in pain, with her black hair spread wide across the white pillow-case in an unaccustomed way for Vanessa, who is used to seeing it neatly pinned up. Vanessa's practical-minded, slang-speaking Aunt Edna wears her black hair bobbed (p. 159), and, perhaps most significant of all, there is the new baby with his "feathery black hair" (p. 163), creating a link between the old lady and her daughter-in-law. Maybe this is a hint that Roderick II can actually restore "order" between the generations?

There are quite a few details in this story that make it typically Canadian on a superficial level. For one, there is the setting of Manawaka, meant to be a small prairie town in Manitoba during the Depression. Another thing is the ancestry of the two sides of the family involved, both Scottish and Irish. In Grandmother MacLeod we are shown a type of "hyphenated Canadian" who is definitely bound to her European roots and the values they carry with them, as opposed to the more easy-going generation of Vanessa's parents, who are still very much aware of these roots (Edna at one point alludes to the difficulties her sister's and her own Irish ancestry pose to Grandmother MacLeod's strictly Scottish attitudes; cf. p. 159), yet do not attach so much importance to them, as their adoption of North American language habits shows.

All this contributes much to the atmosphere of the story, but it is certainly not essential to what we might call its message. There are 'Vanessas' growing up and finding out about the complexity of life all over the world, quite independent of where they live and how many nationalities they stem from: value clashes about order must occur in all growing up.

Treatment of the story in class

In giving this description of the story, I have actually summed up the results of our class discussion. Nevertheless, the procedure in detail looked somewhat less systematic (and more school-life-like!) than the summary suggests. For one thing, the students began their analysis of the story without knowing more than the opening page. This is a procedure I often find more rewarding than having them read the complete story beforehand. It gives more room for really spontaneous remarks (provided this reading of the opening page is done in the classroom and not as homework), and it also serves to make pupils more aware of their own reading process in English. Besides, this way it is often easier to study a beginning as such (uncluttered, as it were, by further details), thus gaining early insight into compositional or stylistic peculiarities that might prove valuable as the reading goes on.[6]

In this case, the opening of the story is written in a particularly lively manner, with plenty of dialogue and striking description of characters. The immediacy of the situation (enhanced by the unaccustomed perspective of the first sentence, "When the baby was almost ready to be born") captured the pupils' interest at once. They were amused by the description of Grandmother MacLeod's first appearance, though they needed help to grasp the significance of the similes used to characterize her. One of the boys spontaneously commented on Laurence's apparent obsession with hair when introducing people, which provided a good start into an interpretation of special features together with a warning to look out for these aspects as the story unfolds.

For the following (double) period, I asked the class to finish reading at least the first half of the story and to make a list of the characters mentioned and what is said about them. This was necessary to get some order into the discussion and to impress on them quite clearly the predominance of Grandmother MacLeod in form and content. Also, at this stage it became necessary to talk about the Canadian background. My pupils did not know very much about where to look for Canadian place names on a map, and since Toronto, Ontario and Manitoba are mentioned, apart from the fictional Manawaka (and some more places in the essay "A Place to Stand On", which would be dealt with next), it seemed advisable to study the map and fill in a few details about Canadian geography and – very roughly – history. The names Neepawa, Manawaka and Manitoba are also interesting because of their Indian sound. All this information is certainly not essential for an enjoyment of the story, but it adds interest because of its 'otherness'. Another aspect of Canadian *Landeskunde* that must be mentioned in the context of this story is the "Canadian way of immigration", which is different from the idea of the melting pot in the United States. Canada has been called a "tossed salad"[7] instead of a melting pot, and many Canadian immigrants have tended to hold on to their original nationalities (or those of their ancestors in the case of immigrant families, cf. Grandmother MacLeod), which has rendered them so-called "hyphenated Canadians". In our story, Vanessa must deal with her Scottish and Irish ancestry and with clashes between the two that seem quite out of order in view of the fact that all the people in question were born and bred in Canada.

For the final (again double) period on "To Set Our House in Order", I asked the class to finish reading the whole story[8] and analyse the shift(s) in the focus of interest up to the end. The evaluation of this homework proved a valuable experience for teacher and pupils alike, since hardly anybody had seen through the rather complex pattern of information and emotions. I was surprised how reluctant the pupils were to focus on the narrator herself, trying to make sense of the bits and pieces of information about various members of the MacLeod family independently of Vanessa's feelings about them. I now think this reluctance was partly on account of a basic need for 'action' in stories as opposed to a gradual development of feelings and insights, which I have often encountered in the classroom. As a matter of fact, several pupils commented that though they did not really dislike (!) the story, they thought there should be more about the baby's birth and the worries of the family, and less about what they termed irrelevant (because dead) people. There is perhaps a point of interest here for teachers who prefer so-called stories of initiation to any other kind of short story in the classroom.[9] In this case, I tried not to stress Vanessa's 'lesson' too much in order not to be too didactic, but of course it was essential for the pupils to grasp the pattern (and message) of the story, if the discussion was to be of any value at all. Actually, after referring back to what is said about that dominant figure, Grandmother MacLeod, with particular emphasis on *how* it is said, it was not really difficult to make the class understand *and accept* that it is a story about Vanessa and what she eventually comes to realize about human behaviour and family relations.

There was a week's time between this final discussion of the story and the next English period. Since the analysis and interpretation of the story had been more difficult than first expected, and particularly since it had of necessity dealt with the story in portions rather than as a whole, I felt it would be useful for the pupils to think again, and more systematically this time, about the story. So I assigned them the following questions, which are basically the type of questions encountered in exam papers:

1) What 'outer action' are we told about?
2) The story is much longer than it should take to tell about the birth of a child, even with complications: what, then, is the story really about? Consider the title as well as the amount of details we are given about certain characters.
3) What compositional and stylistic means does Margaret Laurence use to stress the 'real' focus of interest? Give examples.
4) What strikes you as being 'typically Canadian' (as far as you can tell) in this story? Does this make it a story that could only be set in Canada, or can you imagine a similar story to be set in your own environment? Explain.

It was my evaluation of the pupils' answers that led to the 'summary of results' quoted above.

136

"A Place to Stand On": Brief description of the essay

The title of this essay (first published in 1970) is the last line of a poem by the contemporary Canadian poet Al Purdy.[10] The essay essentially deals with Margaret Laurence's use in her writing of her memories of the world she perceived during her childhood and adolescence. She begins with a quotation from an essay by Graham Greene:

> The creative writer perceives his own world once and for all in childhood and adolescence, and his whole career is an effort to illustrate his private world in terms of the great public world we all share.

Then she proceeds to discuss this statement in terms of her own fiction. She compares her writing to that of contemporary African authors, which is also "the attempt to assimilate the past, partly in order to be freed from it, partly in order to try to understand" it (p. 165). Her early fascination with "the African scene" prevented her from writing "an autobiographical first novel", but ultimately she discovered that there was no way for her to escape writing about the place she had come from, or, as she poignantly calls it, "my own place of belonging". Thus, her writing about "Manawaka" has served her to "come to terms with the past". At the time of writing the essay, she feels that even when her fiction is not set in the prairies or even in Canada, "Manawaka", for her, "will probably always be there, simply because whatever I am was shaped and formed in that sort of place, and my way of seeing, however much it may have changed over the years, remains in some enduring way that of a small-town prairie person." (p. 168)[11]

The essay is appealingly personal in its approach. Here is a serious writer discussing her own views on writing, and not a lecturer making some academic point about the relationship between fiction and autobiography. There is, evidently, this dominant theme, or thread, that runs through the whole piece; there is also a certain order achieved by repeated reference to Greene's statement; but there is also the characteristic loose structure of the English-language essay, which permits the writer to follow up her associations, if not definitely to digress, thus allowing us glimpses of her ideas on such seemingly disparate topics as the significance of modern African literature, the theme of survival, and optimism vs. hope.

The essay "A Place to Stand On" in the classroom

In their study of literature, pupils must be made to deal with different types of texts. It would certainly be boring if they were given an essay on writing by all the authors they come across in the course of their studies, but, used sparingly,

137

this kind of writing is sure to widen their horizon concerning literature. In the case of Laurence's essay "A Place to Stand On", there is the added advantage of the quotation from Graham Greene (with the opportunity to remember another literary name, perhaps to look him up in an encyclopaedia, perhaps even to pick up a novel by him?) and the possibility to apply the ideas put forward here to fiction by other writers, not only in English.[12]

The first step was, as usual, the most difficult one. In order to understand the essay, it was necessary to understand the quotation from Graham Greene with which it begins. We referred (loosely, at first) to the story by Laurence, of course, but at this stage I found it useful to remind the class of Harper Lee's novel about "Scout" growing up into and learning about the society of the American South, in order to widen the scope beyond the world of Margaret Laurence. Harper Lee's "private world" can be seen as mirrored in the family of Atticus Finch, the lawyer (Lee's own father was a lawyer, too) and in the way Scout as the first-person narrator deals with everything that goes on in the (fictional, yet very real) town of Maycomb, Alabama. All this has become a successful novel because obviously the novelist found a means to "illustrate" her "private world in terms of the great public world we all share", i.e. Scout's (or Vanessa's) experiences are only unique in the sense that every individual goes through his or her own unique experiences[13], and not in the sense that a reader must live in the same circumstances or have intimate knowledge of the surroundings before he or she can understand the experience. In this sense, the discussion of the statement as well as the essay that deals with its underlying ideas certainly contributed to the pupils' knowledge about fictional characters in relation to their creators.

It took the class some time to realize that they had already thought about this to some extent when answering the fourth question in the final homework on "To Set Our House in Order" (is it only my pupils who always seem so reluctant to connect?). Once they had realized it, though, they felt prepared to tackle the essay.

It seemed advisable to study the train of thought and to point out the associative style of the essay. Of course some annotations were necessary, although most of the text is self-explanatory. One word (which also appears in the story) caused a considerable amount of consternation, because none of us could find a satisfactory definition or translation of it in any of the (many!) dictionaries we consulted.[14] I am referring to the peculiarly Canadian use (perhaps even confined to the prairies?) of the word "bluff", usually in connection with poplars. There is slight consolation to be found in the following quotation from a story by another Canadian author, Farley Mowat (born 1921); the narrator is a boy who has recently moved to the prairies from Ontario: "I was fascinated [...] by

138

the dusty clusters of poplar trees that for some reason which still escapes me, were known as bluffs."[15]

On the whole, though, the essay was not a difficult text to read and understand. When asked what had particularly struck them as noteworthy, the pupils mentioned Laurence's statement that "Optimism in this world seems impossible to me. But in each novel there is some hope, and that is a different thing entirely." (p. 167) It is a very abstract statement to discuss if you cannot fall back on a whole spectrum of examples. I thought it was just as well to let it alone once it had been re-read and a tentative distinction between the two concepts of optimism and hope been given.

They all seemed to take for granted the main 'message' of the essay, i.e. "the influence of a place on one's writing". This is something that never fails to surprise me when working with advanced pupils: they seem to have known it all all along, hardly anything ever strikes them as unusual or noteworthy. Of course, this is due to their almost complete lack of conscious reading experience on their own; they have not had a chance to disprove literary theories and thus really start thinking about them. So they read Margaret Laurence's discussion of Graham Greene's statement and thought "so what?" – and yet I am sure that it was not lost on them. Is this not what we do so often in the teaching process? We give a student "food for thought" and let it settle, ideally, in its own time. And that is what all essays are for, each in its own way.

Afterthoughts

Despite the fact that some of the experiences mentioned above do not reflect absolute enthusiasm about the way my class responded to the texts, I am quite sure that I will present them to another class soon. As a matter of fact, this time I am planning to use all three Laurence texts from the *Anthology*, beginning with the African story, "The Tomorrow-Tamer". Whereas in the unit described above the concept of "the influence of a place on one's writing" was applied to (at least) two authors, Margaret Laurence and Harper Lee, the new unit would demonstrate how differently it can be used in the fiction of one and the same author.

1 Cf. Bennett, D., Brown, R. (Eds.): *An Anthology of Canadian Literature in English.* Toronto, 1983, Vol. II, p. 138.

2 Schäfer, J.: „Anglo-kanadische Romanciers der Gegenwart". *Die Neueren Sprachen* 83, 1984, 422.

3 See Bennett, D., Brown, R. (Eds.): *Anthology of Canadian Literature*, "The Tomorrow-Tamer", pp. 139–153; "To Set our House in Order", pp. 154–164; "A Place to Stand On", pp. 165–168. All references to page numbers of the texts dealt with are to this edition.

4 Cf. Düsterhaus, G.: „Sinclair Ross: 'Cornet at Night'". *Der Fremdsprachliche Unterricht* 20, 1986, 40–48, who quotes M. Marcus' definition of an initiation story: "An initiation story may be said to show its young protagonist experiencing a significant change of knowledge about the world or himself, or a change of character, or of both, and this change must point or lead him towards an adult world. It may or may not contain some form of ritual, but it should give some evidence that the change is at least likely to have some permanent effects." (41; from Marcus, M.: "What Is an Initiation Story?" *The Journal of Aesthetics and Art Criticism*, 14, 1960, 221–227, here: 222).

5 This conversation is quite similar to "didactic" conversations between Atticus Finch and his daughter Scout in *To Kill a Mockingbird*, including Scout's subsequent confusion.

6 The actual procedure is different, though many of the underlying ideas are related to the approach described here, in L. Bredella: „Lebendiges Lernen im Englischunterricht". – In Schratz, M. (Ed.): *Englischunterricht im Gespräch. Probleme und Praxishilfen.* Bochum, 1984, pp. 188–204, especially p. 195. When working along these lines, a pupil gets the chance to let the beginning of a text "sink in" and also to make a conscious effort at "guessing" what the story will be about. For a more detailed analysis of the method and its underlying assumptions, see L. Bredella: „Leseerfahrungen im Unterricht: Kognitive und affektive Reaktionen bei der Lektüre literarischer Texte". – In Bredella, L., Legutke, M. (Eds.): *Schüleraktivierende Methoden im Fremdsprachenunterricht Englisch.* Bochum, 1985, pp. 54–82.
In the case of "To Set Our House in Order", the first page provides ample guessing material, and experienced readers will notice at once that "human behaviour/relationships" will be the main topic. But my pupils preferred to stick to the 'outer action' at this stage; they were worried about the birth of the baby, and whether that would change Vanessa's home life. This "discrepancy" provides a good topic for later discussion, when the whole text is known.

7 In an address at Chatanqua, New York, on Aug. 3, 1973, Arnold Edinborough, a Toronto writer, said, "Canada has never been a melting pot; more like a tossed salad." (Quoted in a handout from the Canadian Studies Seminar in Toronto, July 1985)

8 The fact that most of them had already finished by then shows that they were really interested in "finding out" (cf. note 6), which in its turn proved it to be a "motivating" story for them, even though it did not fulfil their expectations concerning the plot.

9 For a recent confirmation, cf. G. Düsterhaus, „'Cornet at Night'", p. 40. I am far from excluding this kind of story from my own classes, of course, though I prefer not to put them together for a unit on "initiation". Dealt with from time to time, I am quite convinced that they have a greater appeal to pupils than these may be prepared to disclose. For this reason, I did not stress the aspect of initiation in the story apart from having the pupils recognize it, since it had been dealt with when studying *To Kill A Mockingbird*.

10 "Roblin's Mills (2)". Bennett, D., Brown, R. (Eds.): *Anthology of Canadian Literature*, p. 61 f.

11 In a very interesting recent study on Margaret Laurence, K. Gross explores the impact of her African years on her fiction with particular reference to her novels. This article (which unfortunately was not available to me when preparing the unit) might be of some help to the teacher interested in this particular aspect of M. Laurence's writing: Gross, K.: "Margaret Laurence". – In Bock, H., Wertheim, A. (Eds.): *Essays on Contemporary Post-Colonial Fiction*. München, 1986, pp. 423–443.

12 One very important advantage of reading formal *or* informal essays in class is their potential function as models for pupils' own writing. "A Place to Stand On" gives them a very good example of how to develop a personal comment about a rather complex statement like that of G. Greene. Though not dealt with explicitly here, this aspect was in fact taken into account in our class discussion of the composition of the essay.

13 Cf. what M. Laurence says in her essay (p. 167):
"Writing, for me, has to be set firmly in some soil, some place, some outer and inner territory which might be described in anthropological terms as 'cultural background'. But I do not believe that this kind of writing needs therefore to be parochial. If Hagar in *The Stone Angel* has any meaning, it is the same as that of an old woman anywhere, having to deal with the reality of dying. On the other hand, she is not an old woman anywhere. She is very much a person who belongs in the same kind of prairie Scots-Presbyterian background as I do, and it was, of course, people like Hagar who created that background, with all its flaws and its strengths."

14 I have since found it in *Collins Dictionary of the English Language*. London, Glasgow, ²1986: "bluff [...] 2. *Canadian.* a clump of trees on the prairie; copse [...]."

15 Mowat, F.: "The Coming of Mutt". – In Düsterhaus, G. (Ed.): *Growing up on the Prairies*. München, 1985, p. 80.

Neuerscheinungen

Amerikanische Alltagskultur und Englischunterricht

Hrsg.: Helmut Sauer
Mit Beiträgen von Dieter Buttjes – Rolf Högel –
Helmut Heuer – Jürgen Donnerstag – Amei
Koll-Stobbe – Gerd Kaiser – Ingrid Kerkhoff –
Rudolf Kaiser – Helmut Sauer – Horst Zimmermann – "Be Prepared" – Heinrich Händel
1987. 210 Seiten. Kartoniert DM 25,-
(anglistik & englischunterricht, Band 31)

DENE BARNETT
The Art of Gesture: The practices and principles of 18th century acting

with the assistance of Jeanette Massy-Westropp
1987. IV, 503 Seiten mit zahlreichen
Abbildungen und Zeichnungen.
Kartoniert ca. DM 250,-. Leinen ca. DM 280,-
(Reihe Siegen. Beiträge zur Literatur- und
Sprachwissenschaft, Band 64)

OTTO EBERHARDT
Verkleidung und Verwechslung in der erzählenden Dichtung Eichendorffs

1987. 114 Seiten. Kartoniert DM 50,-
(Beihefte zum Euphorion, 21. Heft)

SABRINA HAUSDÖRFER
Rebellion im Kunstschein

Die Funktion des fiktiven Künstlers in Roman
und Kunsttheorie der deutschen Romantik
1987. 318 Seiten. Kartoniert DM 72,-.
Leinen DM 98,-
(Reihe Siegen. Beiträge zur Literatur- und
Sprachwissenschaft, Band 78)

REINHART KOSELLECK – HANS-GEORG GADAMER
Hermeneutik und Historik

1987. 36 Seiten. Kartoniert DM 16,-
(Sitzungsberichte der Heidelberger Akademie
der Wissenschaften, phil.-hist. Klasse, Jahrgang
1987, Bericht 1)

MONIKA LEMMEL
Poetologie in Goethes West-östlichem Divan

1987. 290 Seiten. Kartoniert DM 69,-.
Leinen DM 95,-
(Reihe Siegen. Beiträge zur Literatur- und
Sprachwissenschaft, Band 73)

LEO POLLMANN
Argentinische Lyrik

im lateinamerikanischen Kontext: Der Fall
Roberto Juarroz
Mit einer deutsch-spanischen Anthologie
1987. 192 S. Kart. DM 64,-. Leinen DM 89,-
(Reihe Siegen. Beiträge zur Literatur- und
Sprachwissenschaft, Band 74)

WOLFGANG RATH
Not am Mann

Zum Bild des Mannes im deutschen
Gegenwartsroman
1987. 85 Seiten. Kartoniert DM 20,-
(Beiträge zur neueren Literaturgeschichte.
Dritte Folge, Band 80)

HANS-MICHAEL SPEIER (Hrsg.)
Celan-Jahrbuch 1 (1987)

1987. 234 Seiten, 1 Abbildung.
Kartoniert DM 140,-
(Beiträge zur neueren Literaturgeschichte.
Dritte Folge, Band 78)

GABRIELA WETTBERG
Das Amerika-Bild und seine negativen Konstanten in der deutschen Nachkriegsliteratur

1987. 224 Seiten. Kartoniert DM 84,-.
Leinen DM 112,-
(Beiträge zur neueren Literaturgeschichte.
Dritte Folge, Band 77)

CARL WINTER · UNIVERSITÄTSVERLAG · HEIDELBERG

Corina Hebestreit / Klaus Peter Müller, Düsseldorf

Background Information on Some of the "New Territories"

It would have been beyond the scope of this volume to give information on all of the countries where English is spoken and where English literature exists, at least to a certain degree. There are the 49 members of the Commonwealth of Nations one would have had to think of: Antigua and Barbadu, Australia, Bahamas, Bangladesh, Barbados, Belize, Botswana, Brunei, Canada, Cyprus, Dominica, the Fiji Islands, the Gambia, Ghana, Grenada, Guyana, India, Jamaica, Kenya, Kiribati, Lesotho, Malawi, Malaysia, the Maldive Islands, Mauritius, Nauru, New Zealand, Nigeria, Papua New Guinea, Sambia, Seychelles, Sierra Leone, Singapore, Solomon Islands, Sri Lanka, St.-Christopher (Kitts-) Nevis, St. Lucia, St. Vincent, Swaziland, Tanzania, Tonga, Trinidad and Tobago, Tuvalu, Uganda, United Kingdom, Vanuatu, Western Samoa, Zambia, Zimbabwe. Most of these countries became independent as late as in the 1960's or 1970's. Membership of the Commonwealth of Nations has grown by thirteen in the last ten years.

There are also a number of British dependencies, or "Dependent Territories", such as the Channel Islands and the Isle of Man, and such territories as Hong Kong and Gibraltar, the one being prepared for a reunion with China, the other now, following a new constitution, a British Dominion and the focus of Spanish claims to sovereignty. In the West Indies there are the dependencies of Anguilla, the Cayman Islands and Montserrat, as well as the Turks and Caicos Islands and the British Virgin Islands, constituting a colony. There are the Falkland Islands (and the Falkland Dependencies South Georgia, South Sandwich, South Shetland, South Orkney) and Bermuda, a self-governing British colony. There are the Pitcairn Island in the South Pacific, Saint Helena and the Gough Island in the South Atlantic. All of these are territories where English is at least one of the languages of intercommunication, if not the only one. (Cf. the maps, where they are all shown, p. 167, 168.)

We have, therefore, confined the background information to those countries discussed in the articles of this volume. Our main sources of information have been *The Encyclopedia Britannica*, *Everyman's Encyclopaedia*, *Fischer Weltalmanach*, and *Munzinger Länderhefte*. Thanks are also due to the embassies and the Commonwealth Institute in London, from which we received additional material.

Geography

Australia is one of the oldest land masses. Its area of 7 682 300 km² is nearly as large as the United States excluding Alaska and Hawaii, and half the size again of Europe excluding the Soviet Union. It is about 25 times larger than Britain and Ireland.

Australia is the flattest of the continents. The average elevation is less than 300 m, compared with the world's mean of about 700 m. Only about five per cent of the continent is more than 600 m above sea level.

The dominating structural division, the vast and ancient Great Western Plateau, merges from Western Australia's coastal plains to cover almost the whole of that state, the greater part of the Northern Territory, much of South Australia and a part of western Queensland.

East of the Great Western Plateau and extending from the Gulf of Carpentaria in the north to eastern South Australia and the shores of western Victoria is the great lowland belt known as the Central-Eastern Lowlands.

The Eastern Highlands, more commonly known as the Great Dividing Range, extend along the eastern rim of the continent from Cape York in the far north of Queensland to the southern seaboard of Tasmania. In some parts, the Great Divide is less than 50 km from the coast. The rugged south-eastern area, known as the Australian Alps, contain some of Australia's highest ground, including Mount Kosciusko (2228 m), their highest point.

Australia's climate ranges from the tropical to the temperate. Slightly more than half of Queensland, 40% of Western Australia and 80% of the Northern Territory are within the tropics. The remainder of the continent, including the whole of New South Wales, Victoria, South Australia and Tasmania, is in the temperate zone.

Early History

Australia's first inhabitants were the Aboriginals, a dark-skinned race of hunters and food gatherers believed to have arrived from Asia at least 38,000 years ago. They scattered in small nomadic family or tribal groups throughout the continent. Like the European settlers, the Aboriginals were attracted to the better-watered country of the coastal fringe, especially the south and the east.

About the time of European settlement, the Aboriginal population is believed to have numbered 300,000. At this stage, they had developed a rich, complex and distinctive culture finely tuned to their environment, but a physically severe and relatively primitive way of life. The directions in which Aboriginal society could develop were limited by their environment and lack of contact with other people.

European Contact

During the second century AD in his map of the then known world, a Greek mathematician, Ptolemy, sketched in the known coasts of Asia, showing what is now the Indian Ocean as an enormous lake and placing a huge unknown land which he called *Terra Incognita* to the south of it. The European discovery 1500 years later that *Terra Incognita* actually existed was a by-product of Portuguese, Spanish and Dutch mercantile expansion into Asia.

The first Englishman to visit the continent was a buccaneer, William Dampier, who landed near King Sound on the north-west coast in 1688. It was not until 1770 that Captain James Cook, of the British Navy, sighted the east coast of the continent. After passing through Torres strait, Cook landed on an island 3 km off Cape York which he named Possession Island. He raised the British flag and formally took possession of the eastern part of the continent.

European Settlement

Although Cook's account of his discovery caused considerable interest in England, no attempt was made to colonise the land until the American colonies were lost by Britain in the American War of Independence. Britain needed alternative overseas settlements for law-breakers sentenced to transportation and to relieve the inhuman overcrowding of its prison hulks along the Thames.

Through immigration and natural increase, the population grew from 34,000 in 1820 to 405,000 in 1850. With more free settlers, public agitation in New South Wales and other colonies forced an end to the transportation of convicts to the mainland in 1840. By then, 100,000 of them had been sent from Britain.

Independence

Self-government became an early objective as the various settlements expanded, and the distances separating them from Britain and from each other caused great administrative problems. New South Wales was granted the first constitutional charter in 1823, with limited legislative responsibility.

The powers provided in the British Government's *Australian Colonies Government Act 1850* made the development of responsible government inevitable. All colonies except Western Australia became self-governing by 1859.

The Commonwealth of Australia – a federation of the six former colonies as states – was declared to come into being on January 1, 1901.

145

Population

Australia's population was an estimated 15,451,900 in December 1983, more than double the 1945 population. The increase reflects, in part, an influx of newcomers through an extensive immigration program. About one in five Australians was born overseas.

Australia is one of the most urbanised countries in the world, with about 64% of the population residing in the eight state and territory capital cities and less than 15% in rural areas. Most of the population is concentrated in the eastern part of Australia. Vast areas are unsuitable for settlement, and consequently Australia has an average of only two people per square kilometre.

In 1981, the number of Aboriginals and Torres Strait Islanders living in Australia was 159,897 – 1.1% of the population. Although there have been many improvements in Aboriginal assistance programs since 1972, most Aboriginals still have low levels of education, poor health, inadequate housing and high unemployment rates.

Religion

At the 1981 census 76.4% of those who stated their religion professed the Christian faith. Non-Christian religions include Jewish (62,126 people), Islamic (76,792) and Buddhist (35,073).

Government

Australia's political institution and practices follow the Western liberal democratic tradition, reflecting British and North American experiences.

Australia is a federation of six states in which legislative powers are divided between the Australian Federal Parliament (located in Canberra) and the six state parliaments. The Federal Parliament has two chambers: the House of Representatives (the Lower House) and the Senate (the Upper House).

Queen Elizabeth II of Great Britain and Ireland is still formally Queen of Australia.

Economy

Before World War II, Australia was largely dependent on primary production. The main expansion in the past 20 years has been in the tertiary sector. During the last two decades, considerable investment has taken place in export-oriented mining and energy projects. Although reliance on primary production has diminished over the years, Australia is still an important producer and exporter of

146

farm products, leads the world in wool production and is a significant supplier of wheat and sugar.

Rural industries now account for about 7% of production, mining contributes about 6%, manufacturing contributes about 20% with the tertiary sector accounting for the balance.

Education

The Federal Government recognises that Australian society is a multicultural society and believes it is important to support the retention of the languages and cultures of all Australians. Funds are provided under the Ethnic Schools Program and the Multicultural Education Program. Two of the specific aims of these programs are to assist in the maintenance of minority languages and cultures and to support the provision of opportunities for children to learn a language other than English spoken by a community in Australia.

Canada

Geographically Canada is the second largest country in the world. Economically it is one of the most industrialized and enjoys one of the highest standards of living. Socially it is one of the most diverse, for the Canadian people have come from every land on the globe. Historically Canada has been part of the French and British Empires, and, like many other countries, has achieved its complete independence only in this century. Politically it has enjoyed democratic institutions for well over one hundred years. It is not an easy country to understand, even for Canadians.

Geography

The very size of the country has always been a threat to its existence. Most of its 24,500,000 people are stretched out in a ribbon along the length of its southern boundary.

The four Atlantic provinces are the northern-most extension of the Appalachian Mountains. Fishing, farming, and lumbering have been the traditional occupations. But offshore is the promise of new riches, as gigantic oil rigs probe beneath the icy waters of the North Atlantic in search of oil and gas.

The Atlantic provinces have been little affected by modern immigration. Most of the inhabitants are descendants of people from the British Isles and have lived in the region for generations or centuries. Poorer than the average Canadian, the people of the Atlantic provinces have a strong sense of independence, a distinctive outlook rooted in their past, and a sense of identity as "Maritimers" – those who live by the sea.

United by geography but divided by history and language, the provinces of Quebec and Ontario form two distinctive Canadian regions and societies. The people of both are concentrated along the banks of the St. Lawrence-Great Lakes waterway.

For almost 400 years Quebec farmers have cultivated narrow strips of land running back from the St. Lawrence. Lumber and minerals are also part of the economy of the region.

80% of the people in Quebec are French-speaking. While most now live in the industrial cities which produce almost one third of Canada's manufactures, the quiet villages and farms and the white towers of the parish church constantly reveal what the province was like for several centuries, and what for some it still is.

But the pulse of the province comes from the large manufacturing cities that sweep around Lake Ontario from Niagara Falls to Ottawa. This "golden horseshoe" is the largest manufacturing region in Canada and one of the fastest growing centres in the world. At one time Ontario was basically Anglo-Saxon in composition. But particularly since the end of the Second World War it has been radically changed by the influx of immigrants who came to work in the factories and built the growing cities of southern Ontario.

The southwestern portion of the Canadian Shield gradually disappears into the wheatlands of the Canadian prairies, one of the great granaries of the world. The prairies were largely settled in the early years of this century. Part of the population is made up of descendants of British, French and American settlers, but the descendants of the myriad of central European peoples who came to build the railways and open the land for settlement now make up half the prairie population. Today the three prairie provinces – Manitoba, Saskatchewan and Alberta – are no longer completely dependent on farming and ranching. Oil in Alberta, and to a lesser extent in the other provinces, potash and uranium in Saskatchewan, and gold and nickel in Manitoba have broadened the economy of the region and provided greater prosperity.

Beyond the Rockies lies British Columbia, a province extremely rich in the products of its forests, waters and mines. With an abundance of hydroelectric power, much of it exported to the United States, it boasts of a rapidly growing manufacturing industry based on its raw materials.

Stretching across the top of the four western provinces are the giant Northwest Territories and the Yukon. Governed partly from Ottawa, but hoping event-

148

ually to become provinces, the north makes up 40% of Canada's area. Yet in that vast Arctic region there are only 70,000 people, many of them Inuit and Indian.

For a long time the distant north was far removed from the mainstream of Canadian life. But the discovery of large mineral deposits and oil and gas fields, the existence of powerful rivers for hydroelectric power, and the brooding presence of the Soviet Union on the other side of the Arctic Ocean have made Canadians look to the north. Canada has been a land of many frontiers; the north is the latest, and perhaps the last.

Population

Less than half the population of Canada is of British stock. Of those who are, many emigrated from Britain and the United States in colonial days. They are scattered all over the country, but form the bulk of the population in the Atlantic provinces, rural Ontario and parts of the prairies and British Columbia.

About 25% of Canada's population is French speaking. There has been little modern immigration from France, and the 6,000,000 French Canadians are offspring of the 60,000 inhabitants of New France conquered by Britain over 200 years ago. Quebec is the heartland of French Canada, but large numbers of French Canadians live in New Brunswick and Ontario, and small pockets exist in other provinces.

One quarter of the population is of neither French nor British origin. Most of these Canadians have come from the countries of Europe, seeking escape from tyranny, war or poverty.

Today more than one Canadian in twenty is of German origin. One in thirty is of Italian, one in forty of Ukrainian, and one in fifty of Dutch descent. Contributing to the rich Canadian cultural mosaic are from 100,000 to half a million people who trace their origins to Austria or Greece, Hungary or Poland, Russia, Sweden, Norway, Portugal, Yugoslavia, and China. Thousands from every other country in Europe mingle in Canadian cities with families from South America, the Caribbean, Africa, the Middle East, India, and Southeast Asia. Until the 1970s most of the immigrants were European, but in recent years "new Canadians" from Asia have been almost as numerous.

History

Almost at the same time, both French and English established permanent colonies in North America. In 1607 the Virginia Company founded Jamestown, and soon hundreds and then thousands left England to settle in the New World, either to improve their fortunes or to escape religious persecution. By the end of

149

the century much of the coastline had been settled, and by the middle of the eighteenth century about 1,500,000 people lived in the thirteen colonies.

In 1608 Samuel de Champlain established the first French foothold on the cliff overlooking the St. Lawrence at Quebec City. But settlers did not flock to Champlain's new colony. By 1760 there were still only 60,000 settlers in New France.

In 1642 the city of Montreal was started at the head of navigation on the St. Lawrence and became the centre of the fur trade. Before long French explorers had reached Lake Superior and Hudson Bay.

The final struggle between English and French for the continent really began in 1754. With the capture of Louisbourg in 1758 and Quebec in 1759, French power in North America was shattered. In the peace treaty of 1763 New France became another British colony.

The Making of a Nation

The first stage in the growth of Canadian independence and democracy came in 1791. In that year the British government divided the old colony of Quebec into the new colonies of Upper and Lower Canada, and gave each colony an elected legislative assembly. However, many matters were still controlled by Britain and a great deal of power was firmly held by the Governor and an appointed council.

Before long, however, Canadian reformers were demanding less control by Britain and more power for the assembly. After a minor rebellion in 1837, the British sent Lord Durham to investigate. Durham wrote his famous report, recommending both that the colonies be given control over most internal affairs and that the powers of the Governor and the appointed executive council be reduced. The 1840 Act of Union created a single province in the St Lawrence-Great Lakes area with a legislature in which Canada East (Lower Canada, now Quebec) and Canada West (Upper Canada, now Ontario) enjoyed equal representation. The union failed to work, however, for differences between French and English helped to paralyze the government of the colony. A federal union of all the British North American colonies appeared as a possible solution. The first of several meetings was held in 1864. Three years later the British Parliament passed the British North America Act creating a federal union called *Dominion of Canada* out of the colonies of the Canadas, Nova Scotia and New Brunswick.

The west was purchased from the Hudson's Bay Company in 1869 and, after a short-lived rebellion by the Metis inhabitants, the then-small province of Manitoba was created in 1870. The rest of the west was organized as the Northwest

Territories and governed from Ottawa, the capital of the new nation. British Columbia joined Canada as the sixth province in 1871. The union was complete. Canada stretched from sea to sea. However, Prince Edward Island, the tiny island colony, remained aloof until 1873. The remote colony of Newfoundland felt far closer to Britain than to Canada, and not until 1949 did she join the nation as its tenth province.

Government

Canada has a parliamentary system of government, similar in many ways to that in the United Kingdom. There is, however, no system of checks and balances as there is in the United States.

The executive branch is composed of the monarch, the prime minister and the cabinet. Queen Elizabeth II is the Queen of Canada, and as such, she is the formal head of state. The real executive power in Canada is held by the prime minister and the cabinet.

The legislature is composed of an elected House of Commons and an appointed Senate.

The Canadian system of government is also a federal system. Power to make laws is divided between the national or federal government in Ottawa and the governments of the ten provinces.

India

India achieved its independence on 15 August 1947. Adopting a new constitution it declared itself to be a sovereign democratic republic on 26 January 1950, the Republic of India or Union of India, composed of 22 states and nine centrally administered areas, known as Union Territories. It is a member of the British Commonwealth.

Population

About 745 million people live on an area of 3.2 million km². Some 82% are Hindus, 12% Muslims. Urban population is about 24%. There are twelve 'million' cities: Calcutta, Bombay, Delhi, Madras, Hyderabad, Ahmadabad, Bangalore, Kanpur, Poona, Nagpur, Lucknow, and Jaipur. The population grows by about 17 million people each year.

Geography

The Indian landscape is greatly varied, but there are three broad divisions: the river plains (the Indus, Ganges, and Brahmaputra are the most important rivers) or the heartland of India; the Himalaya Mountain range in the north; and the peninsula in the south.

There is a wide range in climatic types, but three seasons can be distinguished: a cool, mainly dry winter from November to February; a hot, mainly dry period from March to June; late June to early October is a rainy period.

Economy

In terms of output, India ranks as the 14th industrial country in the world, but it remains a predominantly agricultural country with 71% of the population dependent on, and 36% of its annual value of production from, agriculture.

Indian peasants have no or only very little surplus money, limited technical knowledge and equipment. Half of them own less than 2 ha. In the 1970s only 30% of the population were literate; only one in five villages had safe drinking water; and landless labourers numbered over 30 million. In spite of considerable progress that has been made, India is still a very poor country.

The number of full-time industrial workers amounts to 13% of India's work-force. Unemployment is chronically high.

Education

Education is under the control of state governments, with financial aid from the central government. Primary education is free and compulsory, but the administration is not yet quite able to enforce this. Therefore only four out of five pupils in the age group six to eleven are at school. After the primary stage, the drop-out rate is substantial. Girls are far less educated than boys. In 1951 it was estimated that 16.6% of the Indian population were literate; by 1971 it had risen to a mere 29.5%.

Languages

The 1951 Constitution stated that India's official language would be Hindi, and that English should be used for all official purposes fifteen years from the commencement of the Constitution. The Indian Official Languages Act of 1963 has prolonged the use of English, which is now used for communication between the union and any state that has not adopted Hindi as its official language. At the educational level, most states stress the regional language and English, Hindi not being a compulsory subject.

There has been opposition to Hindi by speakers of the other Indian languages, and by South Indians who prefer continuation of English as the official language. Hindi, however, is the largest single Indian language and it is spoken in

152

the heartland of India. English was regarded as the colonial language when the Constitution was made, and was spoken by only 2.5% of the population. It was the language of an élite, serving at the same time as a *lingua franca* and as an anxiously demanded passport to foreign education and to the mainstream of western ideas. Thus it was for a very long time regarded as an important means of getting away from the narrow-mindedness and corruptness of the regional governments and the close and oppressive air of the Sanscrit learning of the day.

Hindi has to contend with 15 major regional languages, 24 other languages, 720 dialects and 23 tribal languages. But it is, with related dialects, the mother-tongue for 40% of the population. It also serves as the basis of an unwritten 'Hindustani' *lingua franca* which is understood from Pakistan to Bangladesh.

History

That part of the long history of India which can only be dealt with here, begins with the charter given to the British East India Company in 1600. The Company's objective was to do trade by peaceful enterprise and agreement, not by force. Only a century and a half later did the Company realize that it had become a sovereign power and that its efforts to establish a monopoly had led to the possibility of building an empire. Politicians were even slower in grasping the significance of the conquest. Pitt's India Bill of 1784 decreed that the real power over the Indian territories was now in the hands of the Crown, although nominally it still remained with the Company until 1858. In 1823 British supremacy over the native states was finally established and the whole peninsula was ruled by the British. In 1877 Queen Victoria was proclaimed Empress of India.

The Indian history of the 20th century is above all the history of the fight for independence and the separation of the Hindu majority and the Muslims into two fully independent republics.

The Government of India Act of 1935 extended the franchise to 14% of the population and gave autonomy to the 11 provincial governments and a federal government at the centre. However, the Indian princes, who had to accede to the idea and realization of a central federal government, never agreed upon this point, and this part of the Act did not come into force at all. The Indian National Congress, the party led by Mahatma Gandhi, Jawaharlal Nehru and others, agreed to take office in those provinces where they had a clear electoral mandate. This experience modified and tempered their views of how to achieve national independence.

After long negotiations, which remained unsuccessful mainly because it had by now become impossible to reconcile the Hindu and Muslim positions, the British government announced in February 1947 that authority would be transferred in June 1948. But in order to avoid violent upheavals India as a unit disappeared on August 1, 1947, and the two new dominions of India and Pakistan came into existence. Both were completely self-governing and free to frame their own constitutions. Nehru became the first Indian prime minister.

The partition caused mass migrations of Hindus, Muslims, and Sikhs, a civil war in the Punjab, and the Kashmir affair, with the Hindu maharaja of this Muslim majority state calling for Indian intervention and adherence to India.

Nehru's foreign policy of non-alignment greatly influenced emerging Afro-Asian countries in the late 1950s and 1960s. Border clashes with China, however, led to greater dependence on the USA and Britain in the 1960s. There was an Indo-Pakistani war in 1971 which led to the creation of Bangla Desh from the ruins of East Pakistan.

The image of the Congress party became tarnished over the years so that in 1975 even the prime minister, Indira Gandhi, was accused of corruption and debarred from office. By means of emergency laws she remained in office until 1977, when new elections ousted her. Her son Rajiv Gandhi is now prime minister with the comfortable majority of 401 seats from 508 in the lower house or House of the People (Lok Sabha).

Kenya

Kenya became an independent state in East Africa in 1963 and is a member of the Commonwealth of Nations. It is situated astride the equator and has a total area of 224,960 square miles. The country takes its name form Mt. Kenya. The capital is Nairobi. Vast areas in Kenya have a mean annual rainfall of less than 30 in., while a wide belt over nothern Kenya has a mean of less than 10 in.; high temperatures enhance the aridity and rainfall unreliability causes drought to be a main problem in large areas of the country.

The People

Kenya's three fertile and densely populated areas are traditionally occupied by Bantu-speaking and Nilotoc-speaking farming tribes. These are separated by relatively arid belts supporting Nilo-Hamitic speaking pastoralists, e.g. the Masai. The Kikuyu are the largest single group, forming about 20% of the population and living mainly in the highlands south of Mt. Kenya. Smaller Bantu tribes live amongst them. A partly Arab population, the Swahili, is centered on the coastal towns.

The traditional social structure in the territory was one of many largely self-sufficient tribes. There was no intertribal organization beyond occasional

154

alliances against the Masai and other marauders, nor any kingship except in the small state of Hanga among the Luhya tribes. Agricultural and pastoral tribes exchanged grain and livestock, and raiding and warfare between tribes were endemic. The advent of towns, the railway and European farms altered the picture radically. Much of the land was taken for European farms, most of it from the Masai. Farm labour came from the crowded Kikuyu, no longer able to expand their territory once inter-tribal boundaries were fixed. They and to a lesser extent the Luhya spread into the towns and settled as "squatters" on European farms. Christian missions concentrated their efforts on educating these tribes. By the 1960s these tribes then provided a middle class.

The non-African population, though only 3% of the total, has an economic significance out of all proportion to its numbers. Europeans are to be found particularly in professional, commercial or technical employment, in the public services or in agriculture. Indians, Pakistanis and Goans form the largest immigrant group. Population densities present striking contrasts. Extensive areas in the north and east are almost uninhabited, and the distribution is very sparse over the Masai districts of southern Kenya. But densities are very high over the western plateaus, in the East Kenya highlands and in patches at the coast.

Religion

The traditional religions of the Africans of Kenya include cults of a 'High God' and ancestral cults. Beliefs in magic, witches and sorcerers are widespread. Many of the tribes of the coast and the northern deserts have been Muslims for a long period, and Islam is spreading there and in the towns. Christian missions of many denominations operate in Kenya.

Many nativistic cults have emerged, of which the Mau-Mau movement among the Kikuyu was the most important. These are primarily political movements, expressed in the observance of rites which, if not indigenous, have close links with traditional cults.

History

During the 19th century Arab and Swahili caravans in search of ivory penetrated from Mombasa to Mt. Kilimanjaro and thence to Lake Victoria and beyond towards Mt. Elgon. The first Europeans to penetrate into the interior were the German agents of the Church Missionary society. These were isolated journeys, however, and more than 30 years passed before any other Europeans tried to explore the country.

In 1883, Joseph Thomas, the explorer, became the first British traveller to pass through the Masai country, but it was the British East Africa company which undertook the opening up of the land to the west of Mombasa. German interests in East Africa had resulted in Nov. 1886 in the delimitation of the territorial claims of the Sultan of Zanzibar. After recognizing the Sultan's authority over a ten-mile-wide coastal strip between the Ruvuma and Tana rivers, Germany, Britain and France had agreed to divide the hinterland into British and German spheres of influence. In 1887 Sir William Machinnon and the British East Africa association accepted a concession of the Sultan's territory on the mainland for a 50-year period. In 1894 the British government declared a protectorate over Buganda and called upon the company to surrender its charter and concession in return for compensation. The East Africa Protectorate was proclaimed.

At the beginning of the 20th century the importance of the East Africa Protectorate increased. Consequently, regulations were issued in 1897 authorizing the lease to Europeans of land which was not cultivated or regularly occupied by Africans. In 1903 Sir Charles Eliot, commissioner of the protectorate, invited South African settlers to East Africa, who came in large numbers. Because few Africans appeared to be completely occupied all the year around in work on their own farms, it seemed to white settlers that there was no reason why they should not be invited and, if necessary, compelled to offer their services to European farmers. It was not until immediately after World War I, that compulsory labour on either public or private projects was strictly forbidden.

Another cause of African discontent was the decision to confine the native population to reserves. Additional complications arose with the Indian coolies brought to East Africa for the building of the railway. Most of them returned to India after their contracts were completed, but some stayed and later on demanded equal citizenship rights.

World War I and its Aftermath

In 1916 the British advanced into German territory. The war had serious effects on the economy of the protectorate because many settlers joined the armed forces and left their farms unattended. Immediately after the war an attempt to revive the economy was made, but the world depression in 1920 caused many cases of bankruptcy. The settlers, however, did not give up and in the mid-1920s the country's economy slowly recovered. The depression of the early 1930s caused difficulties again but the extension of the railway and the communication-net led to a constant improvement. In 1920 the status of the East Africa Protectorate was changed into that of a colony, and the coastal strip leased from the Sultan of Zanzibar became the Kenya Protectorate. In 1923 a white paper was issued which marked the tentative beginning of an area of "trusteeship" for the backward peoples of Kenya. In 1927 the dispute between Europeans and Indians virtually ceased when the Indians accepted five seats in the Legislative Council. The European settlers were to have their own elected representatives.

World War II and after

The outbreak of World War II again checked development. In Kenya itself the main objective was to achieve the highest possible degree of self-sufficiency. Political progress was not neglected and in 1944 Kenya became the first East African territory to include Africans in its Legislative Council. The number was increased from one to two in 1946, to four in 1948 and to eight in 1951.

Both political progress and economic development received a severe set-back in the 1950s with the outbreak of the Mau-Mau rebellion which necessitated the proclamation of a state of emergency in Oct. 1952. The rising was limited to the Kikuyu tribe and was directed against the presence of Europeans in Kenya and their ownership of land. Jomo Kenyatta was the leading figure. The emergency was brought to an end in 1960.

In March 1957 elections were held on a qualitative franchise for the eight African seats in the legislature. As a result of a conference in London in 1960 Africans became the majority in the Legislative Council of ministers. Two African parties were founded, the Kenya African National Union (KANU) and the Kenya African Democratic Union (KADU). In 1963 KANU took office, with Kenyatta as prime minister, under a new constitution which gave Kenya self-government. In Dec. 1963 Kenya became independent and a year later became a republic with Kenyatta as its first president.

In June 1963 the prime ministers of Kenya, Uganda and the president of Tanganyika pledged themselves to form a political federation of East Africa.

General and Local Government

On Dec. 12th, 1963, with the achievement of independence, Kenya became a member of the Commonwealth, acknowledging Queen Elizabeth II as queen of Kenya and as head of the Commonwealth. Under the independence constitution a Governor-General represents the sovereign and acts on the advice of a cabinet headed by the prime minister who must command the support of a majority of the members in the House of Representatives. The constitution provides for an elaborately calculated balance of power between central and regional governments.

Social conditions

The general standard of living in Kenya showed a continued improvement after World War II, but unemployment and droughts have made life difficult for many inhabitants.

Social insurance is less developed than in European countries, but African family bonds guarantee a certain social security, unless nature and its catastrophes have to be overcome.

Justice

The Supreme Court, which derives its authority from the Kenyan constitution, has full jurisdiction, civil and criminal, over all persons and all matters of dispute in the country. It consists of the chief justice and 11 puisne judges. It is assisted by subordinate courts throughout the country.

Education

The school system caters separately for Africans, Asians, Arabs and Europeans, but there is a tendency towards integration. English is the medium of instruction, at least from secondary education onwards. More than 80% of Kenyan schools are managed by the Roman Catholic and Protestant churches and most are state-aided.

Economy

Following World War II there was an enormous increase in industrial activity in Kenya. The basis of the Kenyan economy is nevertheless agricultural. The main plantation crops in Kenya are: coffee, tea, sisal, wattle and sugar, wheat, maize, barley, oats and pyrethrum. Dairy and cattle farming is also important, as is the growing of cotton. Kenya also produces high quality timber such as podo, cypress and cedar. Mineral production plays a modest part in the economy.

Nigeria

The Federal Republic of Nigeria is a country in western Africa, occupying the basins of the Niger and Benue rivers and extensive adjacent territories. Nigeria consists of four regions, Northern Nigeria, Eastern Nigeria, Western Nigeria and Mid-West Nigeria, and the Federal Territory of Lagos.

Population

The population of Nigeria is mainly Negro, with an admixture of other races.

Languages

More than 100 languages and dialect clusters have been distinguished in Nigeria, but a mere four of them are the mother tongues of 60% of Nigerians: Haussa and Fulani in the north, Yoruba in the west and Ibo in the east.

Religion

Islam was introduced in the 14th century and is professed by 44% of the people; it is supreme in Northern Nigeria, where Christian missions in Muslim areas are prohibited. About 34% acknowledge Christianity and only 22% the old tribal religions, which are rapidly losing their hold although traditional beliefs are not always abandoned by converts to Christianity and Islam.

Western culture has been most readily assimilated by the people of Western and Eastern Nigeria where English is the official language; native institutions have not been protected as carefully as those in the emirates of Northern Nigeria. Education of an English sort, provided by Government and missions, flourishes in the south and among the non-Muslim peoples of the north.

Constitution and Government

The constitutional instruments that came into force on Oct. 1st, 1963, provided for a federal republic consisting of the four territories and the federal territory of Lagos.

The head of state was a non-executive president elected to office for five years. The federal government included the council of ministers, the senate and the house of representatives, the last two forming the federal parliament. The council of ministers consisted of a federal prime minister and a number of ministers who might either hold portfolios or be ministers of state attached to ministries. The prime minister was appointed by the president from the majority party in the house of representatives; members of the council were appointed on the advice of the prime minister. The constitution has been altered or "misinterpreted" by several military governments.

History

The state of Nigeria was officially founded in 1914 by uniting the northern and southern parts of the British protectorate. The country was ruled by a Governor-General and was divided into 4 parts: Lagos, the Northern, Eastern, and the Western Provinces.

In 1922 the British Government established the constitution and for the first time, the principle of direct elections for parliament. The constitution of 1946 granted the provinces certain responsibilities in advising the central government in provincial matters whereas in the constitution of 1951 the provincial administrations were declared regional governments. Three political parties, the National Council of Nigeria and the Camerouns, the Northern Peoples Congress and the Action Group, took part in the conferences which finally led to the establishment of regional parliaments. The Northern Peoples Congress won the majority in the parliament of the Northern region, whereas the National Council of Nigeria and the Camerouns and the Action Group won in the parliaments of the Eastern and Western regions. In 1957 the Eastern and the Western regions became autonomous. The Northern region achieved this status in 1959.

On October 1st, 1959, the whole country achieved its independence as a consequence of the struggle led by nationalistic Nigerians.

On October 1st, 1963, Nigeria became a republic and cut off all connections to the British Crown, but remained a member of the Commonwealth. From 1966 on Nigeria was led by a military government. After violent political disturbances and riots in different parts of the country, the military forces took over; the federal Prime Minister, two regional prime ministers, a federal Minister and a number of high officers were executed. The leader of this military government tried to unite the country under a centralized government. But his government was overthrown and together with his military governors and some army officers he was executed. Nigeria's second military government lasted for nine years. During this period a civil war broke out after the attempt of one region to separate from the state. Finally, a peace treaty was signed and a general amnesty was guaranteed and the country was united again. The reconstruction period after the civil war was succeeded by a period of economic growth. Nigeria became a confederation of twelve states.

On July 29th, 1975, a third military government took over after a bloodless coup. It announced a four-year programme which in the end should have lead to a democracy and the transference of the federal capital from Lagos to Abuja in the central region of the country according to the wish of the population. This government created seven new states. Nigeria then consisted of 19 states. The chief of this government, General Nurtala Muhammed, was killed on Feb. 13th, 1976, in an unsuccessful revolt and was declared hero of the nation. His chief of general staff, General Obasanjo, became his successor and tried to finish the programme begun by his predecessor. On Sept. 21st, 1978, the Government allowed party politics again. On Aug. 11th, 1979, presidential elections took place; five political parties presented their candidates. The new constitution was established on Oct. 1st, 1979, and introduced a presidential system comparable to the American system. On Dec. 31st, 1983, another military government took over in Nigeria.

Agriculture

Agriculture has always been the most important single factor in the Nigerian economy. About 70% of the whole working population work in agriculture and produce yam, maniok, bananas, rice, beans, sugar cane, palm oil, peanuts, caoutchouc, cotton and timber as raw material for the home industry and for

160

export. The Nigerian Agricultural and Co-operative Bank in Kaduna was founded with the aim of granting credit directly or indirectly to farmers. Depending on the region, the emphasis lies on food production, coastal fishing, poultry farming, cattle and pig-breeding and dairy farming. Throughout the country there exist projects for storage, especially for corn, and projects for establishing a transport network to connect the producer with the markets.

Mining Industry

The mining industry plays an increasing role in the Nigerian economy. Among others iron, tin, columbit, calcium, coal and oil are produced. The two main companies are the Nigerian Mining Corporation and the Nigerian National Petroleum Corporation. Nigeria is the sixth-largest oil producer in the world and the second largest in Africa. Nigeria is a member of OPEC.

Industry

In Nigeria more than 2000 industrial companies exist. They have an important share in the gross national product. The Government which prohibits and limits the import of those products which can be produced in Nigeria, tries to increase the share of the processing industry and improve the economic situation. Banks and finance companies were founded to support the industries developing in all parts of the country.

The Education System

The education system is determined by the educational philosophy that the development of the individual child towards a healthy and successful citizen as well as equal educational chances for all citizens have to be guaranteed.

The education system consists of pre-school, primary and secondary as well as university and adult education. Special schools for educationally subnormal children and teacher training also exist. The secondary schools are divided into three-year junior and three-year senior high schools. University is usually attended for 4 years.

Art and Culture

Archaeological discoveries of the Nok culture have proved that the cultural heritage of Nigeria is at least 2000 years old. In the National Museum of Lagos a kaleidoscope of the artifacts of the different peoples of Nigeria can be seen. Among the different expressions of popular art the most well-known is wood-carving, especially in the southern parts of Nigeria. Besides this the casting and decorating of bronze and brass are characteristic of Nigerian popular art. These

161

techniques have been cultivated in Ife and Benin. Nowadays many Nigerian painters and sculptors are acquainted with modern forms of expression and techniques. Some of these artists have an international reputation and their works have been on exhibition in different parts of the world.

South Africa

The Republic of South Africa is a country occupying the southernmost part of the African continent between the Atlantic and Indian oceans. From 1910 to 1961 it was known as the Union of South Africa, comprising the former British colonies of Cape of Good Hope, Natal, Transvaal, and Orange River Colony, which became the four provinces of the Union, the last named known since as Orange Free State. The administrative capital is Pretoria; Cape Town is the seat of legislation.

Ethnic Groups and Languages

Bushmen and Hottentots, the surviving original inhabitants of South Africa, are of non-Negro physical type, with languages which, though related to one another, are unrelated to any other language families.

Nguni, the main element of the South African population, consists of various Negro peoples speaking southern Bantu languages. All the Nguni were traditionally organized into chiefdoms with economies of mixed agriculture and cattle raising. Some of them, particularly the Zulu and Swazi, established kingships and became important military nations in the 19th century.

Various Negro people speaking Sotho dialects, which are closely related to Nguni but lack the Hottentot-derived clicks.

Europeans have lived in South Africa since the founding of Cape Town in 1652 (mainly Dutch, later English and German), speaking Afrikaans or English. Asians were brought to Natal in 1860 mainly as indentured labourers (mainly Indians).

The two principal official languages are Afrikaans and English. At the 1960 census Afrikaans was given first among 58% of the white population and English among 37%, but many people are bilingual.

Constitution

Following the passage of the South Africa Act (1909) by the British Parliament, the Union of South Africa was formed on May 31, 1910, out of the four colo-

162

nies. The Union was a member of the British Empire, and its sovereign independence was later guaranteed by the Statute of Westminster (1931) and the Status of the Union Act (1934). On May 31, 1961, the Union became the Republic of South Africa under a constitution adopted by the Union Parliament. On becoming a republic South Africa ceased to be a member of the Commonwealth of Nations.

The new constitution is virtually the same as that of the Union enacted in 1910. It provides for a State President, an Executive Council of ministers of state, appointed by the president, a Parliament comprising a Senate and a House of Assembly, and, in each provinces, an administrator appointed by the State President-in-Council for five years, an Executive Committee of four members under the administrator's presidency, and an elected Provincial Council which elects the Executive Committee and, like it, serves for five years.

Living Conditions

The standard of living is high for the white population; for most Bantu it remains low but is nevertheless higher than in most African countries.

History

The Cape of Good Hope was discovered in *1488*. Ten years later Vasco da Gama rounded the Cape and sailed through to the Malabar coast of India to open the doors of wealth to Portugal.

By *1600*, the Portuguese Indian trade monopoly was rivaled by the English, French and Dutch. In 1657, soldiers released from service were allowed to start farming in the newly founded settlement. These so-called burghers started the tradition of agriculture. Later a shipload of black slaves from Angola landed at Table Bay. Slaves were imported until 1807 and added an important element to the Non-White population.

After 1671 the small community expanded in search of more sheltered farmlands. Thus began a process of expansion into the interior, more rapid on the whole after 1700, and not arrested until well into the 19th century when the limits of the present-day South Africa were reached.

The legal heritage of the free burghers, mostly of Dutch descent, but with a fair number of Germans as well, was the Roman-Dutch law. Their church was the Calvinist Reformed Church of the Netherlands.

Under the energetic rule (1697–1707) of two governors, Simon van der Stel and his son, Willem Adriaan, the struggling colony solved its original problem of under-production so successfully that chronic over-production of wheat and

163

wine was to plague farmers for the whole of the 18th century. A most significant and spontaneous movement of colonists began at the beginning of the 18th century. Along the trail blazed by hunters and cattle traders, cattle farmers followed, seeking water and good grazing. It was in that time that the term *Boer* (farmer), originally a contemptuous term, became synonymous with Afrikaner. It denoted a people reared on South African soil, and imbued with patriotism centred in the new fatherland into which they were carrying the cultural values of Western Europe as they moved further into the unknown interior. All assisted immigration from Europe to the Cape was stopped in 1707. Ten years later came a further crucial decision to import more slaves. These decisions contributed to the slow growth of the White population.

In September *1795* the Cape of Good Hope surrendered to a British expeditionary force. By this time, the settled White population, despite its European origin, had come to identify itself intimately with the 17th-century Dutch. In January 1806 the British occupied the Cape. Until 1834 the Cape Colony, like other British crown colonies, was governed by senior officials. Faced with the problem of handling a population which was, until 1820, almost entirely non-British, they applied a policy of anglicisation. In 1820 some 5000 immigrants arrived from Britain. Their efforts brought the colony a partly nominated legislative council in 1834, an elected parliament with an executive of officials in 1854, and fully responsible government in 1872. The British settlers also materially altered the composition of the White population. There were now two language groups. Thus the White population of today, which consists mainly of *Afrikaans*-speaking (about 56%) and *English*-speaking (about 38%) South Africans, developed.

In *1834,* the *Great Trek* was started by Boer farmers. It was a deliberate move by thousands of men and women who left their homes to put as much distance as possible between themselves and a British government at the Cape.

The first Boer republic was that of *Natal.* It lasted only four years before it was annexed by Britain in 1843. The events set in motion by the Great Trek divided South Africa into the two independent Boer republics and two British colonies. From 1857 to 1859 the first abortive moves were made towards some form of federation between the republics and even, if possible, the colonies. Britain sought to end the disputes in 1871 by annexing the diamond fields and turning the territory into the Crown Colony of Griqualand West. When diplomatic methods failed, more forceful steps were taken. Britain annexed the *Transvaal* in 1877. This unleashed vehement Boer opposition which was supported by Afrikaners in the Cape Colony. By 1881 the prospect of a federated South Africa had faded; the First War of Independence had reversed the Transvaal annexation, and British arms had suffered defeat at the hands of the Boers at the

Battle of Majuba Hill. This period of Afrikaner awakening coincided with the uneventful development of the 'model republic' of the OFS, and with the rule of the forceful Paul Kruger (1825–1904) as State President of the *South African Republic of Transvaal* from 1883 to 1900.

In *1884* Germany appeared in South Africa. Germany's annexation of the west coast north of the Orange river, now known as *South-West Africa/Namibia* (SWA/Namibia), was an incentive to British imperialism to act. While the republics were being politically and economically confined, *Cecil Rhodes* (1853–1902), diamond magnate of Kimberley and Prime Minister of the Cape Colony from 1890 to 1895, appeared on the scene. Despite concessions by Kruger, and earnest efforts by political leaders in the OFS and the Cape to prevent a tragedy, the *Anglo-Boer War* (also known as South Africa's *Second War of Independence*) broke out on 11 October *1899*. Britain's war on 'Krugerism' lasted 32 months. Peace came on 31 May 1902, with the signing of the *Treaty of Vereeniging*. The war, like the Great Trek, was an event of crucial importance in shaping the course of South African history.

The Boers were compelled by force of arms to become part of a British Empire which, though badly shaken by the Boer resistance, was still at the height of its imperial splendour and almost unchallenged by its rivals, Germany and France. But, on the other hand, the disappearance of the independent republics paved the way for a closer political union in South Africa.

After a certain period of reconstruction a liberal government in Britain granted responsible government to the two former republics, so that colonial parliaments, under Boer leadership, came into being in the Transvaal (1906) and the Orange River Colony (1907) alongside the older Cape and Natal governments. In May *1910* the British Parliament passed the *South Africa Act* which defined the constitution of the Union of South Africa. Thus South Africa took its place as a self-governing dominion within the British Empire. Its first Prime Minister was the Boer general *Louis Botha*. It was only during the war of 1914–18 that South Africa started its own manufacturing industry. The development of the mining economy, 1899–1902, led to a marked shift of population, mostly of rural Afrikaners, to the towns. This process of urbanisation continued during the following generation and beyond. In 1912 the Defence Act was passed establishing the Union Defence Force and in 1913 the Native Land Act was passed which defined and scheduled 8.9 million ha of land in the four provinces to be permanently and inalienably in the possession of Blacks.

The outbreak of war in Europe in *1914* had a profound effect on South Africa. Botha was requested by the British Government to occupy German South West Africa. Botha duly took SWA from the Germans, occupying Windhoek, the capital, in May 1915 and placing it under South African military administration. In 1919, Botha died and was succeeded by General Smuts, who automatically reaffirmed the aims of attaining sovereign independence and complete equality with Britain by constitutional means. In 1927 the historic Balfour Report defined the dominions as autonomous communities within the British Empire, and as members of the British Commonwealth of nations. The status declaration of 1926 became law by virtue of the Statute of Westminster in 1931. The period, from 1934 until the outbreak of *World War II,* was characterized by a dynamic programme of legislation in many fields. The two most significant enactments were the two Acts of 1936 on Black franchise and land.

The *Black Representation Act* removed the Blacks of the Cape Province from the common voter's roll where they had been registered since 1853. Instead they were given the right to elect three White members to the House of Assembly on a separate roll. Black electoral colleges were also instituted in all four provinces to elect four White members to the Senate. Provision was also made for the establishment of the Natives Representative Council to advise the Government on Black affairs. The *Native Trust and Land Act* gave effect to provisions in the Native Land Act of 1913 for the purchase of additional land, to be held in trust for the Blacks, and to provide more living space for the growing Black population. The Acts of 1936 clearly contained the basis of the future policy for South Africa's Black states. When *World War II* broke out South Africa took part in it. The *post-war era* of decolonisation witnessed the rise of Black independence movements in Africa and a growing solidarity among the Non-White nations of the world.

From *1949* onwards the Malan Government introduced legislation to implement the policy of multinational development of the population groups in South Africa. The Group Areas Act of 1949 gave legal status to the traditional residential segregation, and in 1950 a population register was instituted which provided for the classification of the entire adult population according to ethnic groups. In 1960 the representation of coloured people in Parliament was abolished and the Union Council for Coloured Affairs was replaced by a partly elected, partly nominated Coloured Persons Representative Council (CRC) in the same year. In *1960* South Africa decided to adopt a republican form of government, without material changes to the existing constitution. In *1961* South Africa left the *Commonwealth.*

In 1966 B. J. Vorster became Prime Minister. The Afro-Asian campaign against South Africa and the SWA dispute reached a peak during the 1974 UN session with an attempt to oust South Africa from the UN.

In September *1976* the *Turnhalle conference* on the future of SWA/Namibia announced a three-tier system of government for the territory, and an interim multiracial constitution was drafted. This was accepted by an overwhelming majority of Whites during a referendum on 19 May 1977.

In the midst of increasing violence by Swapo terrorists, an agreement between South Africa and the five Western powers (US, GB, W-Germany, Canada and the UN) for a settlement of the SWA/Namibia problem was negotiated in *1978*. It was accepted by South Africa on 25 April, 1978. The agreement provided for free elections in SWA/Namibia under United Nations supervision.

On 26 Oct. 1976 the final documents for *Transkei's* independence were signed by Mr Vorster and Paramount Chief Kaiser Matanzima of Transkei. In 1977 *Bophuthatswana* became the second national state to gain sovereign independence, *Venda* became independent in 1979, the *Ciskei* in 1981.

In June 1976 unrest began in Black residential areas which lasted until February 1977. The first outburst occurred on 16 June *1976* in *Soweto* when the police clashed with thousands of demonstrating Black schoolchildren. On 11 August the violence spread to the Cape Peninsula; in September the situation in some places was chaotic. In the Black townships the youngsters enforced a boycott of schools. At the end of 1976 many schools in these townships stood virtually vacant. After the revolts the Government introduced far-reaching changes in the whole system of Black education in South Africa, e.g. an enormous school building project for Soweto.

In 1978 Mr P. W. Botha took over from Mr Vorster. On 31 July 1982 Prime Minister Botha outlined the main features of the new guidelines for constitutional development which were characterized by a tendency of decentralisation.

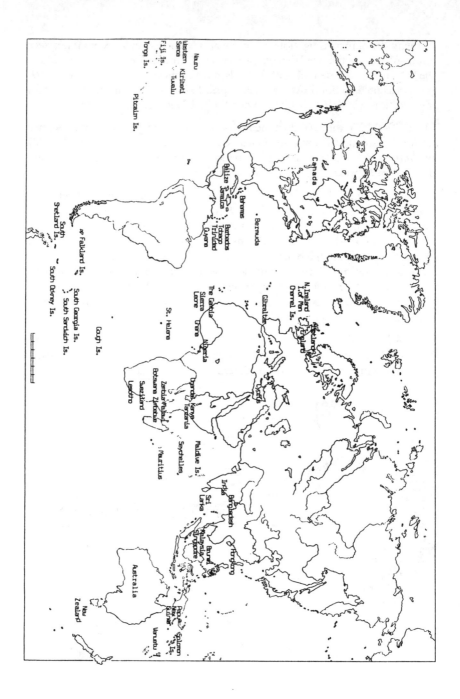

Nauru
Western Samoa
Kiribati
Tuvalu
Fiji Is.
Tonga Is.
Pitcairn Is.

Canada

Belize
Jamaica
Bahamas
Barbados
Tobago
Trinidad
Guyana

Bermuda

South
Shetland Is.
Falkland Is.
South Georgia Is.
South Sandwich Is.
South Orkney Is.

N.Ireland
I.of Man
England
Channel Is.
Gibraltar
Cyprus

The Gambia
Sierra Leone
Nigeria

St. Helena

Cough Is.

Uganda,Kenya
Tanzania
Zambia,Malawi
Botswana,Zimbabwe
Swaziland
Lesotho

Maldive Is.
Seychelles
Mauritius

Bangladesh
Sri Lanka

India
Malaysia
Singapore
Brunei

Hong Kong

Australia

New Zealand

Papua
New Guinea
Solomon Is.
Vanuatu

Corina Hebestreit, Düsseldorf

Classroom Materials

Schoolbooks:

Contacts 9. Projects 1. Enriched Course. 9. Schuljahr für Gymnasien, Realschulen und Gesamtschulen. (Eds. Hans-Eberhard Piepho and Lothar Bredella) Bochum: Ferdinand Kamp, n.d. (Australia, pp. 7–23)

Contacts 9. Projects 1. Basic Course. 9. Schuljahr für Hauptschulen und Gesamtschulen. (Eds. Hans-Eberhard Piepho and Lothar Bredella) Bochum: Ferdinand Kamp, n.d. (Australia, pp. 58–59, India, pp. 116–117, Canada, pp. 133–134)

Contacts 10. Projects 2. Basic Course. 10. Schuljahr für Hauptschulen und Gesamtschulen. (Eds. Hans-Eberhard Piepho and Lothar Bredella) Bochum: Ferdinand Kamp, n.d. (The Third World, mainly Africa, pp. 50–70)

English. Ausgabe G. 8. Schuljahr an Realschulen und Gesamtschulen. Berlin: Cornelsen & Oxford University Press, 1976. (Unit 2: Commonwealth/Immigration, pp. 21–35)

The English Companion. Vierter Teil. (Eds. Heinz Röhr and Dieter Kleine-Horst) Frankfurt/M.: Moritz Diesterweg, 1968. (Unit III: Canada, Australia, South Africa, India, pp. 23–38)

The Highway to English. Vierter Teil. 9. und 10. Schuljahr. (Ed. D. Wilhelm Frerichs) Frankfurt/M.: Hirschgraben, 1963. (Pictures from the Commonwealth, pp. 9–35)

The Highway to English. Ausgabe B. 2. Teil. 3. und 4. Unterrichtsjahr. (Ed. Hans Stoppel) Frankfurt/M.: Hirschgraben, 1968. (Lesson X, Canada, S. 49–52, Lesson XI, Australia, S. 53–56; Lesson XII, Africa, pp. 57–62)

How do you do. Bd. 4. Travelling Faster. Textbook with Dialogues and Pictorial Dictionary. (Eds. Eric Orton and Peter H. Stoldt) Paderborn: Ferdinand Schöningh, n.d. (Australien, pp. 156–159)

Learning English. Neue Augabe B. Teil 2. Stuttgart: Ernst Klett, n.d. (The Commonwealth: Australia, Egypt, India, Africa, pp. 61–86)

Sprachkurs English 3. Unterrichtswerk für Erwachsene. Teil B. (Eds. Doris Jacoby and Mike Caldon) Frankfurt/M.: Diesterweg, 1981. (Unit 4: Australia, pp. 49–70)

Yes. A New English Course. Mittlere Ausgabe. Band 6. Dortmund, Hannover: Lensing/Schroedel, 1983. (Unit 4: Stories and Poems from the Empire and Commonwealth, pp. 78–112)

Anthologies:

Alpers, M., Voges, H., Weiß, G. (Eds.): *Britain and America.* Oberstufe. Bielefeld, ⁶1980.

Althammer, Ch., Weber-Fuchs, V. (Eds.): *The Conflict in South Africa.* München, 1984.

Burton, R., Treacher, P. (Eds.): *Immigrants. Course material for the Reformierte Oberstufe.* Bielefeld, 1975.

Buttjes, Dieter (Ed.): *Panorama. English cultures around the world.* Dortmund, 1987.

Düsterhaus, G.: *Growing up on the Prairies.* München, 1985.

Düsterhaus, G., Franzbecker, R. (Eds.): *Canada – Regions and Literature.* Paderborn, 1987.

Harrison, B. (Ed.): *Britain Observed. 1945 to the present day.* Stuttgart, 1984.

Hermes, L. (Ed.): *Several Englands. Selected British Short Stories.* Frankfurt/M., 1979.

Jarman, F., Whybra, D., Kämmer, G.-D. (Eds.): *Empire and After – Literary Glimpses of the British Empire.* Hannover, n.d.

Jarman, F., Whybra, D. Hase, K. D. (Eds.): *Pink, Black, Brown and Yellow: Multiracial Britain.* Hannover, 1983.

Kaynis, M. D., Schuhmacher, K. E. (Eds.): *Men and Women.* Stuttgart, 1986.

Lehberger, E. (Ed.): *Britain. A Multi-Racial Society?* Stuttgart, 1985.

Lessing, D.: *Eldorado.* Stuttgart, 1985, + *Model Interpretations.* Stuttgart, 1983.

Möllinger, O., Ziegesar, M. v. (Eds.): *Great Short Stories.* Stuttgart, 1986, + *Model Interpretations.* Stuttgart, 1986.

Musman, R.: *Britain and India.* Paderborn, 1978.

Stone, J. B., Masket, L. K. (Eds.): *Stories from the Black Experiences.* Stuttgart, 1981.

Taylor, P. J. W. (Ed.): *Modern Short Stories for Students of English.* Oxford, 1968.

–: *More Modern Short Stories for Students of English.* Oxford, 1981.

Turner, H. (Ed.): *Australian People and Pictures. Ten stories.* Bielefeld, 1966.

Publications Received

Barth, Adolf: *Moderne englische Gesellschaftskomödie*. Von Oscar Wilde zu Tom Stoppard. München, Zürich, Artemis Verlag, 1987, 139 S., DM 19,80.

Die englische Gesellschaftskomödie wird in dieser Einführung als produktive moderne Theatergattung vorgestellt. Weltoffene, herausfordernde Figurentypen wie der Dandy oder Shaws "New Woman", erfolgreiche Geschäftsleute und Künstler beherrschen die lebensbejahenden Spielhandlungen. Zeittypische, von dieser Gattung im Milieu der sogenannten besseren Gesellschaft satirisch dargestellte Konflikte zwischen Schein und Wirklichkeit sowie die Komik der Bühnengestaltung werden bei den fünf Dramatikern Wilde, Shaw, Eliot, Pinter und Stoppard jeweils in der Perspektive ihrer übergeordneten, problembewußten Wirklichkeitsinterpretation erörtert. Trotz des *showbiz* der kommerziellen Theater im Londoner West End: Die hier behandelten Gesellschaftskomödien sind thematisch als *High Comedy* und künstlerisch höher als die Verbrauchsdramatik der Unterhaltungsmedien einzustufen.

Bartsch, Uta: *Alan Ayckbourns Dramenfiguren*. Charakterisierung und Charakteristika. Hildesheim, Zürich, New York, Georg Olms Verlag, 1986, 296 S., DM 34,80.

Diese erste wissenschaftliche Monographie zu Leben und Werk des 1939 geborenen, an westlichen Bühnen meistgespielten englischen Dramatikers wendet sich an Philologen, Theaterinteressierte und Unterrichtspraktiker. Anhand seiner 13 wichtigsten Stücke aus den Jahren 1969 bis 1981 weist Uta Bartsch nach: Ayckbourn ist nicht das literarische Leichtgewicht, als das er lange gegolten hat, sondern ein scharfsichtiger Gesellschaftskritiker, der seinen Platz unter den Großen des Dramas beanspruchen darf. Die Autorin legt die Konzeption der Figuren und die Mittel dar, mit denen sie zu lebensvollen Charakteren und Spiegelbildern unseres Daseins werden, und führt in Ayckbourns vielfältige Thematik einer neuen *Comédie humaine* mit tragischen Zügen ein.

Bradbury, Malcolm, Ro, Sigmund (Eds.): *Contemporary American Fiction*. London, Edward Arnold, 1987, 142 S., £ 9.95.

The scene of contemporary American fiction presents a picture of hothouse artistic growth, the very diversity and contrary pulls of which make any attempt at confident generalizing a risky venture. This collection seeks to make this diversity accessible by charting the main currents in fiction writing in the United States since 1960: the major ethnic writing, women's fiction, the so-called 'postmodern' revolution, as well as persisting, though evolving, realistic strains. At the same time the volume is concerned to show how fiction writing has become increasingly subject to the pressures of publishing, critical theory and film.

Bush, M. L.: *The English Aristocracy.* A Comparative Synthesis. Manchester, Dover/N. H., Manchester University Press, 1984, 248 S., £ 7.95.

This is a study of the peerage, baronetcy and gentry, not within a selected period but throughout their complete life span, aiming to provide an overview that identifies essentials rather than to impart detail. The basic features of an order, not the behaviour of individual members, its long-term development, not its transitory fluctuations, are the book's concern. In characterising the English aristocracy Bush tests the standard view that it was highly unusual by a double comparison: between the English aristocracy and the Continental nobilities, and between the English aristocracy of different periods. He identifies turning points and trends in the history of the English aristocracy, concentrating upon the effect of the Norman conquest, the rise of peerage and gentry in the later Middle Ages, the dominance which the aristocratic order acquired over Crown and society in the course of the 17th and 18th centuries, and its latter-day capacity to survive industrialisation and democracy. The third aim of the book is to examine the aristocracy's impact upon the evolution of the English state and society, assessing the aristocracy's part in promoting or impeding the development of parliamentary government, a professional bureaucracy, a system of regular direct taxation and universal suffrage, and the aristocracy's contribution to the emergence of agrarian and industrial capitalism.

Couper-Kuhlen, Elizabeth: *An Introduction to English Prosody.* Tübingen, Max Niemeyer Verlag, 1986, 239 S., DM 36,--.

Conceived as a textbook for university-level courses, this introduction aims to give a clear presentation and critical evaluation of acquired knowledge in the areas of English stress, rhythm and intonation. At the same time it offers a perspective on new directions in this young and expanding field. Due to the broad scope of intonational function in English, this book deals not only with suprasegmental phonology but also with issues in the areas of syntax, semantics/pragmatics, text linguistics and discourse analysis. However, no specialized knowledge in these fields is required; technical terms and concepts are introduced, where necessary, on the spot.

Day, Geoffrey: *From Fiction to the Novel.* London, New York, Routledge and Kegan Paul, 1987, 223 S., £ 17.95.

By convention, the 18th century is regarded as the era which saw 'the birth of the novel', with Richardson, Fielding, Smollett and Sterne as the great luminaries of the new form. Geoffrey Day argues that this is to read history backwards, making the hunt for the origin of the novel the great literary pursuit, rather than looking at the era in its own terms. Indeed, Richardson and Fielding were affronted that their works should be called 'novels', considering the word pejorative. Day shows that it is much more relevant to consider the 'novels' of the period as experimental forms, arguing that the 18th century produced a wide range of highly inventive original fiction. He provides extensive quotation: from the authors themselves in their prefaces, postscripts and letters, as they identified their intentions; and from the diaries and letters of readers as they wrote about what they thought they were reading.

Deane, Seamus: *Celtic Revivals.* Essays in Modern Irish Literature 1880–1980. London, Boston, Faber and Faber, repr. 1987, 199 S., Pb. £ 3.50.

Seamus Deane begins by locating the roots of modern Irish literature in the 18th and 19th century Celtic revivals as perceived by two commentators, Burke and Arnold. We are then shown the differing attitudes of Yeats, Joyce, Synge and O'Casey. Deane goes on to consider the bequests of these writers to the modern generation, from Beckett to Seamus Heaney. A more recent third literary revival coincided with the return of the political crisis in Northern Ireland – a crisis which confronted writers as various as Thomas Kinsella, John Montague, Brian Friel and Derek Mahon, demanding that they should come to terms with it in their different ways. All the writers discussed are seen first as individuals, then as exemplars of a common fate with its own peculiar risks, burdens and responsibilities.

Fowler, Roger (Ed.): *A Dictionary of Modern Critical Terms.* Revised and Enlarged Edition. London, New York, Routledge and Kegan Paul, 1987, 262 S., Pb. £ 5.50, Hb. £ 12.50.

The distinctive features of the first edition have been carefully maintained, and the book differs from other 'dictionaries of criticism' in concentrating less on time-honoured rhetorical terms, more on conceptually flexible, powerful and contemporary critical terms. Each entry consists not simply of a 'dictionary definition', but an essay exploring the history and full significance of the term, and its possibilities in contemporary critical discourse. In this way, the reader encounters the central preoccupations of contemporary critical thinking, discussed by a wide range of practising critics and teachers representing a variety of theoretical persuasions. Recent developments in literary criticism are covered in over 20 new essays, specially commissioned for this volume from eminent scholars. New topics include *Poststructuralism, Feminist Criticism, Marxist Criticism, Semiotics* and *Psychology and Psychoanalysis,* stressing contemporary theory and criticism. The remaining articles have been rewritten, with particular attention to updating the recommendations for further reading.

Gish, Theodore, Spuler, Richard (Eds.): *Eagle in the New World.* German Immigration to Texas and America. College Station/Tex., Texas A & M University Press, 1986, 252 S., $ 28.50.

In 300 years the German eagle and American eagle have symbolically combined through immigration and colonization to produce unique traditions in art, literature, music, language, and life-styles. The German heritage of nearly one-third of Americans is reflected with particular strength in Texas, one of four states that became home to especially large numbers of German immigrants. *Eagle in the New World* began at a symposium held at the University of Houston in September, 1983, on the occasion of the first German settlement in the New World. The papers which appear here in revised form, constitute, in the main, pairs of "Old World" and "New World" perspectives on the topics dealt with. These include: German emigration from the homeland and settlement in the Texas Hill Country; folk literature as revelation of the attitudes of immigrants as well as some

Germans who stayed at home; the literary topic of the German in America and the literature of German Texas; German-American art; cultural traditions of the German immigrants from the woman's perspective; Texas-German speech.

Gläser, Rosemarie: *Phraseologie der englischen Sprache.* Tübingen, Max Niemeyer Verlag, 1986, 201 S., DM 24,--.

Die als Hochschullehrbuch konzipierte Darstellung behandelt Phraseologismen in
Wort- und Satzfunktion. Die Typologie des phraseologischen Inventars (Nominationen
und Propositionen) gründet sich auf das Konzept von Zentrum, Peripherie und Übergangszone, wobei die Idiome als der Prototyp des Phraseologismus vom Zentrum (ver-
treten durch die Wortarten Substantiv, Adjektiv, Verb und Adverb) zur Peripherie
(Sprichwörter, Gemeinplätze, Routineformeln, Losungen, Gebote, Maximen, geflügelte
Worte und Zitate) abnehmen. Die Übergangszone umfaßt zwischen Nominationen und
Propositionen stehende Phraseologismen (sprichwörtliche Redensarten, Paarformeln,
stereotype Vergleiche, Anspielungen). Als obligatorische Merkmale des Phraseologismus gelten seine Lexikalisierung, Reproduzierbarkeit, syntaktische und semantische
Stabilität; fakultative Merkmale sind seine Idiomatizität, stilistische und expressive Kon-
notationen und seine intensivierende (expressive) Funktion im Text. Hinsichtlich der
Idiomatisierung der Konstituenten wird bei den einzelnen Wortarten zwischen unilate-
ralen, bilateralen und multilateralen Idiomen unterschieden. Erörtert und durch Bei-
spiele veranschaulicht werden der Zeichencharakter des Phraseologismus, diachronische
Beschreibungsaspekte der Phraseologie als Teildisziplin der Lexikologie, die Verwen-
dung von Phraseologismen in Texten der Allgemein- und der Fachsprache und der Phraseologismus als Übersetzungsproblem.

Gross, Konrad, Pache, Walter: *Grundlagen zur Literatur in englischer Sprache.*
Bd. 1: *Kanada.* München, Wilhelm Fink Verlag, 1987, 244 S., DM 48,--.

Die 18 Texte des ersten Teils behandeln in diachronischem Querschnitt wesentliche Pro-
blembereiche wie Regionalität, Nationalliteratur und Identitätsdiskussion vom frühen
19. Jh. bis etwa zum Zweiten Weltkrieg; im zweiten Teil (17 Texte) stehen Aspekte des
literarischen Nationalismus und die Ansätze zur Definition eines eigenständigen Lite-
ratur- und Kulturbegriffes seit den späten 50er Jahren bis in die Gegenwart im Vorder-
grund. Eine ausführliche Einleitung ordnet die einzelnen Texte ihren politischen, sozia-
len und kulturellen Umfeldern zu. Eine nach Sachgebieten gegliederte Bibliographie wei-
terführender Literatur bietet auch ausgewählte Lektürevorschläge.

Haass, Sabine: *Gedichtanthologien der viktorianischen Zeit.* Eine buchgeschicht-
liche Untersuchung zum Wandel des literarischen Geschmacks. Nürnberg,
Verlag Hans Carl, 1986, 366 S., DM 32,--.

Die im viktorianischen England sehr beliebte Dichtung fand zur Charakterbildung und
moralischen Erbauung junger Menschen Einlaß in Schul-, Kinder- und Geschenk-
bücher. Bis zur Mitte des Jhs. spielten bei der Auswahl und Zusammenstellung von
Gedichten für eine jüngere, weiblich-bürgerliche Leserschaft moralische und didaktische

174

Überlegungen eine entscheidende Rolle. Erst mit Palgraves Anthologie *Golden Treasury of the Best Songs and Lyrical Poems in the English Language* (1861) begann eine künstlerisch-ästhetische Bewertung die moralisch-didaktische Funktion des Gedichts in der Rezeption zu verdrängen. Obwohl Palgrave kurze lyrische Gedichte bevorzugte, dabei auf die Dichtung des 18. Jhs. weitgehend verzichtete und wichtige Dichter wie Donne und Blake ausschloß, gelang es ihm mit seiner Anthologie, einen grundsätzlich akzeptierten und lange nachwirkenden Kanon bekannter englischer Gedichte des 16. bis 19. Jhs. zu schaffen. Neben dem durch Palgrave vertretenen Typus der Lyrikanthologie trugen viele Sammlungen themen- und formgebundener Dichtung der viktorianischen Vorliebe für dieses Medium Rechnung. Patriotische und regionale, religiöse und Liebesdichtung, Natur- und Blumengedichte, Sonette und Balladen stießen erfolgreich auf Käufer und Leser, und das trotz der starken Konkurrenz der Romane auf dem Buchmarkt und der schwierigen Copyright-Situation bei der Zusammenstellung zeitgenössischer Gedichte und obwohl sich ihre potentielle Leserschaft hauptsächlich auf wohlhabende Familien, und hier besonders die Frauen, beschränkte.

Hampton, Wayne: *Guerilla Minstrels.* John Lennon. Joe Hill. Woody Guthrie. Bob Dylan. Knoxville/Tenn., The University of Tennessee Press, 1986, 306 S., $ 24.95.

Hampton traces the history of the culture of protest singing in America from the union hymns of the Industrial Workers of the World (IWW), through the topical-political singing of the Almanac Singers and the folkprotest singing of Pete Seeger, the Weavers, and Peter, Paul, and Mary to the folk-rock era of the 1960s. The author organizes his book around key personalities – Lennon, Hill, Guthrie, and Dylan – who sum up eras or genres of protest. He considers these important musicians both biographically and as political heroes, examining in particular the drama of each one's public life and death, and the canonization process that followed. Hampton's nostalgic tour of some of America's best-loved music shows how our protest singers have become cultural guerillas, balladeers for social harmony and camaraderie. Their songs form part of a revolutionary strategy aimed at achieving certain utopian ideals. Paradoxically, however, the heroism that serves as a source of collective identity in the end is also ultimately a source of alienation, where the original participatory dimension of protest singing is undermined by the star system and the cult of originality.

Humm, Peter, Stigant, Paul, Widdowson, Peter (Eds.): *Popular Fictions.* Essays in Literature and History. London, New York, Methuen, 1986, 265 S., Pb. £ 6.95, Hb. £ 15.00.

What are popular fictions? How are the two academic disciplines of literature and history implicated in this concept? Does our inherited notion of 'literature' embrace popular fictions? These questions are explored in this book. All the essays deal with 'popular fictions' which are a prime site for an exploration of the relations between literature, history and ideology. The essays deal with text as diverse as *Henry V, Pickwick Papers, Frankenstein, Rebecca* and *Ginx's Baby* – all texts which were widely sold or read in their day. This fact alone opens up questions of literary and historical placing which cut off the retreat into the immobility of standard literary criticism. Defining 'popular fictions' itself challenges the concept 'literature'. It involves writing a new history of the societies which produced them and demands radical analysis of what popular (or indeed any) fictions tell us. The role of televison and other forms of media in the continuing production and reproduction of popular fictions is also explored in some of the essays. The point of this book, however, is not to rigidly redefine once more what constitutes popular fiction, but to see what happens when proven best-selling fiction is placed within the dialectic of literature-and-history.

Ilson, Robert (Ed.): *Dictionaries, Lexicography and Language Learning.* Oxford, New York, Toronto, Pergamon Press in Association with the British Council, 1985, 135 S., £ 5.50.

Very few people these days avoid dictionaries completely, and almost everyone who has tried to learn a language in formal circumstances will have used one on many occasions. Yet we know little about the uses to which dictionaries have been put by learners and teachers, and much teacher education passes over the use of the dictionary. This may be partly because it is easier to recognize the dangers of misusing dictionaries than the dangers of ignoring them. But anyone in language teaching needs to understand more about them, for they are the most widespread single language improvement device ever invented. One cannot prevent students using them, but one can ensure that they are used wisely. The present collection gives information about various forms of dictionary, as well as discussion of the implications for learners of particular forms of organization.

Lonergan, Jack: *Fremdsprachenunterricht mit Video.* Ein Handbuch mit Materialien. Übersetzt von Ulrich Rösner. München, Max Hueber Verlag, 1987, 140 S., DM 28,--.

Der Band dient als praktische Methodik für den Einsatz von Video, mit zahlreichen Unterrichtsvorschlägen aus dem Englisch-, Französisch- und Deutschunterricht. Er informiert in erster Linie über: videospezifische Übungstypen und Lernaktivitäten; Auswahl und Einbindung von Videosegmenten in die praktische Spracharbeit; und den Umgang mit Videogeräten und -materialien. Die vorgestellten Übungen decken verschiedene Lernstufen und -bereiche ab; sie sind für alle Schultypen und Kursformen geeignet.

Malouf, David: *Harland's Half Acre.* Ringwood/Victoria, Penguin Books, Australia, 1985, 230 S., £ 2.95.

Harland's Half Acre is a novel rich in passion and incident and with the obsessive, sometimes violent claims of family life. It is the story of Frank Harland who, from his poverty-stricken upbringing on a dairy farm in Queensland, nurtures his artistic genius until the time comes when he can take possession of his dreams; and it is also the story of Phil Vernon, the only child of a wealthy Brisbane family, whose life is inextricably tangled with that of Frank Harland.

176

Neumeier, Beate: *Spiel und Politik*. Aspekte der Komik bei Tom Stoppard. München, Wilhelm Fink Verlag, 1986, 278 S., DM 48,--.

Ausgangspunkt dieser Arbeit ist das im Rahmen der Mischformen der zeitgenössischen Literatur verstärkte Interesse an den Spielarten des Komischen. Insbesondere anhand des Dramenwerks von Stoppard können Aspekte der Komik im Gegenwartstheater paradigmatisch aufgezeigt werden, vom Spiel mit literarischen Vorlagen bis zur Satire auf politische Realitäten. Bei der Analyse von Stoppards Stücken deckt sich die chronologische Abfolge mit den erwähnten Tendenzen, die ihrerseits zu den oppositionellen Polen eines Spektrums der Komik in Bezug gesetzt werden können. Dieser Korrespondenz von zeitgenössischer Theaterentwicklung im allgemeinen, Stoppards Werk im besonderen sowie theoretischer Komikforschung wird im Einleitungskapitel nachgegangen, um hieraus den Ansatz der Arbeit entwickeln zu können. In zwei unter den Oberbegriffen Spiel und Politik gefaßten Teilen folgt die Interpretation der einzelnen Dramen, wobei die textverarbeitenden Formen der Travestie und Parodie als Ausdruck von ästhetischem Konstrukt und Formen der Realitätskritik als Ausdruck einer satirischen Haltung mit den inhaltlichen Analysebegriffen verbunden werden.

Nickel, Gerhard: *Einführung in die Linguistik*. Entwicklung, Probleme, Methoden. 2., überarb. Auflage. Berlin, Erich Schmidt Verlag, 1985, 190 S., DM 28,60.

Die vorliegende Einführung kommt dem Bedürfnis nach einer kurzgefaßten, leicht verständlichen Gesamtübersicht über das inzwischen weitverzweigte Gebiet der Linguistik nach. Der Band führt an den ganzen Komplex der Linguistik in ihrer historischen Entwicklung heran und erfaßt auch die Verflechtungen mit anderen Fächern. Die Probleme und heutigen Methoden der Linguistik werden unter den wichtigsten Gesichtspunkten erklärt und umrissen. Der Band wurde für die Neuauflage nach dem neuesten Stand überarbeitet und, wo nötig, verändert und ergänzt; neuen Strömungen in der Linguistik wurde Rechnung getragen.

Poole, Richard: *Richard Hughes*. Novelist. Bridgend/Mid Glamorgan, Poetry Wales Press, 1987, 253 S., £ 12.95.

Hughes (1900–76) is best known for his remarkable bestseller about childhood, *A High Wind in Jamaica* (1929), now recognised as a modern classic. *In Hazard* (1938), his second novel, has been compared to Conrad's *Typhoon*. In his latter years, he worked on a series of novels, called *The Human Predicament*, a massive project in which he explored the social, economic, political and moral forces which shaped the period 1918–1945. Although only two of these novels, *The Fox in the Attic* (1961) and *The Wooden Shepherdess* (1973), were completed, Hughes's achievement has been widely praised. No other 20th-century novelist has so successfully transposed history into fiction. This is the first biographical and critical study of this major author. The first part deals with the extraordinary life of this remarkable man, who was a successful playwright before he left Oxford University, who wrote the first radio play, who undertook amazing adventures in the Balkans and Morocco, and who, for nearly the whole of his life, exhibited a deep attachment to Wales. The second and longer part of the book is a detailed examination of Hughes's work: his plays, poems, short stories and the novels.

Schrick, Annegret: *Jane Austen und die weibliche Modellbiographie des 18. Jahrhunderts*. Eine strukturelle und ideologiekritische Untersuchung zur Zentralfigur bei Jane Austen. Trier, WVT Wissenschaftlicher Verlag Trier, 1987, 300 S., DM 48,90.

Die vorliegende Studie weist nach, daß es eine weibliche Modellbiographie des 18. Jahrhunderts gibt. In zeitgenössischen normativen didaktischen Texten wird nicht nur der Normenkatalog dargelegt, mit dem die Frau aus der Schicht der *gentry* konfrontiert wurde, sondern vielmehr werden die Normen umgesetzt in einen musterhaften biographischen Ablauf mit spezifisch weiblichen „Wendepunkten". Die „Geschichte" der Modellbiographie beginnt zu dem Zeitpunkt, als das junge Mädchen zu strikt ritualisierten Anlässen als heiratsfähig ,angeboten' wird. Die vergleichende Analyse läßt keinen Zweifel daran, daß Jane Austen in der Romanbiographie ihrer weiblichen Romanfiguren nicht ein mehr oder minder ,schrulliges' Verhaltenskonzept entwickelt, sondern von dem Bezugstext der Modellbiographie ausgeht. Ihr Verhältnis dazu ist quasi parodistisch, womit zugleich die kritische Freiheit als auch die Begrenztheit ihres narrativen Vorgehens beschrieben wird. Neben einer Anzahl von Realisierungsmomenten erweist sich, daß Jane Austen die Inhalte und Strukturen der Modellbiographie gleichzeitig infrage stellt. Doch da die Autorin mit dem Trick des Glücks arbeitet, erspart sie sich eine letzte konsequente Stellungnahme: „zufällig" stimmt die Herzensentscheidung ihrer Zentralfigur mit gesellschaftlichem Wohlverhalten überein.

Schulze, Rainer: *Höflichkeit im Englischen*. Zur linguistischen Beschreibung und Analyse von Alltagsgesprächen. Mit einer Zusammenfassung in englischer Sprache. Tübingen, Gunter Narr Verlag, 1985, 279 S., DM 58,--.

In den letzten Jahren hat es eine Anzahl von Versuchen in der Linguistik gegeben, dem Zusammenhang von Höflichkeit und Sprachverwendung auf die Spur zu kommen. Doch waren diese Arbeiten in ihren jeweiligen Zielsetzungen weitgehend theoretischer Natur: Man denke hier z.B. an die Entwicklung von Höflichkeitsmaximen und -prinzipien (Leech, R. Lakoff) aus den sprachphilosophisch fundierten Gesprächspostulaten (Grice). In all diesen Darstellungen herrscht Einigkeit darüber, das theoretische Konzept der Höflichkeit für die Beschreibung und Analyse von *face-to-face*-Interaktionen nutzbar zu machen. Dieses Ziel verfolgt die vorliegende Arbeit, indem sie eine primär linguistische Beschreibung von Höflichkeit im alltagssprachlichen Englisch anstrebt und sich um eine Präzisierung einzelner Komponenten des Höflichkeitskonzeptes bemüht. Die Analyse besitzt exemplarischen Charakter und deckt anhand von versteckt aufgenommenen Verkaufsgesprächen u.a. auf, daß Alltagsgespräche in der Regel als eine Abfolge interaktiver Muster, d.h. als ständige Balanceakte zwischen selbst- und partnergerichteter *face*-Arbeit zu interpretieren sind.

Schwarz, Ingrid: *Narrativik und Historie bei Sir Walter Scott*. Eine strukturale Analyse der Waverley Novels am Beispiel von "Old Mortality". Frankfurt/M., Bern, New York, Verlag Peter Lang, 1986, 318 S., sFr. 66,--.

Die traditionelle Scott-Forschung hat in der Analyse der Waverley-Romane bislang einen wünschenswerten Grad der wissenschaftlichen Intersubjektivität ihrer Ergebnisse sowie die notwendige Transparenz der Erzähldynamik vermissen lassen. Zum Abbau dieser Defizite geht es im vorliegenden Buch um eine Untersuchung der Waverley-Romane im Sinne strukturalistischer Methoden. Dabei wird allerdings nicht verabsäumt, auch die Entstehungsbedingungen des Scottschen historischen Romans mitzureflektieren. Als Exempel dieser präzisions- und begründungsorientierten Vorgehensweise schließt die Arbeit mit einer ausführlichen Strukturanalyse des Romans *Old Mortality*.

Spaunhorst, Franz-Peter: *Literarische Kulturkritik als Dekodierung von Macht und Werten am Beispiel ausgewählter Romane von Upton Sinclair, Frank Norris, John Dos Passos und Sinclair Lewis*. Ein Beitrag zu Theorie und Methode der Amerikastudien als Kulturwissenschaft. Frankfurt/M., Bern, New York, Verlag Peter Lang, 1987, 381 S., sFr. 72,--.

Die amerikanische Kultur ist umfassend nur mit Hilfe eines kulturtheoretischen Konzeptes zu analysieren, welches sich für empirische wie hermeneutische Disziplinen der Amerikastudien/*American Studies* eignet. Die vorliegende Untersuchung geht davon aus, daß 1. Kulturen sich durch spezifische Werteraster unterscheiden, welche die Kommunikation prägen, 2. in jeder Kultur Machtverhältnisse herrschen, die sich ebenfalls in Kommunikation ausdrücken. Dementsprechend wird ein Grobmodell von Kultur als gleichzeitig macht- und wertgeprägter Kommunikation entwickelt und mit Hilfe eines daraus abgeleiteten Verfahrens gezeigt, daß literarische Texte als kritische, Macht und Werte dekodierende Analyse kultureller Epochen gelesen werden können.

Todd, Janet: *Sensibility*. An Introduction. London, New York, Methuen, 1986, 169 S., Pb. £ 5.95, Hb. £ 16.95.

In *Sensibility* Janet Todd charts the growth and decline of sentimental writings as a privileged mode in the 18th century. She shows how sentimental writing is riven with contradictions: while it applauds fellowship, it also expresses a yearning for isolation and, while it stresses the ties of friendship and family, it does so at the expense of sexual feeling, which grows menacing and destructive. By the 1770s, as the idea of sensibility was losing ground, 'sentimentality' came in as a pejorative term. Todd ends her study of sensibility by detailing the various attacks on the cult, from radicals and conservatives, feminists and Christian moralists; from Coleridge who saw it as unmanning the nation to Jane Austen who considered it an elaborate sham.

Truchlar, Leo (Ed.): *Für eine offene Literaturwissenschaft*. Erkundungen und Erprobungen am Beispiel US-amerikanischer Texte/*Opening Up Literary Criticism*. Essays on American Prose and Poetry. Salzburg, Verlag Wolfgang Neugebauer, 1986, 139 S., DM 45,--.

Der Titel dieser Sammlung deutsch- und englischsprachiger Aufsätze hat appellativen Charakter und leitet sich aus der Vorstellung der Verfasser ab, am „Entwurf einer Literaturwissenschaft" mitzuarbeiten, die für die Betroffenen einen „Kommunikationsprozeß" darstellt, welcher „ästhetische Erfahrung von literarischen Texten und ihre gesellschaftliche Funktion wie ihre anthropologischen Aspekte berücksichtigt". So werden die amerikanischen Texte von Marilynne Robinson, Hisaye Yamamoto, Mary Rowlandson, Mary Jemison, Hannah Dustan, Paule Marshall und Robert Coover – ergänzt durch literaturdidaktische Überlegungen zur Short Story und einem Beitrag zu 'Feminist Criticism' – bewußt zwanglos und ‚informativ' behandelt und die Aufsätze somit als „Versuch einer Annäherung" an Text und Leser verstanden.

Weinreich, Regina: *The Spontaneous Poetics of Jack Kerouac*. A Study of the Fiction. Carbondale, Edwardsville, Southern Illinois University Press, 1987, 180 S., $ 16.95.

While a legend has developed about the man Kerouac, there has not been a thorough study of what he wrote. Weinreich is the first to explore Kerouac's place in American literature by establishing the total design of his work. She contends that Kerouac wrote with this "grand design" in mind, that he thought of his works as "one vast book" (a "Divine Comedy of Buddha") he called The Legend of Duluoz. Weinreich finds that Kerouac's linguistic experimentation leads to a poetic unity rather than the linear unity commonly associated with legends. She discusses the nature of his "spontaneous bop prosody", relating it to the work of Thomas Wolfe and Henry Miller. Kerouac himself compared his "loose style" to that of a jazz hornplayer sounding one long note. While this explains his method, Weinreich seeks further to define the unity of his works, from *The Town and the City, On the Road,* and *Visions of Cody* to *Desolation Angels* and *Vanity of Duluoz.* Weinreich feels the autobiographical nature of Kerouac's opus links him to other 20th century American writers, following a distinctly Whitmanesque tradition. She goes on to argue that Kerouac's autobiographical fiction led to the discovery of a unique voice, one that is significant in contemporary American letters.

Weinstock, Horst (Ed.): *English and American Studies in German 1985.* Summaries of Theses and Monographs. A Supplement to Anglia. Tübingen, Max Niemeyer Verlag, 1986, 178 S., DM 98,––.

The authors' summaries in this issue cover book-length studies that appeared in 1985 or earlier. Most of the German-language treatises and doctoral dissertations summarized are in fact available in book form. For typescript dissertations unpublished but officially deposited, the titles to the summaries locate the universities of origin for interlibrary loans. Owing to an increasing number of publications by diverse hands and in mixed language medium, *EASG* reports on anthologies, casebooks, Festschriften, manuals, the *Shakespeare-Jahrbuch* (Bochum), proceedings of *Anglistentage,* conferences, seminars, societies, and symposia. The volume retains the previous arrangement in four sections. Section II on "English Literature" also contains summaries of theoretical and comparative studies as well as of works on non-British literature in English. Section III includes both American and Canadian literature. The indices assemble the authors and editors (I), the contributors to collectanea (II), and the authors and subjects treated (III).